Client-Centered Evaluation

MW01049998

EX LIBRIS

Alex Wood

EX LIBRIS
Alick Wood

Client-Centered Evaluation

NEW MODELS FOR HELPING PROFESSIONALS

Martin Bloom
University of Connecticut

Preston A. Britner
University of Connecticut

Allyn & Bacon

Boston   Columbus   Indianapolis   New York   San Francisco   Upper Saddle River
Amsterdam   Cape Town   Dubai   London   Madrid   Milan   Munich   Paris   Montreal   Toronto
Delhi   Mexico City   São Paulo   Sydney   Hong Kong   Seoul   Singapore   Taipei   Tokyo

Executive Editor: Ashley Dodge
Editorial Product Manager: Carly Czech
Senior Marketing Manager: Wendy Albert
Marketing Assistant: Craig Deming
Editorial Production Service: Jerusha Govindakrishnan/PreMediaGlobal
Editorial Project Manager: Beth Kluckhohn/PreMediaGlobal
Production Manager: Fran Russello
Cover Administrator: Jayne Conte
Cover Image Credit: Fotolia, Computer generated graphics © Tupungato
Cover Designer: Suzanne Duda

Copyright © 2012 Bloom and Britner, publishing as Pearson Education/Allyn & Bacon, One Lake Street,
Upper Saddle River, NJ 07458. All rights reserved. Manufactured in the United States of America. This
publication is protected by Copyright, and permission should be obtained from the publisher prior to any
prohibited reproduction, storage in a retrieval system, or transmission in any form or by any means, electronic,
mechanical, photocopying, recording, or likewise. To obtain permission(s) to use material from this work, please
submit a written request to Pearson Higher Education, Rights and Contracts Department, 501 Boylston Street,
Suite 900, Boston, MA 02116, or fax your request to 617-671-3447.

Many of the designations by manufacturers and seller to distinguish their products are claimed as trademarks.
Where those designations appear in this book, and the publisher was aware of a trademark claim, the designations
have been printed in initial caps or all caps.

Library of Congress Cataloging-in-Publication Data

Bloom, Martin
    Client-centered evaluation: new models for helping professionals/Martin Bloom, Preston A. Britner.—1st ed.
        p. cm.
    Includes index.
    ISBN-13: 978-0-205-83258-3
    ISBN-10: 0-205-83258-X
1. Social service—Evaluation.   2. Evaluation research (Social action programs)   I. Britner, Preston A.
    II. Title.
    HV41.B4497 2012
    361'.06—dc22

                                                                          2010052470

10 9 8 7 6 5 4 3 2 1

Allyn & Bacon
is an imprint of

PEARSON

www.pearsonhighered.com

ISBN-10: 0-205-83258-X
ISBN-13: 978-0-205-83258-3

CONTENTS

PREFACE

This book is about client-centered evaluation of practice, in which we propose ways clients can have a profound impact on nearly every step of the evaluation process. These include defining their own goals and objectives; helping to choose or devise the measures used; sharing ideas on collected data and their interpretation; informing the helping professional to what degree a given outcome matches what the client had aspired to; and, managing to maintain positive results when the client is on her or his own. This last point is really the heart of client-centered evaluation of practice. And we propose all of this without the use of statistics or other artificialities in the name of science. This new approach to single-system evaluation is suitable to the beginner in the helping professions (that is, and undergraduate student or a new case worker), as well as more advanced and experienced students and helping professionals.

Because this approach is new (although it builds on what we have done before), we invite faculty, students, and practitioners to write us with their reactions and suggestions. We really believe in the client-centered approach to evaluation, and this should include a user-centered approach to help construct better methods of thinking about and performing evaluation.

What you will find in this book is briefly described in the flow diagram (on p. 9). This includes:

- An introduction to client-centered evaluation of practice, as contrasted with traditional approaches that are, in effect, evaluator-centered.
- A discussion of theory as connected to evaluation methods as connected to the raw ingredients of everyday practice situations.
- A focus on empirical evidence as the basis for practice and evaluation.
- A review of graphing methods as a universal language of the helping professions.
- A review of methods of information retrieval for the contemporary helping professional.
- Discussions of the several ways to measure: individual rating scales, behavioral observations, standardized rating scales, and qualitative methods including narrative writing approaches to self-monitoring.
- A consideration of cautions in doing evaluation, such as obtaining unobtrusive and non-reactive measurements.
- A practical presentation of evaluation designs, basic and advanced, that emphasize the client-centered approach.
- A pain-free discussion of the analysis of data; no statistics are used, and yet we propose a multi-dimensional approach to analysis.
- A consideration of putting all of these pieces together as we make decisions on helping our clients help themselves.

Students will have access to a Web site with glossary terms and additional research and evaluation tools. The instructor's resources will include ideas for advanced educational projects, lectures and discussions, additional cases examples, lecture slides, and a test bank.

We hope that you will find the client-centered evaluation of practice to be useful to you and empowering for your clients or future clients.

Martin Bloom

Preston A. Britner

ACKNOWLEDGMENTS

Professors learn. They learn from colleagues, clients, students, and strangers. We express special appreciation to our colleagues of long standing, Joel Fischer, Tom Gullotta, John Orme, and Waldo Klein, and to the many practitioners and clients who have shared their insights and stories. (We should note that no real names of clients are used in the book, but that many of the examples stem from our direct experiences with clients.) We also thank the many students who have lived through our classes, contributed astute comments and asked vital questions, and made us better evaluators because of it. We have also benefited from anonymous (and not so anonymous) reviews, for which we are very grateful. But most of all we acknowledge with love and appreciation our families: Lynn; Bard, Victoria, Rhys; Laird, Sara, Paul, and Beth (MB); and, Suzanne, Sam, Serena, and Colin (PAB).

Client-Centered Evaluation of Practice (C-CEP) and Single-System Designs (SSD)

In the first part of this book, we will introduce the basic ideas about client-centered evaluation of your practice, using single-system designs as the main tool.

This means that we are going to take seriously the statement that what is important in any kind of helping practice is that the client's goals are met, and for this we need the client to be involved in almost every step of the way. This is also a good practice, as your other instructors will teach you.

The use of single-system designs means that you can take these tools with you into the field with your client—a single person, a married couple, a classroom of children, whomever—and use the laws of logic to demonstrate that positive changes have occurred, and in some situations, that you have caused those changes. If positive change does not occur, it is important to have this information in order to consider trying something else.

This is the kind of powerful evidence that is required by society so as to continue to underwrite your job, whether you are a social worker, counseling or clinical or school psychologist, educator, allied health professional, or any form of helping professional.

So, enjoy this venture into evaluation; it will stay with you the rest of your professional life.

Introduction to Client-Centered Evaluation of Practice

A NEW APPROACH TO EVALUATING PRACTICE

So, you want to become a helping professional in the realm of human services, and not a researcher? Then why are you sitting in a classroom, rather than serving on the front line, meeting clients at a family agency, or school, or nursing home, or soup kitchen, or wherever? Good point. But many professional associations, including counseling, education, nursing, occupational therapy, psychology, public health, and social work, among others, require students to take classes in evaluation of their own practice, as well as methods of practice and such. They require these classes for very good reasons; helping professionals not only have to learn the ropes (of practice), but they also have to be able to determine whether what they have done in fact works for the client (evaluation).

So important are these considerations that many professional associations have built them into their codes of ethics (Association of American Educators Code of Ethics, Principle II; American Occupational Therapy Code of Ethics, principle 3 [implied]; American Psychological Association Ethical Principles of Psychologists and Code of Ethics, 9.02; Code of Ethics for Nurses, provision 4.4; NASW 2009 Code of Ethics, 4.01.C; and others).

It is not simply that the helping professions are doing this out of the goodness of their hearts—they probably are—but that they also hear the drum beats from many funders that require agencies to demonstrate that they are using the best available information to guide their practice, and that they are evaluating whether these practices work well on behalf of the clients. Welcome to twenty-first century professional helping and evaluating your practice. Actually, that is not exactly right. We will be talking more about evaluation *from the point of view of the client* because this is where evaluation really belongs. Let us explain.

In all of ordinary life, we make decisions for ourselves and our families and friends on the basis of our on-going evaluation of the situation. When things go wrong or when difficulties arise that we are not able to resolve on our own, we usually go for help. "Hey, (friend), I can't seem to meet any guys with 'relationship' potential; what am I doing wrong?" "Doctor, I have this sharp pain in my left side that doesn't go away." Or, (to a family social worker or counselor), "We seem to be arguing about everything, and our marriage seems to be breaking apart."

Your friend may reveal her secrets of success as her method of helping you solve your difficulties. The doctor may prescribe some medicine or treatment, and things change in your body. Or the counselor may suggest some marital intervention to change the negative patterns of communication.

Whatever these helping professionals or friends do, *we* must tell our friend, our doctor, or the counselor when *we* feel good (or not) or have our impasse resolved (or not). *Evaluation of an outcome of service ultimately belongs to the clients whom we serve.* When we started to take this

---

Case Study

Phillip, a 10-Year-Old Boy Who is Diabetic and Obese Who Just Wants "to Be Like the Other Guys in My Class"

We are going to present an overview of client-centered evaluation of practice by illustrating it with a case study, as we will do in most of the chapters in this text. We'll be using case examples from many fields, with different numbers of clients, involving various modes of helping—and various ways to evaluate these situations. We will present these case studies so that you will be able to see the situation from the client's point of view, as well as that of the practitioner and the evaluator.

Let's begin with a story about Phillip, an obese 10-year-old boy with diabetes whose condition has life-threatening potential. Let's imagine that you are interning at a social agency where his parents, who are also obese, come for help, having been directed there by their family physician. We will take one specific concern and use it as an example of client-centered evaluation of practice. In later chapters, we'll go into more detail on the several elements in this process.

It's difficult being a 10-year-old boy when you are told by your parents (and doctor) that you have to do many things to control your diabetes while you can't do other things that your peers do all of the time. It's frustrating and depressing, and it affects the image you hold about yourself as being damaged or not as good as other kids. Sometimes events on one day bring this home to Phillip more sharply than on other days, but lately he has been very depressed. So, with mixed feelings—does going to a social agency really mean you're crazy?—he went with his parents to your office.

This story is heavily clouded with complexity as all stories about people are, but we'll keep it simple so as to focus on the client-centered evaluation of practice with this one element, namely Phillip's image of himself. The first question to be raised is, who is the client? Phillip is a minor, with parents as guardians. Yet, Phillip is the only one who can indicate his own state of mind. So, on this question, we will call Phillip the client who not only identifies the problem but also will be able to inform you when (and if) the problem is resolved and remains resolved. (In other questions, such as timely delivery of medications or performing exercises regularly, his parents can take primary responsibility for Phillip's actions, and hence are the clients toward whom your services are directed regarding these activities.)

point of view seriously, suddenly the world of evaluation began to look very different. We can only compare it to the scene in *The Wizard of Oz* in which Dorothy, who has been living in a sepia-colored world, is caught in a tornado, wakes up in the Technicolor splendor of Oz, looks around in amazement, and says to her dog, "Toto, I've a feeling we're not in Kansas anymore." Well, some of you may still be in Kansas, but as far as this evaluation book goes, you're not going to be in that state (of mind) anymore.

EIGHT STEPS IN EVALUATING PRACTICE

In this section of the chapter, we will introduce you to an eight-step process of practice and evaluation.

1. Identify the Client Who Defines the Goals in the Case

*The first component of client-centered evaluation of practice is to identify the client because the client defines the **goals***. (Terms in **bold italics** are defined in the glossary at the end of the book.) Let's say you engage Phillip in conversation, and he tells you tearfully how depressed his is, being so restricted for the sake of his health. You empathize how difficult this can be and ask what sort of image he would like to have of himself, recognizing that diabetes will likely be with him forever. He replies that he just wants to feel like he imagines everyone else does. "What does everyone feel about themselves?" you ask, and Phillip replies, "I guess they feel pretty good most of the time."

You begin to clarify what this means in a way that Phillip and you can both agree on: "Ok, Phillip. Let's imagine a step ladder with five rungs. The top rung, or step 5, is the best feelings about yourself you can have. What should we name this?" Phillip suggests "feeling very good most of the time." "The bottom rung or step 1 is the worst feelings you can have about yourself," you say. Phillip suggests calling this "rotten." Then you fill in the other steps: Step 4 is "pretty good"—this becomes the level or goal that Phillip seeks to attain and sustain. Step 3 is "just OK, some good, some not so good." Step 2 is "not so good."

You remind Phillip that steps on a ladder are equal distances apart, and he nods in agreement. You give Phillip a small calendar and ask him to write down one number each day, just before he goes to bed, that indicates how he felt overall about himself that day. Phillip says he understands, and in fact he comments that if he had been doing this for the past few weeks, the numbers would have been 2s and 1s. This young man is not a happy camper.

2. Select Intermediary Objectives and Their Specific Targets

*The second component of client-centered evaluation of practice is to take this goal and break it down into workable components or intermediate stages called **objectives***. You ask Phillip what goes into making up his image of himself, and he thinks about this for a while and says, "I'm really fat, and I just look so different from the other kids. And I get chosen last for every sports team in gym because I just can't hit or field very well. And I get tired fast, I guess because of my diabetes." Phillip mentions other things that affect his self-image. You ask which are the major ones, and he cites those identified above.

You start talking about weight (a more neutral description than "being fat") because you know that this is also a concern of his parents and the doctor. He is taking in more calories than he is expending in activities. Phillip says he knows what you are going to talk about—exercise. You ask, "What about exercise?" Phillip explains that this is what his parents are after him to do all the time on an exercise machine that they just bought. And he hates to exercise. It makes him feel tired, and he hurts all over. You nod in understanding, saying that you have a friend who doesn't like exercise machines either, but he finds a lot of other ways to exercise, like walking through the park nearby, shooting a basketball, and listening to music while pretending he is conducting the band. He gets in an easy hour of exercise a day and really enjoys it. You can see Phillip thinking about your story, figuring out what things he likes to do that would count as exercise, like helping in the family garden (his mother would love that, and he might get some extra allowance), riding his bike around the block, and maybe practicing throwing the basketball toward the hoop so he might get a little better at that. He says he isn't so sure about exercising an hour a day; his doctor suggested a half hour, and maybe he should start there.

Notice what happens next: The objective concerns the concept of weight loss, which is one element related to Phillip's goal of a positive self-image. But you will focus on some specific empirical proxy suitable for Phillip. In fact, let's call these empirical proxies *targets*, as we specify exactly what Phillip will do to deal with this objective of weight loss, that is, expending more energy (calories) than he is consuming. (Exercise alone will not reduce weight without a parallel program for eating the right foods in the right amounts.) For example, we might operationally define riding his bike around the block (summer weather permitting) three times in a row, which takes about 30 minutes. In bad weather, he could clean up his room (which always seems to need it) or help his father haul newspapers, bottles and cans, and trash to the local transfer and recycling station. (Let's assume that these would be equivalent physical activities that burn off calories.) He would start eating carrots and fruits as his snack food, rather than cookies and the like. (His mother is already preparing meals aimed at being healthier than what she had been used to making.) Thus, we have translated the idea (or concept) of weight loss into an empirical target, such as performing so many minutes of physical activities combined with eating a healthy diet. This will lead to weight loss, other things being equal.

3. Identify Evidence-Based General Practice From the Literature and Evaluation-Informed Specific Practice From Working With the Client

The third component of client-centered evaluation of practice involves two steps: The first step is to identify and use evidence-based general practice and individualize it as needed to fit the context of your given client. Clearly, there will be an information-retrieval step in the intervention: What methods have worked best with minimal harm to clients in similar situations? (See Chapter 5.) Once you have sifted through this information and made your choice of the best available information, you will still have to figure out how to tailor this general information to fit your given client. Phillip may be from some ethnic minority background. Will the information from non-minority populations be useful? Phillip's parents are both obese and diabetic. How does this information affect what you know from the general literature?

The second step of this component is called evaluation-informed specific practice. It occurs when you actually apply your individualized plan of action and observe the effects on this specific client. What evidence do you have that this plan is working? By looking at the data being collected over time, you get one indication. (You will also get feedback from the client about how well the program is working.) You may observe that the target is: (a) being attained on or ahead of schedule; (b) being attained but behind schedule; (c) showing no clear positive change; (d) showing some indication of deterioration; or (e) showing strong indication of deterioration. Each of these observations informs the practitioner about ways of responding, either to leave matters stand or to make suitable modifications.

4. Collect Data in an Ongoing Basis and Plot Data on Graphs

The fourth component of client-centered evaluation of practice is collecting ongoing information on these targets and plotting the results on graphs. Phillip starts out being cooperative on data collecting, but soon needs a bit of prodding from his parents. Let's say you obtain the following 14 numbers that Phillip recorded on his calendar: 1, 1, 1, 2, 1, 1, 1, 1, 2, 1, 2, 3, 2, 2. A string of numbers by themselves is not very exciting; you need a context to have them make sense. Graphs provide that context. Let's look at the various notations on Figure 1.1. These are basic to any graph.

There is a vertical axis called Y, on which the various steps or intensities of the target are named: A dot placed in the graph at the level 5 means Phillip felt very good about himself most of the time that day. A dot at level 1 means Phillip felt rotten most of the time that day. And so on for all the other three levels that Phillip defined.

The horizontal axis, called X, identifies the time periods, days in the case of Phillip, in which some intensity of the target is identified. So, on day 1, Phillip wrote on the calendar that he felt rotten. On day 16, he wrote 3, meaning that it was just OK, some good, some not so good.

Putting the string of numbers together like this means we can see a moving picture of Phillip's 2 weeks between the first introductory session and the second session when you introduce the intervention. This string of numbers represents a ***pattern of targeted events***. We will eventually compare this pattern of results against later patterns. The first pattern is termed ***baseline (A phase)***, a period of time when systematic observations are made with no intervention. By tradition, it is identified as A on the graph. The second pattern is called ***intervention (B phase)***, a period of time when some systematic intervention is made, along with the continuation of the systematic observation. Tradition again has suggested B as the name of one distinctive intervention; C, D, and E (and so on) could be other distinctive interventions. (We will save a few letters for special purposes later.) For example, in a school setting, a time-out procedure might be instituted as the planned intervention; or, a support group might be found for parents whose children are obese. Each of these phases is labeled and distinguished by a dashed vertical line between them. (By the way, do not draw these dashed lines on top of any data point as you will not be able to tell to which phase it belongs.)

It is important to note that this evaluation model will work with any type of intervention you choose to use, from behavior modification to a summer program for school children, so long as the targets are clearly defined, the data are collected systematically, and the intervention is operationalized fully so as to be repeatable. (We'll discuss the place of theory in practice in Chapter 3.) The intervention phase represents your translation of a theory (if one is used) and available empirical evidence (data) into the specific actions that constitute your attempt to help. The specific details of the intervention should appear in the case report related to this graph. This way, you will know exactly what you did that went right (or wrong) so as to use this information in your continuing effort at professional development.

5. Construct Clear Benchmarks to Know When the Results Are (or Are Not) Successful

The fifth component of client-centered evaluation of practice is to construct an empirical goal or benchmark to know when results of the intervention have been successful (or not). This is a critical point for the client-centered approach, so let's consider the possibilities. First, recall that Phillip has defined step 4, being positive about oneself most of the time, as what he would like to attain as his desired goal. You would likely add that he should sustain that level of positive self-feeling for a reasonable time as well, rather than be in a temporary upswing in mood. (More on

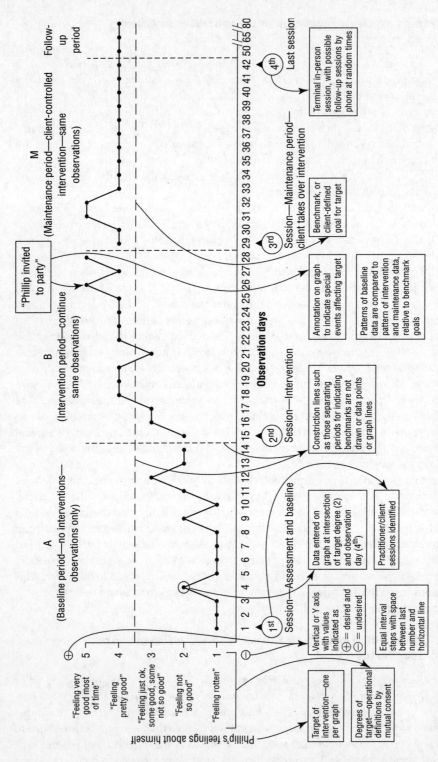

FIGURE 1.1 Basic elements of a graph—expanded interpretation (hypothetical data)

this point in Chapter 3, when we discuss how to aim at a goal and sustain that goal.) This is an empirical benchmark that the client has defined for herself or himself.

A second way of knowing if the results of intervention have been successful or not, especially when your client cannot articulate his or her own goal, is to look outside of this situation. Consider the norms from a standardized scale that specify positive and negative ranges of scores on self-image for a boy of Phillip's age. (We'll come back to this discussion of standardized scales in Chapter 8.) These norms represent scores derived from large numbers of children who were independently identified as having low self-esteem. These scores are compared to the scores of another large number of children who exhibited high self-esteem (e.g., DuBois, 2003). Norms become a kind of benchmark and can be useful in cases in which the client has trouble specifying a goal. You can draw a line on the graph between the low and normal self-esteem norms, and then observe where Phillip scores over time. (We drew a hypothetical line like this on Figure 1.1.)

Both of these ways can be useful in understanding the progress of the case. Both of these approaches involve the use of a graph to make this judgment, and you and the client can see the evidence of what has happened during the intervention phase. Most books on evaluation of practice stop here, but in our opinion, evaluation really begins here.

6. Engage the Client in Determining If the Client's Goals Have Been Attained During Intervention

The sixth component of client-centered evaluation of practice is to engage the client in making the determination whether the observed change in the target is, in fact, what the client wants as goal attainment. In Phillip's case, it may be easy to go from the graph to a discussion that asks to what degree he sees these data as representing the attainment of his objective.

However, this is not always as clear. Consider, for example, an older adult client forced to go to a nursing home for skilled care and being away from her family and friends. Yes, she is getting the care she needs, but is this the goal she would seek? She might define such a living situation as not living at all according to her wishes. Or a pair of newlyweds. She came from a conservative background and doesn't want to have sex as often as her husband does. After much discussion with the counselor, they agree to a goal of three times a week, far too often for the wife and far too infrequent for the husband, so when that goal is achieved empirically, it still may not be satisfactory to the parties involved. Or the high school student whose grades are poor, and his parents are going out of their minds trying to convince him to shape up before he starts applying for college. The school academic advisor works out some compromise situation in which the student has to do his work without the "aid" of his MP3 player (at full blast) to get his parents off his back. He manages to do this, but misses his music terribly. These are just some of the many possible situations in which empirical evidence of success has been attained without having comparable approval by the client as to the meaning of the change in his or her life.

The determination of empirical success takes place at the end of some intervention phase, when the evidence seems clear, and the client is willing to sign off as fulfilling his or her goals. But this is still not the end of client-centered evaluation.

7. Introduce a Maintenance Phase in Which the Client Is in Complete Control of the Intervention on His or Her Own

The seventh component of client-centered evaluation of practice occurs when the client on his or her own can manage to sustain the same successful outcome as in the intervention (B) phase. We will call this **maintenance phase (M)**, meaning that the client can be trained to be in independent control over the successful management of the target he or she identified (to the extent possible). Children may need the continuing support of their parents; people with various types of physical and mental disabilities may also need ongoing support. But even in such cases, the clients should participate to the extent possible in their own management of a successful outcome.

We will discuss this in Chapter 13, but let's consider the situation of Phillip. Without going into any practice details, let's say that you used some form of cognitive-behavioral method to help Phillip boost his self-esteem, such as self-talk to encourage positive thoughts, or thought stopping of negative thoughts. With training, Phillip has been able to learn these methods and the results appear to be quite positive on the graph. (See Figure 1.1.) Philip agrees at the end of intervention that things seem to be going well. Then the maintenance phase begins. Your task is not

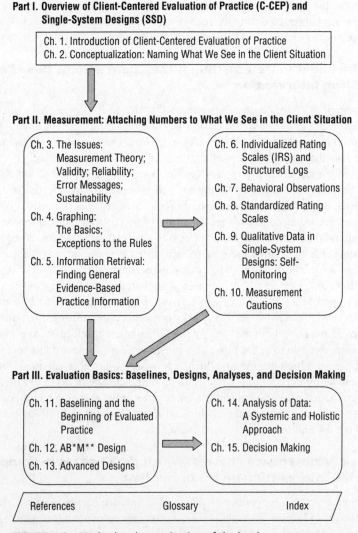

Part I. Overview of Client-Centered Evaluation of Practice (C-CEP) and Single-System Designs (SSD)

> Ch. 1. Introduction of Client-Centered Evaluation of Practice
> Ch. 2. Conceptualization: Naming What We See in the Client Situation

Part II. Measurement: Attaching Numbers to What We See in the Client Situation

> Ch. 3. The Issues:
>   Measurement Theory;
>   Validity; Reliability;
>   Error Messages;
>   Sustainability
>
> Ch. 4. Graphing:
>   The Basics;
>   Exceptions to the Rules
>
> Ch. 5. Information Retrieval:
>   Finding General
>   Evidence-Based
>   Practice Information

> Ch. 6. Individualized Rating
>   Scales (IRS) and
>   Structured Logs
>
> Ch. 7. Behavioral Observations
>
> Ch. 8. Standardized Rating
>   Scales
>
> Ch. 9. Qualitative Data in
>   Single-System
>   Designs: Self-
>   Monitoring
>
> Ch. 10. Measurement
>   Cautions

Part III. Evaluation Basics: Baselines, Designs, Analyses, and Decision Making

> Ch. 11. Baselining and the
>   Beginning of Evaluated
>   Practice
>
> Ch. 12. AB*M** Design
>
> Ch. 13. Advanced Designs

> Ch. 14. Analysis of Data:
>   A Systemic and Holistic
>   Approach
>
> Ch. 15. Decision Making

> References   Glossary   Index

FIGURE 1.2   Method and organization of the book

to intervene as such, but to teach Phillip how to intervene as needed on his own. Indeed, this is what life is about, but people with various forms of mental and social distress need some assistance in order to get back on track. The intervention period has shown that Phillip is on track. Now, let's see if he can run the train by himself. You introduce the self-instruction, and then you step back. Phillip reports the data at the end of the next month. It looks like the prior pattern of success, and Phillip says he now thinks he can do it on his own.

Looking at this hypothetical drama of Phillip, we have two patterns of successful outcome (one in B and one in M). At both times, the client says he agrees that this is an attainment of his goals. How likely is this kind of result to happen by chance alone? The more times it happens like this, the less likely is it to be happening only by chance.

8. Analyze Patterns of Data to Coordinate With the Client's Statements

An eighth component of client-centered evaluation of practice may occur, as desired or required, when some form of analysis is performed to back up the client's opinions and a visual review of the data. There are at least five major ways to analyze data from *single-system designs* that we will discuss in Chapter 14.

What is important here is that each of these analytic approaches offers a different piece of the whole situation, and we recommend that practitioners perform as many of these methods as feasible in order to get a more nearly complete picture of how the client is doing. The mathematically or statistically challenged readers of this book will be happy to learn that the level of such required expertise is about at beginning college level. So, enjoy the trip to Chapter 14 without fear.

Chapter Summary

There is a kind of flow of events in evaluating practice in any of the helping professions, and it is this flow that we seek to reflect in the following summary of this chapter. (See Figure 1.2.) Every helping professional has to conceptualize (i.e., name what we see in the client situation). Every helping professional has to measure client events by attaching numbers to what we see in these happenings. Every helping professional has to plan for the intervention and design how to document the change (positive change, one hopes!) that has occurred. Every helping profession is, or ought to be, a client-centered profession throughout every aspect of helping. This is what we seek to attain and why we have written this book.

That's the story, told in brief. There are some complicating factors to be discussed throughout the book, but if you understand these basic steps, the details will take care of themselves (as solvable by logical reasoning in the course of practice).

C H A P T E R

2

Conceptualization: Naming What We See in the Client Situation

Case Study

Introduction to Conceptualization—Ben and Kat Washington

One of the paradoxes of the helping professions is that we discuss specific people and concrete problems in abstract and general terms. Why? For several important reasons. First, abstractions magnify the issues so we can see them better. We take abstract and general ideas (we'll label these *concepts* in a moment) and go to the literature to find out what others have thought and done with similar problems. Second, using abstract and general ideas, we may discover some aspects of the unique client problem that we had not thought about, but which may help to resolve the issue. Third, using concepts diffuses the high level of emotions that often bring clients to our door, so we can see other aspects of the situation that may have eluded them. We don't disregard the strong feelings that clients have, but we can put them into a perspective that may be the strong card that helping professionals have to play.

So, come along as we meet *your* clients. They came to the door of your agency holding hands, which was itself quite unusual for a family social agency flooded by people with problems. They were a striking couple, very young, married for only about a year, and they seemed very much in love. His tattoo of a dragon encircling his entire left arm emphasized his huge biceps. Her various facial jewelry did not distract from her bright smile. They are a physically handsome and distinctive looking couple. But they did, indeed, come to the right place.

They married almost the day they got out of high school, at age 17. He went to work at a bike shop—when there was work to be done—repairing wheels and gears, going for test rides (which he loved; he loved any kind of biking), and getting covered with grease. She picked up several part-time jobs and started taking courses at the junior college at the beginning of a long

(Continued)

13

dream of becoming a nurse. They rented a tiny apartment in the worst part of town, and they thought they were in paradise.

Unfortunately, even paradise comes with snakes. They began to argue about many things, such as not having enough money. She wants to quit college and get a full-time job to earn more money; he says that, in the long run, it would be better for her to continue moving toward a nursing career. He feels badly about not having a higher-paying job, but he likes where he works. They argue about having children. She loves kids and wants some of her own as soon as possible; he wants kids, sort of, but not right away when they have so many financial issues. They argue about sex. He wants more, and she says that she enjoys sex, but not as much as he does, and Ben recently has been getting more insistent on having sex. They have no shyness in discussing their use of contraceptives. They also argue about religion. She is quite religious, and he thinks it is a bunch of "nonsense" (not his exact and more vivid term).

You sit there listening, taking a few notes, and asking some questions to clarify matters. After they finally stop to catch their breath, you ask if these are the major concerns they have. Yes, they agree, and wait quietly for you to solve them all immediately. Thus begins the case of Ben and Kat (short for "Katherine") Washington.

We have constructed this situation in order to emphasize client-centered evaluation in practice, starting from this brief introduction to one form of the helping process. Let's see how we can get from here to there, from the concrete reality of the presented case to the various abstract tools you will eventually need to understand it and evaluate your success in dealing with the Washingtons' concerns.

GOALS: DESCRIBED IN TERMS OF CONCEPTS, PROPOSITIONS, AND THEORIES

All of the presenting concerns were hurled at you, a family counselor intern, in rapid order, without many details, and so you ask which of these do the Washingtons feel are most central to the reasons they came to this agency? They look at each other for a few moments, bend their heads toward each other, and whisper. Then Kat says, probably the financial problem is the most important, but that has much to do with the nursing education plan, too. Their families are poor and can't afford to help them. And she recognizes that without more education, there would not be many entry-level situations that pay well. Ben wants the sex issue to be considered, as one of his chief pleasures in life and an ever-renewable resource for this couple. Kat finally agrees to have sex be discussed as part of these interviews, but she says that Ben is being demanding again.

Concepts

Let's get into the mind of the counselor at this point (in a much simplified case situation) to see what ideas are being formed regarding the Washingtons. There are a cluster of ideas around the topic of money: work; earnings; recurring bills to pay; other expenses, especially schooling; part-time vs. full-time jobs; and the like. Each of these words describing ideas emerging from the conversation are something you will turn into a *concept*, an arbitrary construction around events or happenings in the world that are important to these people. For instance, Ben goes to the bike shop, works on broken bicycles as directed, and receives pay once a week for however many hours he was there. These are the realities of his life, but for you as practitioner, these events are translated into a general and abstract term or concept, "work." (By the way, you may come across the term *construct*, which is generally seen as higher order of *concept*. We'll consider them interchangeable but stick with *concept*.)

Why do we form concepts when we have perfectly good words to describe these activities? Because these general and abstract terms can be linked to other such terms to form sentences that are helpful in understanding the client's situation. It turns out, for example, that Ben's and Kat's combined earnings barely cover their recurring and special expenses, and this worries them enormously because they promised their parents they would not ask for money (which the parents couldn't give in any case) when they got permission to marry at such a young age.

Moreover, when concepts are combined with other concepts, sometimes explosive things happen. Let's look at this process more closely. To begin with, concepts are neither true nor false; they just exist as words naming abstract and general ideas. Concepts are not real things in the sense that the dollar bill in your wallet is real or the reality that you hope you have enough of those dollars to get through school. Now, on to the explosive part.

Propositions

As soon as sentences are formed from two or more concepts (and linking terms), they become testable. We can look at experiments in the real world and see whether or not what the sentence or ***proposition*** asserts is true. Is this the way that the world operates as described in this proposition of two or more concepts? For example, let's construct a proposition regarding Ben and Kat, but notice the change in level of language, from everyday language to conceptual language.

> *Prolonged imbalance of earnings compared to expenses leads to psychological stresses that may affect the continued well-being or survival of a group. (Proposition 1)*

This is the way you will see propositions expressed in the literature. Now, let's look at the proposition in a different way, where we distinguish concepts and connector terms to make the proposition clearer:

Proposition 1

> [concept #1] *Prolonged imbalance of earnings compared to expenses*
> [connector term] leads to
>
> [concept #2] *psychological stresses*
> [connector term] that may affect
>
> [concept #3] *the continued well-being or survival of a group.*

Or, more briefly: Prolonged financial imbalance leads to stresses that may affect group survival.

These several concepts have been put together in such a way as to predict a future state of some group (like Ben and Kat, a two-person group)—such as a possible breakup—after going through an intermediate state—such as high stress. Kat and Ben did not have such a notion of possible breakup in their minds at all, but the set of concepts dealt with an abstract series of events that included this possibility as a final outcome. This proposition may or may not be a fruitful guide to the future, but it puts the daily happenings that the couple is experiencing in a different light. It also urges decisive actions to prevent this chain of events from unfolding. This is a lot of powerful information packed into a prediction (or hypothesis).

But more is known about the situation. What shall we do with all of the other things Ben and Kat mentioned—and which, therefore, must be important to their lives? For example, Ben talks about feeling guilty about not bringing in enough money to pay for their expenses. Kat says that's why she wants to quit the two classes she is taking to go to work full time, a plan with which Ben disagrees. You can see by the way they discuss this issue that it is something that can't be ignored. But how should we take into consideration the many things they talked about in a flood of words?

Theory

Let's see if it is possible to put some of these other ideas into propositional form. Breaking down a definition of *theory*, we will talk about a *local theory* involving a system of specific events, such as in a client situation, as contrasted to a *general theory* like behaviorism, Freudian theory, cognitive-behavioral theory, and the like, which deal with more general abstractions and that describe many possible events. Thus, local theories will contain local propositions, those dealing with the specifics of a client situation. General theories will contain general propositions, such as "reinforcing a response will likely lead to a repetition of that response in like situations." Let's try to make use of other relevant information from our conversations with Kat and Ben to construct other propositions in a local theory. We'll first introduce a definition, and then we'll suggest a second proposition. This definition simply tells us how words are being used in this situation:

A "stronger partner" in this marriage is the one who brings in the larger amount of earnings so as to pay the bills. It does not involve physical strength. Next, proposition 2:

> *When the stronger partner does not earn enough money to pay the bills, that partner will compensate his or her weakened situation by becoming more demanding in other domains (e.g., sex), which may be unwelcomed by the other partner. (Proposition 2)*

Now we have two propositions interrelated by shared terms, such as earnings, and imbalance of income and expenses (using different words for the same ideas). We are also using a lot of the major ideas that Kat and Ben were saying, so nothing much in their conversation is wasted. This interrelated set of propositions begins to form a logical theory, even though it is a local theory. What we need next is a conclusion drawn from these two propositions.

> *Therefore, only when former (economic) difficulty is resolved will the latter (sexual conflict, etc.) will be resolved. (Proposition 3)*

We don't know if proposition (3) is true or false, but we can test it in the course of our work with the clients. At the moment, it seems like a reasonable guide for our actions in the case. This is exactly what local theories are intended to do. A suggested order of intervention has emerged from these abstract ideas—economics first, then interpersonal issues. It also offers a new possibility that if the first problem were solved, it may automatically reduce problems in other areas. We don't know this for sure, but the ordering among concepts in these propositions makes it a possibility to be tested.

In sum, we have identified two interrelated goal concepts (i.e., finances, sex); we have put them into a propositional context with relevant other concepts; and, we have interrelated the propositions to form a local theory. From this local theory, we can formulate a plan of action in this case. All of this looks so easy and simple on the printed page, but what exactly are you supposed to do with this conceptual and theoretical information? Here is our suggestion:

1. Every complex case situation will have many ideas and many concepts connected to it, and it will be beneficial to get a handle on the situation by using concepts, propositions, and a local theory to guide your thinking and actions. Concepts summarize a large number of words and gestures clients make during the course of an interview. So as not to be drowned in words, find the common meanings among them and formulate concepts that represent them.

2. Once you have a small set of concepts that appear to describe the major themes of the client's concerns, then combine these concepts in sensible ways. That is, what seems testable? Does concept A lead to concept B or concept C, and how is concept D related to these? There are no right answers, only suggestive ones.

3. If you get stuck, look at the logic of a general theory. For example, from behaviorism: What appears to be reinforcing the client to repeat some unhelpful behavior (concept A) rather than another constructive behavior (concept B)? For example, what keeps Ben at an ill-paying job? Or, from the cognitive-behavioral perspective, does the client have some inaccurate mind-set about what causes the unpleasant behavior and can this be modified? For example, does Kat have to take two courses each semester in order to get to her goal? These big-picture ideas from general theories can give some order and direction to your local theory.

4. Remember that local theories are not complex constructions of a thousand details; they are very close to the big pieces of reality that you have learned about the client's life and concerns. You have put them into your own conceptual language to think about them, to go to information retrieval devices to see how others have handled the same kinds of issues, and to plan a specific strategy of action to help achieve the client's *goals*.

5. When all else fails in your construction of a brilliant local theory, then just imagine telling a colleague what is going on with your client and what this means to you in terms of an action plan. You may be pleasantly surprised at how sensible your discussion is. As Dr. Benjamin Spock wrote in his ever-popular book on baby and child care, "Trust yourself. You know more than you think you do."

OBJECTIVES AND TARGETS: THE AIMS OF OUR PLANS OF ACTION

With the local theory, we have some theoretical ideas about the case, but it is time to focus. The couple mentioned that with their combined income, they were barely able to meet weekly expenses, let alone special expenses like tuition and books. You ask them to think about a specific *objective* like an amount of money that would be needed to pay for routine and special expenses viewed over a year's time. You provide a checklist of routine expenses and ask them to add the special but expected expenses, such as those connected with schooling.

Ben expected this kind of question, and he pulls out their financial record book that they had been keeping. To make a long story short and simple, let's say that the couple and you figured they needed about $15,000 a year, or about $300 a week. This is a very modest budget, but they thought it fit their lifestyle and was within their capability, given their background and education. What brought this situation to a crisis for them is the fact that they netted only $250 and $225 for the two prior weeks.

There was a moment of silence while you digested these facts. The goal they brought with them to the agency involved financial solvency. There were a number of intermediate stages—specific objectives in this case—each of which would contribute to that goal: locating a new job; earning a higher wage; obtaining health insurance (which they currently did not have); possibly modifying Kat's educational plans; among others. Let's examine these.

Ben sighed, and admitted that his job was not very good, although he loved the work itself. Silence. Kat was looking at Ben adoringly but with expectation. (They must have had this conversation before, but without a third party present.) "OK," Ben eventually said, "I'll start looking at the job advertisements online." You mention a few other paths toward job-seeking, and he makes a note in his record book. You add that he should check into any benefits a job offers, like health insurance. This is something neither of them had considered before, and they agree to do this.

Kat asserts that she can get a full-time job, too, and Ben frowns at her. (Another conversation they must have had.) You suggest waiting to see what Ben turns up before changing Kat's plans. Ben nods in agreement. You add that it may be useful for Kat to look into extending her educational career by a semester, until they are on their financial feet. Kat ponders this a moment and then nods in agreement. That would mean taking only one class, not two, paying lower fees, but still remaining on the college track. Ben reluctantly agrees.

EMPIRICAL EVIDENCE AS BASES OF PLANS OF ACTION

We will discuss two kinds of empirical evidence. The first is from the evidence-based literature on studies researchers have conducted on given problems in order to know what works, what looks promising, and what does not work. The practitioner should choose from the "what works" category whenever possible, from "what looks promising" when no other guidelines are available, and never from "what does not work"—no matter how much publicity an intervention may have received in the popular press. (An example of the "what does not work" approach was an anti-drinking program in which police officers talked to classes of children about the problems associated with alcohol use and abuse. The program was empirically shown to have no positive effect, even though it was popular with parents and teachers, touted on many car bumpers, and was an inexpensive way for administrators to show they were "doing something" about underage drinking.) We will return to this kind of evidence in Chapter 5 where we discuss information retrieval methods.

The second kind of empirical information comes directly from client feedback. You introduce some intervention; what happens? This local empirical information is vital for you to modify your intervention, if necessary, depending on the course of events following your intervention. Let's explore this second kind of evidence.

You pull out a pad of graph paper, and make two graphs. In the first (Figure 2.1), you label the vertical axis as Ben's job. This is the target for change. You could just write on that vertical

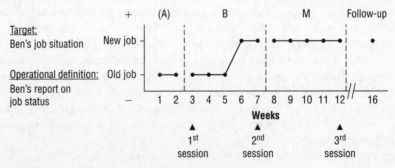

FIGURE 2.1 Ben's job situation (hypothetical data)

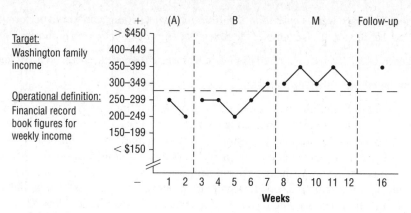

FIGURE 2.2 Washington family income (hypothetical data)

axis "same job" at one point and "new job" at a second point. Or you could use symbols, like 0 = same job; 1 = new job, just to distinguish the two situations. On the horizontal line are time periods, in weeks. From the information Ben has been providing, you indicate on the graph that he has had the same job for the preceding 2 months. This is the reconstructed baseline or reference pattern of events. If and when Ben gets and retains a new job, you will put 1s in the succeeding time periods. Simple and clear-cut evidence.

In the second graph (Figure 2.2), you label the vertical axis as family income (from Ben and Kat together), and from their financial record book you add the relevant information from the past 2 weeks. You also add in a dashed line the benchmark they are aiming at, $300 a week. This is an important part of the graph, as it embodies the valued goals these clients are seeking. They study the graph and recognize that the past few weeks have been financially bad, but that there were some weeks before when they did earn about $300. You ask whether they see any pattern in the ups and downs of their earnings. Pause. No, they don't see anything in particular, but they'll keep their eyes on these patterns. Graphing sometimes helps clients to focus on possible problems or their causes. The same graphs will help you in determining your plans of action: Is the evidence such that you will continue your *intervention* that seeks to help the client move toward the goal? Or should you modify the intervention to make it more effective (an outcome element) or more efficient (a time element)? Or should you start considering a termination date for a successful and stable intervention?

In sum, constructing graphs with clients may help them focus on specific *targets*, and the desired target levels within them. Having a benchmark to aim for adds another piece of guidance for clients. Sometimes having a graph to look at the past and present is itself an encouragement ("look, I'm making progress . . ."); in other instances, it may help the client identify that they need to work harder.

DEFINITIONS, OPERATIONAL AND CONCEPTUAL: AGREEING ON THE TERMS OF THE PLAN OF ACTION

The glossary contains a very specialized dictionary of the terms we have used throughout the book. It may be helpful to know how this glossary was constructed, not only with the help of a trusty college dictionary but also in terms of what you would have to do to use these terms. Dictionaries contain conceptual definitions (something defined in terms of other concepts), whereas the glossary contains **operational definitions** (what actions you would perform to exemplify this concept). Here's an example: the *American Heritage Dictionary* definition of *concept*.

A general idea derived or inferred from specific instances or occurrences. (concept, n.d.)

Now, here is the glossary definition of *concept*.

This operational definition is embedded in a conceptual framework so that you know roughly what we are discussing, along with an example (when possible).

A concept is an arbitrarily constructed general term derived from some class of events (such as how a client presents herself and the troubling situation that brought her to your agency; e.g., she may sound depressed to you). Concepts serve as building blocks for larger conceptual terms (e.g., propositions, theories) and as links to the information network where you can find evidence-based practice ideas. Concepts are neither true nor false, but merely better or worse guides to reality. For example, the concept "depression" refers to some but not necessarily all of these physical (e.g., slumped posture), psychological (e.g., persistent unhappy feelings, unpleasant thoughts), and social factors (e.g., ineffective in ordinary social roles), and so on. Having this concept enables you to locate effective methods of intervention, although you should evaluate the specific outcomes with your client. Keep open to other relevant concepts that describe more fully your client situation.

OK, so the glossary definition is a lot longer. The critical question is this: Is it helpful to you as you deal with that term? We believe that the operational definition would be more useful in helping you and the client agree on what is happening in this situation and how things are changing.

Chapter Summary

This chapter has provided a brief overview of conceptualization as you would use it in practice. We will add more details in later chapters, but if you grasp this basic picture, you will have understood a very important aspect of professional helping: Concepts provide the head work; practice is the hand and foot work. Both are necessary.

Measurement: Attaching Numbers to the Client Situation

Everything depends on accurate measurement of the client's presenting concerns and the environments in which they occur. In Part II, the longest part of the book, we look at every basic angle of measurement.

- Connecting abstract guiding concepts to the concrete realities that make up a client's life by means of precise measurements or observations
- Drawing "moving pictures" of client events over time on graphs
- Finding the information we need to construct a viable plan of action, representing the evidence-based general practice
- Measuring specific individual concerns, possibly starting from structured logs surrounding these concerns
- Measuring the concrete behaviors, which we can observe
- Using standardized rating scales that have proven useful in similar problem situations, to compare our client against some known group
- Using qualitative information to inform us about the whole client in a complex environmental situation
- Recognizing the cautions we have to use in making sense of any information we collect

Each measurement helps to ensure that a client-centered evaluation of practice really reflects that client and our efforts to serve them as effectively as possible.

The Issues: Measurement Theory; Validity; Reliability; Error Messages; Sustainability

MEASUREMENT THEORY: CONNECTING CONCEPTS TO THE CLIENT'S REALITY

Practice involves helping clients to help themselves, solving problems, or attaining goals. As we argued in Chapter 2, **concepts** and **theories** help us make logical guesses about what is going on in our client's situation. They may or may not be fruitful ideas, as we shall see. Theories are translated into strategies for action in the real world, which is the crux of practice. In this chapter, we will show how to connect these conceptual materials to the real-world events in our client's life. In this way, we can test whether our conceptual musing leads to positive practical solutions to the client's concerns.

Let's return to Kat and Ben Washington (discussed first in Chapter 2). We suggested some hypotheses and a **local theory** about some of the events going on in their lives. Let's reexamine the first hypothesis or **proposition**:

> *Prolonged imbalance of earnings compared to expenses leads to psychological stresses that may affect the continued well-being or survival of a group. (Proposition 1)*

Now rearrange the parts of the hypothesis as follows:

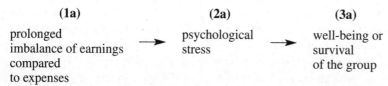

(1a)		(2a)		(3a)
prolonged imbalance of earnings compared to expenses	→	psychological stress	→	well-being or survival of the group

This conceptual mapping seems pretty abstract, and you are probably asking, how do we know about any of these things? Good question, the answer to which is to *connect (a) conceptual or theoretical terms to (c) events in the real world by means of (b) objective observations or measuring devices.* Here is a diagram of what we mean:

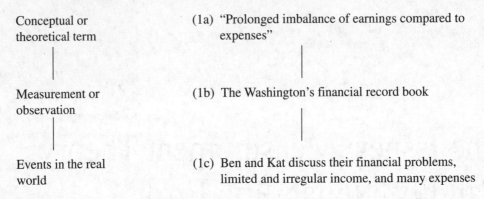

Conceptual or theoretical term

Measurement or observation

Events in the real world

(1a) "Prolonged imbalance of earnings compared to expenses"

(1b) The Washington's financial record book

(1c) Ben and Kat discuss their financial problems, limited and irregular income, and many expenses

The lines connecting each level (1a to 1b; 1b to 1c) represent some procedures that connect one to the other. This seems straightforward when it comes to considering the connections among income or expenses, financial record books, and discussions about not having enough money to cover expenses. But now consider the next concept.

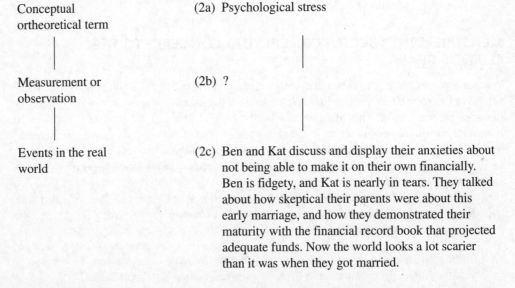

Conceptual ortheoretical term

Measurement or observation

Events in the real world

(2a) Psychological stress

(2b) ?

(2c) Ben and Kat discuss and display their anxieties about not being able to make it on their own financially. Ben is fidgety, and Kat is nearly in tears. They talked about how skeptical their parents were about this early marriage, and how they demonstrated their maturity with the financial record book that projected adequate funds. Now the world looks a lot scarier than it was when they got married.

You will notice that we did not enter a measurement device to indicate the extent of psychological stress on the couple. The simple observations of tears and fidgetiness somehow do not capture the full meaning of this concept, psychological stress. In fact, you may not be sure that you understand what stress means to them, and you would like to have some help from experts in this field on how to measure it—both to see if it exists in a problematic state as the couple suggests, and to understand how it changes over the course of the **intervention** period. (We will come back to this point in Chapter 5 on information retrieval.) And eventually, you will need some **objective**, like a measure of some manageable level of stress in their lives, as a benchmark to aim for in your intervention. This way, both you and the clients may agree that this is what they are seeking, and you all can tell when that manageable level is attained.

We will discuss various methods over the next few chapters on obtaining some approximation of that abstract concept, psychological stress. These methods will vary from the subjective and private to the objective and public. But all of them will supply certain vital information. What we see is that we go from an abstract concept (like prolonged imbalance of earnings compared to expenses) to the reality to which it refers (such as their records of wages, the various bills they have to pay, etc.) by going through some means of systematically and objectively observing the reality on the one hand, and then linking with the abstract world on the other hand. (In the Washingtons' case, it is the financial record book of income and expenses.) This middle-level observation or measurement connects both the abstract and the real. It provides the tools to give operational meaning to the concept ("prolonged imbalance . . .") and, at the same time, it directs us what to do in the real world—to look at their wage slips and bills by looking at the measurement tool, in this case the financial record book.

Thus, measurement and observation are vital tools for the practitioner, as well as the researcher or evaluator. Think of them as vital connections between your theoretical knowledge and what your eyes tell you about the client's life situation. Choose these connectors wisely, and they will serve you well.

In the following sections, we are going to discuss some basic ideas in measurement, what is true (validity), what is consistent (reliability), what may be wrong (measurement errors), and what holds up over time (sustainability of outcome). These are so basic that we really can't talk about evaluation without considering them.

VALIDITY

In dictionary language, *validity* means several things, from being well grounded—that is, there is something in reality that corresponds exactly to the statement about it—to being a conclusion that is logically derived from its premises, which is to say, a valid argument in logic. In the sciences and social sciences, we have a definition of validity that is at first glance simple and easy: some measure is valid if it measures what it is supposed to measure.

What is a measure supposed to measure? Unfortunately, that's the hard part of the scientific definition because the only way to know about anything in reality is to use some observation or measurement tool that assumes the reality that corresponds to our measurement of it. Let's explore this circular dilemma.

If we have a rating scale with the title "contentment," then presumably it is supposed to measure something about a person being contented to some degree ("not at all" to "very much"). But what if the creator of the scale is devious and has really designed that rating scale to measure the level of depression in a person. She may be using the fake title so as not to scare off a client who is feeling unhappy with his current state of affairs. (After all, "depression" sounds like a mental illness, and the client probably doesn't think he is that sick, just a little unhappy with his current experiences.) So, do not depend on the title of a measuring instrument to mean what it says; look at the content of the instrument to see what it intends to measure.

What if there are several instruments that assert they are each measuring "contentment," but all of them use different questions or look at different client behaviors, each in a different way? Are they all measuring the same thing, "contentment," or is each instrument measuring something different? Clearly they are measuring different things, but what are they measuring?

If you are thinking that validity is a difficult idea to pin down, you are correct. What scientists have done is to agree among themselves as to how measures are to be used—with caution, when using two or more instruments with the same title word, and in fact, when using any measuring instrument. It will be instructive to look at conventional ways to consider validity (see, e.g., Bloom, Fischer, & Orme, 2009; Greenstein, 2006; Wiersma & Jurs, 2009) because we will then be introducing something new.

Face Validity

Face validity means that, on the face of it, a measuring instrument appears to measure what it says it measures. Sometimes this is called faith validity because you are accepting a lot on faith. Yet, if an instrument doesn't appear to measure what it is supposed to be measure, the client might not feel comfortable about taking the test.

Content Validity

Any instrument contains a small sampling of all possible statements about the topic. But, is this sampling a reasonably accurate representation of the whole? There is no way of knowing this for sure, and this introduces error to the entire validity process. The best thing to do is to have a good *operational definition* of the *target* of the intervention, and then see if the specific items on the instrument tap into as many aspects of that definition as possible. This is called content validity.

Criterion Validity

If your measure of the target predicts to a person's performance on some defined outcome, this is called criterion validity, and it gives meaningfulness to your instrument. This can occur in two ways: First, concurrent validity means that a measure predicts a person's current performance. This can be done by giving or completing the measure and also having someone independently observe the behavior being measured. Could a high correlation (association) between them happen by chance? Yes, but it's not likely, especially if the measurement is repeated over time.

Or, you could use two measures concurrently, one a well-known and previously validated measure, and the second, your new measure, and then correlate the two. How do you know the well-known measure is itself valid? By correlating it against an even better known and previously validated measure, *ad infinitum*. In short, there is no real way for a measurement to be validated without scientists just saying that such and such an instrument is the criterion against which they are testing new measures. Why bother developing a new measure when a well-known and previously validated measure already exists? Good question. Maybe because the new one is shorter, easier to use, costs less to deliver, and so on. But even so, what if the correlation is low and the new measure is in reality more valid than the standard? Is there any real way of knowing? (Not by this route.)

The second form of criterion validity suggests a different route. Predictive validity refers to an instrument's ability to predict some future event. For example, if a measure of a serious level of "depression" predicted which people in a large group attempted suicide and which did not, then it would have predictive validity. After a measure was found to have this kind of predictive quality with a group of persons with a given characteristic, then it could be used to conduct preventive work with a completely different individual who shared similar characteristics with the group. We don't know if this correlation is true for the individual as it was for the group, but it may provide some guidance in dealing with this client. Then, the use of evaluation-informed specific practice with a specific client, using a strong evaluation design (see Chapter 14) can give us some confirmation on the usefulness of our practice decision.

Construct Validity

Construct validity is a traditional way to consider validity by linking scores on a measure or instrument to what a theory says is supposed to happen. This means that a numerical score is correlated with ideas in a conceptual network with regard to observable events: It is exhibiting what was supposed to be present (convergent validity) and/or not exhibiting what was not supposed to be present (divergent validity). To refer back to the previous discussion about a conceptual level linked to an observational or measurement level, construct validity means that the observation or measurement accurately reflects the concepts involved. The clearer the conceptual mapping and the measurement are, the easier it is to determine the construct validity. But there may be a number of relevant conceptual mappings and several measuring instruments purporting to measure the same thing. Which among these are the right theory and the right measuring instrument? It's hard to say.

Hiding behind all of these discussions of validity is the assumption that there is a reality "out there" that can correspond to however we want to measure it. For example, we assume that there is something out there called "depression" for which there are many different kinds of measures of depression. In fact, there may not be such a "thing" as depression—at least psychiatrists in different countries with different cultural contexts indicate very different proportions of people with this condition. However, it is reasonable to assume that such a condition should be normally distributed around the world, so that "depression" as a medical condition exists in the minds of the interpreters of symptoms in a given country, and not in "reality" as such. Likewise, not so many years ago there was such a thing as the "mental disease" of homosexuality, but it was voted out of existence (by a slender margin) by the professional psychiatric organization. So, what is the truth?

Client Validity

Perhaps the reason that predictive validity seems to be so useful in testing the truthfulness of an assertion is that it ultimately rests with the people and situations involved, and this leads us to consider one more—new—test of validity from the point of view of a client-centered evaluation (Bloom, 2010). We call this *client validity*. In the best-case scenario, you are working with an intelligent, cooperative client who is eager to resolve some challenge (problem, potential), which he or she has joined with you to address. How will you know whether the client has attained his or her *goal*? Ask the client. Actually, we will be suggesting in Chapter 12 that you ask this question twice, and gather objective information to confirm the client's answer. So client validity involves a major commitment on the part of the client and the practitioner, but it is the same commitment they formed when they agreed to work together to resolve some client concerns.

There are situations in which this version of client validity would not be as appropriate, such as with young children, persons with certain mental disorders, and under social circumstances (e.g., domestic violence) which might force a client to report things that are not true. We will address these kinds of issues in Chapter 10, because there are approximate solutions.

RELIABILITY

Reliability refers to the consistency of measurements of a given situation. The methods used to measure reliability are relatively easy, but there are some challenges involved. For example, two observers watching the same child behave in a classroom might report some of the same things and some different things, perhaps because of where they were standing or what they understood that they were supposed to be observing (i.e., different interpretations of their same directions given in terms of abstract concepts). Moreover, the same person may ask the exact same question of a client on two different occasions and get different answers. (After all, conditions may change in that client's life, and there is no reason that the client has to be or feel the exact same way.) And if the questioner asks a question twice in slightly different wordings to the same respondent, there may be different answers. Maybe the client didn't understand a term being used, so the interviewer rewords it for clarity. Again, there may be different answers.

All reliability measures should be as independent as possible (so that one measurement doesn't influence the other measurement—think unkindly of two "independent" observers who are peeking at each other's scoring of the same child).

Interobserver Reliability

This is the major form of reliability that is possible in single-system designs. (We'll talk more about *single-system designs* [SSDs] in Chapters 12 and 13, but for now think of them as methods of continually observing some target before, during, and sometimes after an intervention, so as to compare logically the differences among them.) It involves two trained observers independently rating the same person using the same form at the same time, and afterwards comparing for equivalent judgments. If the correlation is very high (e.g., over 90% on a defined behavior or scale), then we can be reasonably confident that they are using the ratings in a consistent way (Friman, 2009). To calculate interobserver reliability, divide the number of agreements by the number of agreements and disagreements (and multiply the result by 100 to calculate the percentage). Consider the following example.

In a study of cooperative behavior in a nursery school, two observers were watching the same child for the same period of time using the same instrument (a checklist of when a cooperative behavior occurred). They also wrote a brief note as to what occurred. Afterward, the two observers sat down and compared forms. Let's say there were 20 observation intervals (of 10 seconds each beginning when the second hand was on 12 and again when it was on 6), and the observers either checked once in that interval on the form if some cooperative behavior was observed or left it blank if none was observed. They had a moment to write a note if needed. This means that the two observers could agree on: (1) the number of intervals during which cooperative behavior was observed, and (2) the number of intervals during which cooperative behavior was not observed. But (3) they also could disagree on a given interval, if one observer saw a cooperative behavior and the other observer did not. So, instances of (1) and (2) are counted as agreements, and instances of (3) are counted as disagreements, in the following formula:

$$\frac{\text{Agreements}}{\text{Agreements} + \text{Disagreements}}$$

Let's put in some numbers here: Let's say both observers saw 6 occasions when cooperative behavior was exhibited, and 9 occasions when it was not. However, one or the other saw cooperative behavior (when the other observer did not) on 5 occasions. How did they do?

$$\frac{6+9}{6+9+5} = \frac{15}{20} = .75 = 75\% \text{ Reliability score}$$

This score might be adequate for short time periods, while it would be very good for longer ones (Hunsley & Mash, 2008). It would also suggest that the observers needed more training sessions to get better consistency in observing and in the operational meaning of the questions (Chesebrough, King, Gullotta, & Bloom, 2004).

There are several other forms of reliability, and we will mention them briefly, and ask readers to go back to their statistics books for the details of their use.

Test-Retest Reliability

Test-retest reliability refers to measuring the same client with the same measure under the same circumstances on two different occasions. Actually, it really means approximating these "same" things, which are impossible to duplicate exactly, but the degree of difference from the original means that the results are to that degree less reliable.

Alternate-Forms Reliability

In alternate-forms reliability testing, we use different forms or different questions that we believe to have been constructed using the same specifications, such as the same content areas tapped, the same length of question, comparable instructions for use, same time allotted, and so on. A high correlation between these two sets of forms probably means that clients are responding in the same way to both sets—even though the questions are entirely different. Then we can use one form at one time, the other form at another time, and hope that the resulting answers are reliable. Do we ever know this for certain? Probably not without a lot of experimental testing of forms, but again we take a lot on faith when it comes to science.

Internal Consistency

Imagine a long scale with many items. It is theoretically possible to locate sets of different items on that scale on which respondents answer in the same way. Such sets would demonstrate an internal consistency form of reliability. In this way, you have alternate forms without having to construct two different sets of questions from scratch. You can use such devices when looking at odd and even questions. Or you can perform what is called the Coefficient alpha (or Cronbach's alpha) or the KR-20 statistics—the average intercorrelation among items weighted by the number of items. See any statistics book for details on these procedures.

ERROR MESSAGES IN MEASUREMENT

There are, unfortunately, several types of errors in measuring anything. One type is called random measurement errors, such as when one client interprets the wording of a question in one way, while another client interprets the wording differently, even though they actually have the same opinion. The clearer our questions are, the fewer times we should encounter this kind of error.

The second type is called systematic measurement errors, which happen consistently in a particular way that influences the measure. For example, you ask a person to take a standardized scale measure of depression, and she does so just before bedtime; it may be that this is when she is most unhappy and thus scores unusually high on the scale. In contrast, if you and she could figure out how to take measures of her feelings at random times —like when a programmed wrist alarm or mobile device like a cell phone prompts her at a random time during the day to fill out the scale—the emerging pattern would probably more nearly resemble her actual feeling state. A systematic error, reading a problem as larger or smaller than it really is, affects both the baseline phase as well as the intervention phase, which can lead to practice decisions based on erroneous information.

Dealing with these kinds of errors is difficult to do, and you have to be continually vigilant to make sure you don't accidentally fall into these traps. The same considerations apply to any questions you ask clients: Be as clear as possible in your questions, try to get representative information, and obtain independent confirmation when possible.

TIME AND SUSTAINABILITY

From the perspective of client-centered evaluation of practice, it is essential that the client not only be able to negotiate his or her own satisfactory intervention—that's the *maintenance (M phase)* idea—but that this successful venture must be maintained for a sufficient time so that the helping professional and the client may feel confident that it will remain successful thereafter. This raises the difficult question of how long is long enough to be confident that the successful change is permanent (or relatively permanent)?

We wish we could give you a simple answer, but there are no commonly agreed upon rules for this game. We will make a commonsense suggestion, on the basis of thin air and not much else. Take the length of time of the intervention (B) phase, in which the practitioner and client have negotiated a successful outcome. It can become a Smoot unit of measure. Oliver Smoot was an MIT student. In 1962, when his fraternity brothers used him as a unit of measure, end over 5′7″ end, to measure the length of the bridge over the Charles River, the results showed 364.4 Smoots, plus or minus an ear (error factor).

In any case, the B phase becomes a kind of Smoot unit of measure for how long you might keep in touch with your client in the M phase, when the client is negotiating his or her own intervention. In ordinary situations of family disputes, and the like, one B time length in the maintenance phase may be enough. If the situation is serious and threatens the stability of a group, then consider two B time lengths. If the situation is life threatening, then three B time units may be enough for the formal maintenance phase, but you also might want to have some significant other keep tabs on the client—maybe forever.

Chapter Summary

Your practice will include generous amounts of the events clients are experiencing as problems or potentials. You will have received lots of ideas about those problems and potentials in your theory and methods classes. And in this chapter, we talked about ways of trying to connect the events of everyday life to the abstract concepts (and ultimately, to the empirical evidence these concepts generate) so as to be guided in your practice. For example, let's say a client tells you that she feels unable to ask her boss for a justified raise in pay. You might consider where else such an inability emerges, by generalizing that one fact to other similar situations: is she able to ask for what she wants from friends or family as opposed to doing what they want her to do? It sounds as if she is not assertive on her own behalf. This category term is probably a concept (assertiveness)—and there you are, a whole vista opens up about related problems and possible solutions. As more facts come in, the web of concepts may grow. You can make sense of this flood of information through the use of general concepts; they subsume many life instances. Check out the information retrieval devices and see what others have done (successfully) to address this kind of issue. Then individualize this information to fit your specific client, and go to work.

Graphing: The Basics; Exceptions to the Rules

Case Study

Rick Alverez and His "Walking Support Group"

To his Anglo classmates at school, he was known as Al (short for Alverez), a very shy Hispanic youth who was always near the bottom of the class in every subject. To his parents, he was known as Ricardo, a stubborn youth who was the source of yet another generation of problems because he was skipping school, just as his three older brothers had done before they dropped out—or were pushed out. To his friends, he was Rick, a lively, talkative youth, full of energy and determination. You were about to meet him in person, along with his family at your social agency.

The agency had long known the Alverez family. The five children (Rick has a younger sister in addition to his three older brothers) had been in summer camps for years, and recently, Mrs. Alverez came to a series of free workshops on "ordinary family concerns" such as how to discipline children, how to talk to teenagers about sex and drugs, and other pertinent topics. She enjoyed the discipline workshop very much and tried to convince her husband to join her, to no avail. Mr. Alverez has a job as foreman of the city sanitation crews, and makes a reasonable wage, but with his large family, it is still a struggle. He blames Ricardo for his own troubles at school, just as he had blamed his older sons.

Then the family received notice from the school truancy officer obliging them to meet with him and to get help from the local family service agency about possible issues causing this situation. So, the Alverez family came unwillingly to your office, the parents talking rapidly in Spanish between themselves, the son saying nothing at all. Your year of college Spanish didn't quite extend to everything they were saying.

(continued)

You welcomed them into your office and asked them to sit down. There was an arc of six chairs and a small coffee table in the middle. Mrs. Alverez sat next to her husband, Ricardo sat as far away as possible, and you sat in between them. You begin by recognizing that it is difficult to come to a social agency with this concern, but you needed to hear more about it in order to try to help them help themselves. Mrs. Alverez started talking about Ricardo in relationship to his three older brothers who had also had school dropout problems and . . . but here she was interrupted by Mr. Alverez speaking rapidly in Spanish, and Mrs. Alverez stopped talking.

You wait a moment. Silence. Then you thought it better to change the topic and you address Ricardo, asking how things are going at school. "Fine." Does he have any special concerns with teachers or other students? "No." He is staring at his shoes. His mumbled monosyllabic answers infuriated Mr. Alverez, who launched into a lecture of his son's stubbornness and the futility of this meeting. More silence.

Then you ask the parents about Ricardo's grades. Mrs. Alverez reports "below average, but his test scores show he should be doing much better." Then you ask Ricardo about his goals in life; does he have any ideas about a career? "No, never thought about it much"—and here Ricardo looked at his father for the first time—"except I am going to do well for myself." Mr. Alverez gave him a withering glance and turned his chair and stared out the window. You thought you just saw the premature end of this case, in which family problems seemed to be at the heart of Ricardo's school troubles. So, gathering up courage, you suggest that you would like to meet with Ricardo alone and with the parents alone in later sessions, and much to your surprise, they all agreed.

A week later you met with Ricardo, and after a lot of very short answers and careful study of the floor, he finally enters into the flow of conversation. "Hey, call me Rick, OK? Like my friends do."

So Rick began his side of the story that started when his older brothers received the same kind of attack from their father. One by one they eventually dropped out of school to get a job and be away from the family. One brother had even had a mental breakdown, which scared Rick considerably. School really wasn't that bad, Rick reported, although he got hassled a lot. "By whom?" you ask. A moment of silence. "By Anglos." You (an Anglo, let us say) nod your understanding, and Rick continued. Some of his Hispanic peers were too busy trying to stay afloat, and of the friends he did have, many had dropped out already. Rick was thinking this might be the easiest path to follow.

You ask how his other friends were managing to stick it out at school. He said they all had career aspirations; he did, too, he added. "What plans?" you ask, and Rick's answer was rather vague. However, it was the major topic when he talked (endlessly, until his parents objected) on his cell phone with his friends. But Rick noticed that his friends didn't seem to get upset the way he did.

You wonder out loud to Rick: It might be helpful to invite his friends to the agency to talk about these things, how they manage not to get upset; it might lead to some specific ideas on how to get Rick through school, too. Maybe? Rick is silent for a while, then nods yes, and finally brightens up. "Yes," he said, "yes."

Another week passes, and you hear the loud joking and carrying on by the three teenagers before they get to your office. They enter, wrap themselves around the furniture, dig into the potato chips and bottles of water you provided, and then they become awkwardly silent. Your move.

By prior consent, you discussed briefly the reason for the visit, to help Rick prevail at school, not simply stick it out. You mention some of the family issues, because Rick had been discussing them with the other two—Mario and Freddy (Fernaldo)—for months. The boys nod in understanding, and then mull over the question, how to help Rick get through school and make the best of it. After some false starts—Mario suggested dragging Rick to school, and so on—you begin to think you had lost this battle. But then Freddy gets a good suggestion going, of arranging to meet at Rick's house to walk to school together, and then eat lunch together (when possible), and then walk home together to talk about the day's events (although that was not totally possible, as Mario had a job). You compliment the boys on the ideas and suggest that they keep a record of how it goes. In fact, you sketch a kind of log book in which Rick records who goes with him to school and what happens on the way there and back. The boys look interested in the log book. Mario says "now we'll have to deliver, because it is going to be written down." You said you would call them on Sundays to remind them as well. When the session ended, the trio marched out in triumph.

GRAPHING BASICS: THE RULES

We'll leave Rick and his friends at this point, although we'll come back to see how things are going throughout this chapter. We want to discuss graphing, the topic of this section, using Rick's information. Essentially, we want to know what's happening, that is, whether each of the *targets* are moving in a desired direction and the overall effect on Rick, his progress in school, his family, and his friends. We will build on what you read in Chapter 1 (Section D: "data collection and plotting data on graphs").

For simplicity, we will construct three graphs in detail, and refer to different portions of the graphs in order to illustrate the basics, what goes into a comprehensive graph, and how it can be used in practice. (See Figures 4.1, 4.2, 4.3, and a summary Figure 4.4.)

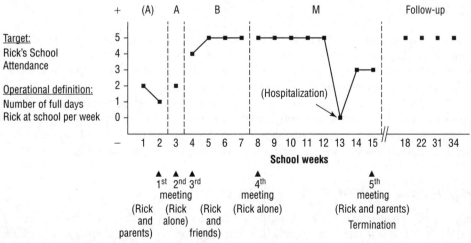

FIGURE 4.1 Rick's school attendance (hypothetical data)

Rule 1: Draw a Graph with Horizontal and Vertical Axes

Leave a small space between the end of the vertical axis and the beginning of the horizontal axis so that putting data points on that bottom line will be clearly visible. Put equal time intervals, as relevant to the situation (e.g., hours, days, weeks) on the horizontal axis. Put equal target intervals on the vertical line as relevant to the situation (e.g., percentages 0–100%; proportions .00 to 1.00; actual numbers indicating frequency of the occurrence of that target; or whatever might be relevant).

Rule 2: Labeling the Graph

Target #1 is labeled by its named *concept* (e.g., school attendance) and its *operational definition* (e.g., number of days Rick attends school the whole day during a given school week). Because there are 5 days of school, then the numbers on the vertical axis will run from 0 times attendance to 5 times attendance. It is critical that a + be placed on the end of the vertical axis indicating the desired end; in this case, attending school for 5 days is desired (by the powers that be, even if not in Rick's eyes).

Next, label the top of the graph by its phases, or periods of time in which one kind of activity occurs. The basic phases are *baseline A phase* (observation only); the *intervention B phase* (or C or D, etc., if other distinctive interventions are used); and, a *maintenance M phase* (when, after appropriate training, the client is essentially carrying out the successful intervention entirely on his or her own). It may be useful to distinguish a training phase in the intervention period because it may take some training for the client to get up to full speed in using the intervention, and we might expect initial intervention scores that are still like baseline data. In some cases, a *follow-up phase* might be used, during which time random call backs by the practitioner are used to see how the client is doing on his or her own. Note the break in the time line with follow-ups because the time intervals will not likely be the same as those used in the intervention period.

The phases are distinguished by a vertical construction line between them, but be careful not to put that construction line on top of any time unit (because then we could not tell whether that time unit fell into the A or B phase). Similarly, a construction line separates the intervention phase from the maintenance phase. It may be useful to add a construction line between the training period and the full-blown intervention.

Rule 3: Adding Data Points to the Graph

As in any graphing, a dot is placed at the intersection between some time unit and some degree or amount of the target condition at that time. For instance, in week 3 (before the intervention started), Rick attended school only two times. So we put a dot at 2 in week 3. On week 12 during the intervention, he attended all five days; here is a 5 at week 12.

There are several additional points on placing these dots. First, be careful and accurate; use graph paper with lines (or use a simple graphing program on your computer). A little care now will save a lot of headaches later. Add data on a continuous basis (for 5 school days, so that time units 6 through 10 represents the second week of school, skipping the weekend days).

GRAPHING EXCEPTIONS TO THE RULE

Unfortunately, clients are not as predictable as case examples in textbooks that present nice, neat data. So, be prepared to deal with exceptions to the rules, which is to say, keep as close to the spirit of the rules as possible while using as much of the relevant information as possible. Be creative but have good reasons for changes you make in the rules. (After all, rules are created so that everyone will have a level playing field in understanding each other.)

Missing data: Sometimes you won't get a continuous record on the client's targeted behaviors. Things go wrong. If only a few data points are missing from the record book (e.g., Rick was sick two days, represented as a 3 rather than 5 days attending school on the 14th week), you can use the whole data set, and recognize that this 3 is a reasonable exception to the higher scores he had been getting. If you collect enough data points, one or two exceptions won't harm the whole pattern; but if you have only a small number, then those exceptions will be harmful to your analysis. Use your judgment, but err on the cautious side.

If many days are missing, or if the record is spotty, or if one day is consistently missing for each of several weeks, then you have another problem on your hands. Something is going on, and it is hard to account for what's happening. Maybe Rick was in the hospital for four days and kept at home for the fifth day. Maybe Rick has to care for his younger sister on Mondays when his parents are at work, because no one else is available. Or maybe Rick is cutting classes. Unless you know for sure, it may be best not to use these data and instead to start over again.

USING GRAPHS TO MONITOR DATA AND INTERPRET OUTCOMES

We now present a finished set of graphs reflecting events in Rick's life. First, we previously introduced the plotting of data on school attendance in Figure 4.1. Second, we'll use another graph on Rick's grades (Figure 4.2) and go over the interpretations of data on an ongoing basis, just like the practitioner would do when receiving this information weekly. Third, we'll discuss a more complex graph, on self-efficacy (Figure 4.3). Finally, we'll look at these three graphs at the same time, because they all refer to the same time period for the same person in the same circumstances. We can ask, how do events related to one target change in relation to events in some other targets (Figure 4.4)? Reading multiple graphs gets a little complicated, but is very interesting because there may be several ways to interpret the same package of graphs, resulting in several ways of acting on this information with the client.

Back to the second target, Rick's grades (Figure 4.2). Just to make life easier, let's say that this graph contains the weekly averages of all of Rick's grades in various subjects. (Imagine that you did the footwork necessary to obtain all of this information by teachers' permission, and averaged it, using the typical 4.0 grade point system in which A = 4.0, B = 3.0, C = 2.0, D = 1.0, and F = 0. You record the baseline information, and then obtain weekly information from

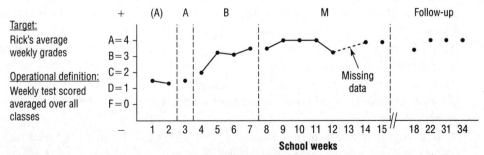

FIGURE 4.2 Rick's average weekly grades (hypothetical data)

the teachers' grade books with their permission and perhaps the coordinating assistance of Rick's school guidance counselor.)

Instead of looking at the whole graph all at once, cover up the right-hand side and move that cover one week at a time, which is like what would happen in real life, if you were collecting data weekly. Each time, we will ask the same question: What did you observe about Rick's grades, as of this week? This means an accumulating picture of grades, starting with two weeks of baseline in which we reconstructed Rick's grades, indicated by the reconstructed baseline symbol (A), instead of the symbol A which is used for baseline data collected concurrently. Each week of intervention is indicated, as usual, by a B. Ready? Here goes:

Week 1 (reconstructed baseline): grade average of 1.4 out of 4.0. which is something like a D+. Not very good, especially for a guy who is supposed to be quite bright (on confidential intelligence tests).

Week 2 (reconstructed baseline): grade average of 1.2. Thought it couldn't get much worse from Week 1? Think again. So, what you have is a reconstructed baseline (from his teachers' grade books—a highly reliable source) of a young man in a lot of academic trouble. Rick says this is fairly typical of his grades for the past year.

Week 3 (baseline): Rick averages 1.6.

Week 4 (intervention): Rick averages 2.0. Rick says this is his highest set of grades since he can remember. This is somewhat encouraging news, but the grades are still low. You mention this to Mario and Freddy in your weekly Sunday calls to remind them to walk to school with Rick. Are you worried about the strength of your intervention? Thinking of any changes?

Week 5 (intervention): Rick averages 3.4, or a B+. You ask the teachers to check again. Can this be so? Yes, it is. Rick has a big smile as he comes to see you for his weekly meeting. What are you thinking about in connection with these grades?

Week 6 (intervention): Rick averages 3.2. He says one test was very tricky, and he didn't do as well as he should have. We have to expect some ups and downs in average scores, and this is still pretty good, given Rick's extensive record of poor grades.

We are going to intervene at this point, for heuristic purposes: Let's say that at this meeting, you introduce the maintenance phase in which Rick performs the same intervention that the practitioner did. That is, Rick will call his friends as reminders. The same record keeping is maintained. Do you think Rick is ready for this?

Week 9 (maintenance phase): Rick averages 3.8, which is close to an A-level across all of his classes. Everyone involved is getting very interested in his rapid improvement: teachers, friends, classmates (who more or less ignored him up to this time), and parents. What do you think is going on with these grades? Or in Rick's life?

Week 11 (maintenance phase): Rick again averages 3.8. No change. Still excellent. What can this mean?

Week 14 (maintenance phase): Rick gets a straight A average in all of his classes, 4.0. Cheers all around. The teachers are amazed and tell you so. One says she always knew he could do it. You smile.

Week 15 (last maintenance phase): Rick repeats his 4.0 average. It is not a fluke. He really is doing well at school, and says how much he likes it.

Again, we are going to intervene in this story: You terminate this part of the service, and suggest that you'll check in every now and then to hear how it is going. Rick nods in agreement, and leaves whistling.

> Week 18 (first follow-up call): Rick reports his grade average is 3.6, quite good, but he hasn't been feeling too well lately and maybe that is making him less effective. He doesn't know. What do you think? Will Rick maintain his high grade point average?

> Week 22 (second follow-up call): Rick reports a 4.0 grade average. You compliment him on his successes. Are you sure this good news will last?

> Week 31 (third follow-up call): Rick reports another 4.0 grade average, with a false "coolness," but you can tell he is bursting with pride. Keep going, Rick.

> Week 34 (last follow-up call): Rick reports a grade average of 3.8 with a touch of embarrassment, but he is confident in himself like he has never been before, and he is ready for the next level of schooling. You wish him well for a bright future.

OK, that's how it happened, week by week. Now let's look at the graph in Figure 4.2 again and ask what you knew (about how things were going) and when you knew it. Grade averages were going up slightly in weeks 3 and 4, but really took off in weeks 5 and 6. Probably at that time, you knew something important was happening, so in week 6 you asked Rick, were these cumulative grades attaining his goal? He replied that they were greatly improving and he was happy about that, but they still weren't as good as he wanted. That was enough of a positive reply to have you terminate your part of the intervention, and turn over the whole show to Rick—as he would have to do eventually. He was happy to be in charge of his own life with regard to this target.

You were following events in Rick's life by receiving and plotting data in weeks 7–10, and you knew these were important changes. You asked Rick in the 10th week whether this grade pattern attained the goals he wanted, and he answered, "yes!" with great enthusiasm. You probably would not have bothered with follow-up phone calls, except that your research class instructor insisted—and, secretly, you were excited to hear his continuing good news.

Next, let's turn to Figure 4.3, on self-efficacy. What is self-efficacy? It is a concept based on Albert Bandura's cognitive-behavioral theory (e.g., Bandura, 1986). Briefly put, this general theory suggests that a person needs information, skills, and motivation in order to perform some action (like work diligently on his class assignments), but one more factor is needed above all: self-efficacy, the belief that one can in fact do this particular task successfully. The teachers supplied all the information and skills needed, and the "walking support group" reinforced Rick's own motivations to get ahead in a good career. But only Rick could develop his self-efficacy, and this is what the practitioner was trying to augment in discussions with Rick.

Bandura's theory suggests several ways to do this: First, you could engage the client in some small aspect of the whole and show him or her that this aspect could be performed successfully. The more mastery the client shows, the more his or her self-efficacy grows. Second, Bandura suggests pointing to successful efforts by similar people (such as Rick's peers who are showing mastery in related topics, using methods that are known to Rick; in this way, Rick comes to believe that he can do what they are doing). A third and much less powerful method is to tell Rick that he is smart and that he can do it. Pep talks apparently don't last long. A fourth

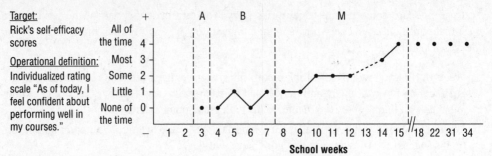

FIGURE 4.3   Rick's individualized rating scale scores on self-efficacy

way involves reducing tensions that prevent the performance of some task by physiological means, like taking a deep breath before starting an exam.

In talking with Rick, you realized that he had little confidence in himself as being able to master the school work, in spite of his good scores on intelligence tests. That is, he had low self-efficacy. You planned a method of working with him on simple school tasks that were parts of larger ones and showed how he was, in fact, mastering them. The results of your work with Rick are shown in Figure 4.3, using a five-point constructed scale where his confidence ranged from 0 = none of the time to 4 = all of the time. Rick and you worked out these anchoring terms, intending them to be equal steps apart. And he reported his feelings of self-efficacy by phone to you once a week, averaging the self-efficacy of each school day. (We'll discuss these kinds of scales in Chapter 6.)

What do you see in Figure 4.3? Rick is slow to warm up to the idea that he can, indeed, master his schoolwork successfully, even when he is seeing pretty good grades. "Just luck," he says and remains glum for a few more weeks. Eventually, his good grades take effect, and he realizes that he can do the assignments quite well. He gets some appreciative comments from his teachers, and, amazingly, from classmates. Once this sinks in, he remains very high on self-efficacy.

Now, let's do something that is quite amazing. Let's look at all three graphs at once, which is like reading a score of music in which many instruments combine into one melody (in Figure 4.4). What can we glean from the three of them all together? Attending school does not seem to be the real problem, as the presence of his friends walking to school seems to be a simple and inexpensive solution. At the same time, his average grades are creeping up over the term, until he becomes one of the top scholars in the class, much to the surprise of everyone, including Rick. This latter point is borne out in Rick's persistent low self-efficacy, a question about his belief in his own ability to perform well, even with a lot of contrary evidence at hand. Eventually, he recognizes what he has done, and he gains an invaluable ingredient of thinking that he can perform very well on these class tests. Different instruments may start to play at different times, even as the whole melody comes together.

Everything looks great, but then this is a made-up example for a textbook, and would you expect anything less? But we do hope that the graphing approach makes sense to you.

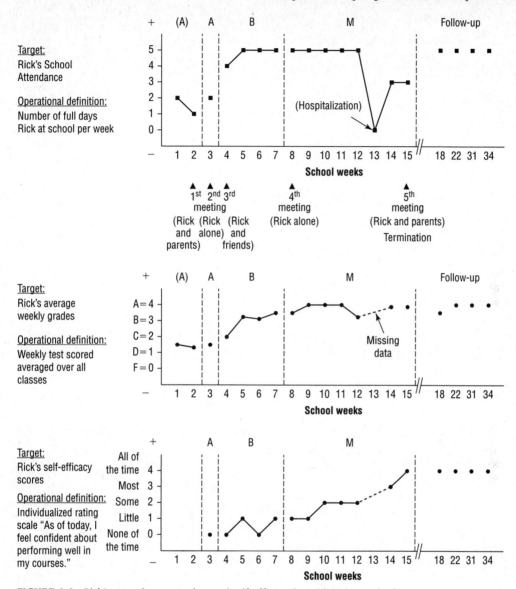

FIGURE 4.4   Rick's attendance, grades, and self-efficacy (considered together)

Chapter Summary

Look back at Figure 4.1, and see if you can identify all of the parts of the graph and how they fit together as you are intervening in the case. This is the best summary of the chapter.

Information Retrieval: Finding General Evidence-Based Practice Information

Case Study

Finding Information on Self-Efficacy for Rick Alverez

An infamous bank robber was once asked why he always robbed banks, and he replied, "that's where the money is." So, when we suggest that you go through your university or college library, it is because that is where the knowledge is that you need for any specific case. Libraries have direct and indirect access to the entire world of information. These days, it is also true that you can connect with your library—or another library or Web of libraries— at home or at the café with your trusty laptop computer. That little box in front of you gives you access to essentially every piece of information you ever might need.

A helping professional has to understand the concerns facing the client *and* the context in which these concerns occur. We must ask questions about these concerns and contexts in order to understand the client and how to help him or her. Initially, the helping professional's question is a fishing expedition: "What concerns bring you here today?" This kind of question either lets the client define the territory or context where his or her concerns are located, or allows the client to go directly into the concern itself.

You are likely not the first helping professional to tackle a given client issue, so tapping into the knowledge base of researchers and practitioners will lead you to evidence-based practices, or at least help you find promising approaches and avoid ones that that have failed in the past. To help your client, you may want to retrieve information about engaging

(continued)

clients, reviewing what techniques have been successful with clients like your own, whether there is a good measure (validated, easy, and freely accessible) of the behavioral outcome your client wants to change, and so on. Indeed, there are many questions in each case that could be informed by a search of the right databases. All you have to do is search using the right questions in the right order.

This chapter will focus on these questions and some possible answers. We will do this in two parts: First, we will stroll through *information space*, in connection with the Rick Alverez case from Chapter 4. We will demonstrate our smart strategies to find specific answers to questions, while mentioning some of our not-so-brilliant stumbles along the way. Finding the exact information you need is not always easy; it takes practice. Second, we will summarize the more successful strategies (and suggest how to avoid things that tripped us up). All of this is to set the stage for you to go to your professional librarian and practice learning how to use the most current tools available to you.

Let's start the stroll with a few helpful terms: Information space is simply the domain in which the information you are seeking exists—if it exists at all. Information space contains concepts or ideas; the physical objects like books and journals are simply the containers of those ideas. To find concepts in information space, we have three tools: (1) the right words to use—this is where a thesaurus of key words for a given field of study is most helpful; (2) the right *kinds* of words—this refers to levels of abstractness (for which a thesaurus might also be helpful); and (3) the right way of combining words; for this bit of magic, we will employ Venn Diagrams—those overlapping circles by which you can include some combinations of terms while excluding others.

The first step is to find the right words to use in an information search. It is likely that you will begin your information search using a common or lay person's language that you share with clients, which is fine. Always communicate with your clients in words they can understand. However, when you begin your search for evidence-based practices, you will need to use terms that scientists have used in similar circumstances. Fortunately, there are tools, for example, the *Thesaurus of Psychological Index Terms* (American Psychological Association, 2007, with even more recent updates online at http://www.apa.org/pubs/books/3100084.aspx), that translate your lay language terms into the concepts used in the scientific literature. The *index term* is the concept under which all of the related terms are included and where the information you seek is to be found. For example, the index term, SELF-CONCEPT, is used for a variety of other terms, such as ideal self, identity, and self-image.

This APA thesaurus is well structured for our purposes because it also defines terms at a lower or higher level of abstraction, as well as related concepts at the same level of abstraction. For example, a narrower or less-abstract term for the index term SELF-CONCEPT would include self-esteem. Likewise, if you started with a term like self-esteem or self-respect, then the broader and more abstract term would be SELF-CONCEPT. The idea is like the genus-species hierarchical relationship from biology.

Once you have your client-relevant concepts that are also used in the scientific literature, then you begin your actual search for specific information. You can find the exact area for what you need by keeping in mind Venn Diagrams, those overlapping circles, each of which names a distinctive concept (see Figure 5.1). Circle A (self-concept) overlaps with circle B (academics), and the overlapping portion contains materials relevant to both A and B (that is, the part of self-concept that is involved in that person's academic situation). If you

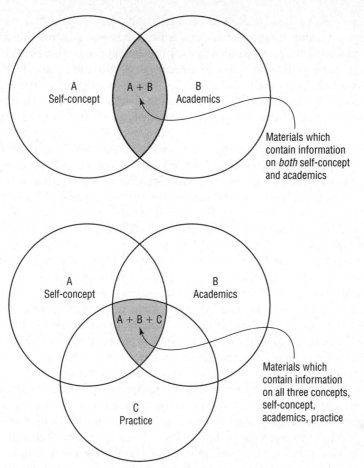

FIGURE 5.1   Illustrations of Venn Diagrams

need only A and B materials, then it is useful to exclude A-only and B-only materials. The general rule is that adding (or subtracting) concepts (e.g., A + B + C – D) to your search question will give you more specifically relevant information, namely those materials that only discuss A combined with B combined with C, while excluding D and everything else that does not involve all three concepts.

Search programs vary in the mechanisms they use for locating specific information, but many databases (especially the library subscription ones, like psycINFO) use Boolean terms: "or" for the "+" or the adding of circles; "not" for the "–" or exclusion of circles; "and" to get at the intersection or overlap of circles. So, in a database that uses Boolean logic, if you wanted literature that addressed both A and B together, you would search "self-concept" AND "academics." Other search programs (especially the free open-access ones, like Google) return the most relevant items first, so you should order your search terms in the order of centrality to your client question; the Boolean and, or, and not terms aren't used in these programs. In our example, that might be: self-concept, academics, and then maybe other terms like evidence, intervention, practice, or the like.

(continued)

Now, let's go back to the Rick Alverez case. We chose to consider "self-efficacy" because it is an important term, and it may not be familiar to you as a practitioner. You probably encountered the concept in your introductory psychology classes, but now the question is to *use* the term to guide practice. What we are going to do is to run a search on this term and report what we found, successes and failures. There is no one right way to search for information, but as we discovered, there are plenty of ineffectual search paths. Here is our *search question*: How can self-efficacy be used to guide practice with Rick Alverez and his school problem?

We started with Google, that huge search engine, which can locate an incredible number of things. (Other search engines like Bing or Yahoo! would work the same way, and each of these engines has its advantages and disadvantages.) We innocently typed in "self-efficacy" and found 3,350,000 hits and about half that number of advertisements. We quickly turned to Google Scholar, which filters out everything except scientific information. When we typed in the search term "self-efficacy," we found merely 506,000 hits (as of the day of this search; numbers change continuously). (Google Scholar is free and available to anyone with an Internet connection; it includes more sources than the scholarly databases, and it delivers many free, full-text resources. This free access may be relevant to practitioners who can't access some of the subscription databases we will discuss in the chapter.)

Obviously, these are far too many to search through, but as long as we were there, we looked at the first page of listings, and found citations to several classic items by Albert Bandura, the creator of this concept. If you don't know much about the term, it would be worth reading some of these—from one-page capsule versions to Bandura's definitive book, *Social foundations of thought and action: A social cognitive theory* (1986).

However, we stuck to our task of retrieving information about using the self-efficacy concept in practice; this is a vital point, as one can easily get drowned in a sea of interesting information. We found some recent citations very closely related to the case of Rick and his academic problems. Imagine Venn circles with these labels: A = self-efficacy, B = academic concerns, and C = practice. Now, look for articles with the overlap of A + B + C, which should be just what you are targeting. Some of the articles we found are here:

Bandura, A., Barbaranelli, C., Caprara, G. V., & Pastorelli, C. (1996). Multifaceted impact of self-efficacy beliefs on academic functioning. *Child Development, 67,* 1206–1222.

Bandura, A., Barbaranelli, C., Caprara, G. V., & Pastorelli, C. (2001). Self-efficacy beliefs as shapers of children's aspirations and career trajectories. *Child Development, 72,* 187–206.

Notice that our specific search terms are not the same as in the actual titles. We wanted the "*effects* of self-efficacy on academics," and we found "self-efficacy beliefs as *shapers* . . ." and "Multifaceted *impact* of self-efficacy beliefs. . . ." We had to carefully read these titles in order to recognize how close they were to our combined search terms. In a word, we had to be very sensitive to synonyms. (Wouldn't your eighth grade English teacher be proud of you now?) With Bandura mentioned among the authors, we were extra sure the papers would be relevant to our search.

By the way, some articles can be read on and/or downloaded to your computer, whereas others cannot be (without paying a fee). If you can't access a full-text article that appears relevant, free of charge, your librarian will help you discover what articles are available to you at your school or agency. We recorded these citations accurately because we knew we would be using them to look up the articles in the library and to write this chapter citing them. Take the time to do this, and you won't waste time retracing your steps to relocate the citation when you need it.

OK, back to the search. Let's say that with some half million Google Scholar hits, we thought we might do better than the above citations, to give us step-by-step directions to apply the self-efficacy idea to our practice. So, instead of merely thinking about combined terms A + B + C, we actually typed in those terms in the second search attempt— just the words, no quotation marks, separated by commas. (Each information retrieval tool has its own rules for how to retrieve information correctly. Read the instructions carefully, and then practice. You will get more comfortable, more accurate, and faster over time.) The question was more refined, and we knew this would be sharply limiting the numbers of hits. Yet any one hit should be right on the mark—a point to consider as you frame your search questions.

Here are the key terms for our second search: self-efficacy, practice, academic. This brought us to a Banduran website with all kinds of information about the concept and related matters including some interactive links. For example, one heading screamed: "Not sure what self-efficacy is?" And it led the viewer to some brief basic questions and answers. There were many current articles, including some of the development of academic self-efficacy that would be worth checking. For example:

Alfassi, M. (2003). Promoting the will and skill of students at academic risk: An evaluation of an instructional design geared to foster achievement, self-efficacy, and motivation. *Journal of Instructional Psychology, 30*, 28–40.

For us, this turns out to be a free full-text article, in contrast to the teasers shown on other Web sites, usually an abstract and a first page (only), which is where many of these citations lead. The evidence from this Alfassi paper supports the effectiveness of the structured environment program, which may give you some ideas to adapt as you construct your intervention plans for Rick.

We were not satisfied with this article in the sense that it did not offer any specific proposals for action with a client. So we checked into the Cochrane Collaboration (www.cochrane.org), an international not-for-profit organization that has reviews of studies on health care "in plain language." There are subcategories on various health areas, and ways to search for specific topics. We clicked onto Search and Browse (among many options) and entered the search terms, self-efficacy, practice, academic, which turned out to be too specific (i.e., there were no hits on the A + B + C terms). We modified the search to one concept, self-efficacy, and found 9 citations, of which one was particularly interesting:

Dale, J., Caramlau, I. O., Lindenmeyer, A., & Williams, S. M. (2008). Peer support telephone calls for improving health. *Cochrane Database of Systemic Reviews, 2008*, Issue 4, Art. No. CD006903. pub2 . doi: 10.1002/14651858.

This review of seven randomized control group trials showed that peer support was helpful in the health area, although more study is needed. Note that this is an evidence-based idea that might be useful in thinking about sustained arrangements to help Rick or other clients in similar circumstances. See also the Campbell Collaboration for reviews of the effects of behavioral and social interventions (www.campbellcollaboration.org).

EVIDENCE-BASED GENERAL PRACTICE AND INFORMATION-INFORMED SPECIFIC PRACTICE

We were still not satisfied that we had found the best available information as the source of evidence-based general practice, so we turned to psycINFO, a huge subscription database from the American Psychological Association, with over 2.7 million records. (Our university library had a subscription, so we could use this database for free.) psycINFO led us to the APA Data Databases, where among the many choices, we selected PsycArticles, because it is a subset of the whole database that contains full texts, which is useful if you want immediate information. Again, we were faced with many choices, but it seemed to make most sense to clique on full-text journals in PsycArticles, because we wanted specific details on methods. We selected *Psychological Bulletin*, a well-known journal that contains research review articles summarizing specific fields of interest. This would be very useful in a quest for evidence-based general practice ideas. This journal goes back for more than 100 years, and the user can pull up the tables of contents for any issue. We found one interesting paper in a fairly recent issue:

Roseth, C. J., Johnson, D. W., & Johnson, R. T. (2008). Promoting early adolescents' achievement and peer relationships: The effects of cooperative, competitive, and individualistic goal structures. *Psychological Bulletin, 134*, 223–246.

This is a study of 148 independent studies over eight decades on more than 17,000 early adolescents in 11 countries. It showed that higher achievement and more positive peer relationships are associated with cooperative rather than competitive or individualistic goal structures. This suggests the cooperative "walking support group" was an inspired idea by one of the three boys, and that the intervention plan was on a reasonable path. (Yes, you are right; we should have discovered this review study when we were searching for the best available evidence in designing the practice intervention, but in our story, the practitioner was benefiting from the spur-of-the-moment idea of one of Rick's buddies, and there wasn't time to check it out then.)

It is also possible to enter a specific search sentence in *Psychological Bulletin*. So, with great optimism, we entered the search sentence "self-efficacy as practice tool in academic settings," and found one item. You could look at finding one item and think it is too little information; or you could say that the computer has done a lot of leg work for you to find this specific fit. We tend to favor the latter view.

Poropat, A. E. (2009). A meta-analysis of the Five-factor model of personality and academic performance. *Psychological Bulletin, 135*, 322–338.

Notice that only "academic" is mentioned in the title. The search program looked at the whole paper to find self-efficacy. But titles are short-hand abstracts and, whereas the abstract of this paper sounded interesting, it did not seem to focus on the intersection of our three major terms; thus, we chose not to pursue it. There has to be a good fit between article titles and your search terms; otherwise you may be spending more time and effort than it is worth. (If you have the time to explore paths and options, it can be a good learning experience—but not if you have a specific task at hand.)

Then, we tried other search terms: Self-efficacy; Hispanic (or Latino or Latina); Academics—and found no relevant references. [Again, search programs vary in how they handle key word terms. You may be able to enter "Hispanic" and get all related terms or you may need to type "Hispanic* or Latin*" (with * as a wildcard to include anything with the root Latin, like Latin American or Latina or Latino), depending on the database.] Then we tried still other search terms: self-efficacy; grades; social support—and found no relevant references. The overlapping Venn circles that led to nothing told us a lot of important information, that there wasn't anything specifically on our search question about Rick's situation. In fact, this means that the practitioner is probably in advance of the researcher, and has to use his or her own judgment on top of whatever evidence does exist.

We thought it would be wise to consult Educational Resources Information Center (ERIC) with its huge database on all things to do with education. The home page indicated that there was an ERIC Thesaurus, so we clicked on this and recognized the distinction between descriptor terms and key terms. Descriptors are the index terms for ERIC, but one could enter with one's own key terms and hope there is a connection. We chose to go with descriptor terms and clicked on Search and Browse, which had many choices of where information was stored. We went to the Individual in the Social Context as best reflecting what information we needed, and then saw the term *dropout*. Some bells rang as we realized we had not even considered this part of Rick's story, so we explored that term, and clicked on *dropout prevention*. To conduct the actual search, we had to limit our field of requests, that is, we could ask for free full texts from ERIC (click); publication dates—recent (the last 10 years) (click); publication type—any form (click); for what educational level?—we checked high school; and then, finally, clicked search.

In an instant, 732 items appeared, 10 at a time. No, we did not go through all of them, but we received some important help, by being directed to ERIC's What Works Clearinghouse (WWC), a branch of ERIC that reviews studies according to strict empirical rules for eligibility into their recommendations sections. The High School Puente Program encouraging Hispanic youths to get to college by tutoring and other means sounded very interesting, until we read further that none of the 11 studies examined in this paper met the criteria of the WWC for inclusion of recommended programs. OK, so if we are serious about using strong evidence-based practices, then we would not employ this material at this time.

We continued the ERIC search and found one WWC Topic Report on Dropout Prevention (Sept, 2008) that examined 84 studies that were eventually reduced to 4 programs that met the WWC criteria on dropout prevention methods to keep youth in school and progressing academically. Clearly, these four programs are worth exploring for applicability in Rick's situation. We'll leave these details to your practice classes. Our general point is that with ERIC (and other databases), you can find: (1) ideas that work; (2) ideas that are promising; and (3) ideas that do not work. This gives you important information that can help you design your own intervention.

Because there were mental health issues involved in Rick's situation, we looked into MEDLINE, the information arm of the National Institute of Medicine. (Note: The larger PubMed includes MEDLINE and even more databases related to public health). Most of this huge database concerns illnesses and related matters, but some are on Health Topics, which we clicked, and found 800 topics on conditions, diseases, and wellness. We looked into the category Disorders and Conditions, and clicked onto Mental Health and Behavior. There were still many choices to be made, and we clicked onto Teen Development, and then Body Image and Self-Esteem as being the closest topics we could find regarding Rick. We found a subcategory, School Stuff (clearly written for adolescent users!), and indeed, we found 5 Facts About Goal Setting. These were specific suggestions for being effective in setting goals, written directly to teenagers, by experts in the field. We could also see these being used by practitioners to guide their plan of action for all of the Ricks out there.

All of this searching took about 3 hours (including note taking); we intentionally set a time limit because a practitioner's time is always in short supply so that he or she has to do the best with whatever information is available.

What would you have gained from the information we presented above? This is an important question because we have to convince you that it is worth the effort to retrieve information for practice.

First, you (the student practitioner) probably would have gotten a clearer sense of the term, *self-efficacy*, by reading definitions of it in several places.

Second, you would have recognized that it was a widely applicable term—useful whenever we needed to help a client learn to perform some specific task as a way to achieve his or her goal.

Third, the concept turns out to have been widely studied in research projects and received considerable support. In a phrase, it is one solid basis for evidence-based general practice.

Fourth, the search led to no applications for your specific client, but there were several close approximations that you might have adapted:

   a. Peers are important in helping a teenage client, as a support group.
   b. Having a structured intervention might be helpful, such as building in a mechanism by which Rick's two friends know what to do and when to do it, in order to get him to school.
   c. There appears to be no evidence that Hispanic youth need special interventions to affect their behavior, although conflicts with the general culture may pose difficulties apart from academic challenges. Use culturally sensitive practice methods.
   d. Because there were no specific directives for action, you probably would have used the general Bandurian theory on self-efficacy as a guideline, and made specific adaptations with the particular client.
   e. This gives greater urgency to evaluate your specific practices with Rick, to see how well those adaptations were actually helping him.

Chapter Summary

In this section, let's summarize some suggested search strategies using the vast resources of the Internet, and a few pointers on avoiding pitfalls. What are the best ways to obtain key information?

1. *Identify the controlling events in the client situation.* These are the structures or forces determining the problem or potential for the client, and that are most in need of intervention. Make sure that you and the client have a clear understanding of his or her goals to be attained. Consider terms that are narrower or broader regarding your target, or terms related to your targets of intervention.

2. *Formulate a search sentence* that reflects specific events in the client's situation, which are translated into concepts that researchers use in reporting evidence on those topics. These concepts are the key terms for entering the literature and searching for answers. If you are using databases and Web sites from established organizations like the American Psychological Association, then you are probably safe to accept their authority on strong empirical evidence; in contrast, information provided by free Web sites without institutional or organizational affiliations needs to be carefully and critically evaluated.

3. *Learn the specific structures and rules to use any given retrieval tool.* Practice, practice, practice, so as to speed up your search time when you have real case situations and little time to spare. Learn by experience which information retrieval tools are most relevant for your work, and give them particular attention to learn the nuances. Google Scholar is free and available to anyone with a Web connection; it includes more sources than the scholarly databases, and it delivers many free, full-text resources. The subscription service databases (like psycINFO, Social Work Abstracts, ERIC, PubMed and MEDLINE, which we discussed; Scopus and Web of Science in the sciences; LexisNexis for legal and policy matters; and EBSCOhost, JSTOR, and other aggregate databases) are available free to members of many university communities but fewer practice agencies; they yield more discipline-focused returns and are viewed by some academics as more rigorously screened, although concerns about "how scholarly is Google Scholar?" have been challenged of late (see Howland, Wright, Boughan, & Roberts, 2009). If you start to spin your wheels going nowhere in information retrieval, it is time to talk with your librarian again.

4. *Use only titles that are a good fit to your search statement.*   Record the full citation for future use: author, title, journal, year, volume number, pages. If you can't access it full text, check to see if your library carries that journal, or has interlibrary loan. There is a ton of information out there, so be selective on what you choose to invest your time and energy examining. Use advice, such as from ERIC's WWC, on which are the strongest papers. However, where there does not appear to be any information that is exactly like you need, be prepared to use good information on related topics—with care.

5. Where possible, *use review papers on the best available knowledge for a specific topic.* This is a good approximation of evidence-based general practice.

6. *Translate the concepts from the review paper into specific actions that the client and practitioner can perform.*   For example, Bandura (1986) describes four methods to increase a person's self-efficacy—by mastery of small portions of the overall task, by seeing that other people like himself can do it, by someone telling him or her that he or she can do it, and by physiological means like breathing deeply before going into a scary situation like a test. These are all fairly abstract, and the practitioner has to translate them (or at least some of them) into words and actions that the client can understand and accomplish.

7. *Evaluate your practice.*   Read a good book on the subject!

Individualized Rating Scales (IRS) and Structured Logs

INTRODUCTION TO INDIVIDUALIZED RATING SCALES (IRS): NATURE AND CONSTRUCTION

To get started in thinking about ways to measure specific attitudes, beliefs, or actions using individualized rating scales, let's begin with you, so you get a feel for what it is like to respond to such a device. This is the sixth chapter of the book, and presumably you've read and discussed in class some earlier chapters.

So, tell us, how's it going? Specifically, how do you like this client-centered material on evaluation of practice? You could write to us (the book authors) with your feedback. But let's try a different approach. We will suggest a set of comments about possible attitudes toward this material, ranging from very bad to very good. [In the real world of practitioners and clients, you would work out these items together to make sure the items were clear and about equidistant from each other (as on a step ladder).] Here goes:

1. This is the worst possible material I have ever tried to read and comprehend.
2. I don't like this material, but at least I get the general idea.
3. This material is more or less OK; I think I understand it.
4. This material is pretty interesting, and I understand most of it.
5. This is the best stuff I have read since *The Lord of the Rings* trilogy, and I'm even thinking ahead about how I can use it.

This is an ***individualized rating scale (IRS)***. It has a specific focus on the subject being discussed with a corresponding attitude toward it. It has an equal interval scale of possible attitudes, favorable to unfavorable. The rater is asked to make one judgment. Unfortunately, this is not a perfect example. Maybe the only person who ever rated our book a 5 is the spouse of the second author (PAB), and PAB is not so sure that she ever really read the book. Or a son of the author (MB) scores it a 1, but MB thinks that he was kidding. These answers represent cautions in dealing with an IRS, from overenthusiastic responders to jokesters. But in general, an IRS is very versatile, easily used, and can involve the client in his or her own helping process. Moreover, there are some kinds of questions or judgments that *only* the client can make, such as internal feelings or beliefs. Thus, IRS tools can be very helpful to you.

Table 6.1, below, presents some examples of IRS. Let's discuss these so as to consider different aspects and problems with IRS.

TABLE 6.1

1. Feelings of Road Rage (RR)

1	2	3	4	5	6	7
Never feel RR		I find myself getting angry at bad driving on occasion		I get angry at bad driving quite often		I feel RR every time I'm in my car

2. Worry about granting late hours for my teenager (by a parent)

1	2	3	4	5
Never	Occasionally	About half the time	Frequently	All the time

3. Shyness about speaking in public

1	2	3	4	5	NR
Never	Rarely	Sometimes	Often	Frequently	(Not relevant)

4. Thoughts about my dying (from a person in Hospice)

1	2	3
Occasionally	Quite often	Most of the time

5. (Same person as in 4.) How debilitating are your thoughts on dying?

1	2	3
Rarely	On some occasions	Quite a bit, as related to my frequent pain

6. Self-Efficacy (the belief that I can perform a certain action for which I have the knowledge, skill, and motivation)

1	2	3	4	5
I have full self-efficacy on this specific action		I have some self-efficacy, some of the time		I totally lack self-efficacy

7. (Manager of a neighborhood association) How likely is it that we will experience serious conflicts over the establishment of a group home for the mentally disabled in this neighborhood?

1	2	3	4	5
No conflicts likely				Serious conflicts likely

Now, let's discuss these examples.

1. Road rage is becoming a serious ingredient in automobile accidents, given more drivers, longer delays in traffic, and a culture that values speed. This seven-point scale gives a respondent a wide range of options and makes it possible to gain an admission of a little road rage at bad driving on occasion. This may be enough to encourage some approaches of self-control, without labeling the client as "one of those people" whom he or she dislikes. There are four anchoring points, which give the respondent three unnamed places in order to qualify their answer, which might also be a way to save face.

2. Late hours for one's teenager. There are social pressures on parents to be protective, while also allowing increasing independence for their teenagers. All five points have anchors (presumably given by the parents-as-clients), so a decision must be made without dodging the issue. Discussing the five options means that a parent with the teenager may come to terms with the issue of protectiveness vs. teenage autonomy and self-responsibility, so that a measuring device on attitude change can also serve as an intervention tool.

3. Shyness on speaking in public. Again, this is a classic five-point scale with full anchor illustrations, plus an NR (not relevant). For example, because this IRS might be used in a public-speaking class, some students may be there to learn public speaking rather than deal with shyness, and so the scale may not be relevant to them.

4. and **5.** The person in Hospice is in a terminally ill state and is being cared for—not to be "cured" but to be as comfortable as possible, so as to be able to communicate with loved ones for whatever time is remaining. We used only a three-point scale to make choices less taxing. (Presumably the client would have aided in constructing these anchoring points. This kind of scale for which the client provides anchors may help the practitioner who may be more fearful in talking about death than is the client.)

6. Self-efficacy: A five-point scale with three anchors. This allows people who hesitate to use any extreme score (1 or 5) to show a high or low level (2 or 4). If we have a client who can deal with a more complex scale, we might use nine points so as to give a finer discrimination on the degree of self-efficacy. There are no norms for IRS, of course, so it is important to plot these data on graphs and compare the patterns of scores in the baseline and the intervention phases so as to know how change is occurring for this one person.

7. Neighborhood association: This five-point scale has only two anchors on the extremes. Such an anchoring choice requires the respondent to be fairly sophisticated in indicating degrees of the target. Even so, we are leaving a lot of wiggle room for a respondent. That may not be good for obtaining comparable answers from other administrators, so it may be better to have more anchoring points.

In general, it is possible to accommodate whatever target you are seeking to measure to some form of an IRS with anchors. Obtaining the client's cooperation in constructing this scale is very important, especially in defining the targets and their anchors so that reliable and valid judgments can be made using those anchors.

INTRODUCTION TO STRUCTURED LOGS: NATURE AND CONSTRUCTION

Wait a minute. This IRS may not do justice to the situation of your learning how to evaluate your practice. The IRS is not nuanced enough to capture the whole experience as the client lived it. Experiences are processes, with some parts moving ahead satisfactorily and some parts appearing muddled. Every person is confused or satisfied in his or her own way, and we need another kind of personal measuring device to capture this complex flow of events. A personalized, yet structured, log may be your answer.

What is a ***structured log***? Logs are not diaries: "Dear Diary, I just met 'Mr. Right.' He's tall, dark, and handsome. Well, not exactly handsome, and not too tall or dark either, but I really feel he is the one for me. All my friends hate him. . . ."

Logs are structured journals kept by the client (and possibly by relevant others, such as a partner or another helping professional working on the case) to record the unique circumstances surrounding the client's problems or potentials. This package of recorded events may help the practitioner to understand the situation more fully and to pinpoint the problems as the client is experiencing them. These are data from the inside out, so to speak, unlike most other data collection methods.

Second, structured logs can bring together the dynamics of a situation in which the client's problems or potentials occur, what went before, what happened concurrently, and what happened afterward. The structure of the log may help clients recall events in clearer detail and thereby reduce forgetting. The log presents a unique context to capture more nearly the whole situation, whereas other modes of data collecting usually provide only pieces of the whole. Of course, we have to ask the right structured questions to get a view of this flow of events. And it might be possible to get some hints about causal patterns among these events so as to design an intervention to modify them, but this is rare.

Third, logs can enable clients to participate in their own treatment by describing events as they occur to them in a holistic fashion. This may be the most thorough information clients can provide practitioners in the sense of supplying enough detail to flesh out the bare bones of other measures. Structured logs are in the hands of clients, and they remain a record of events that matter to them. It is possible to provide space for clients to speculate about these patterns of events, and thus become a problem solver in their own lives, as they work cooperatively with the practitioner. Indeed, after the treatment has ended, some clients may find it useful to keep track of their situation by continuing to use structured logs and make their own interpretations.

Fourth, structured logs attempt to break down a problematic situation in ways that may ultimately help clients gain insight and perhaps change their unrealistic or maladaptive ways of behaving. In one study, for example, clients in severe pain were acting in ways that contributed to their own pain; by means of a structured log, practitioners were able to suggest ways of reducing those maladaptive behaviors (Turk, Okifuji, & Skinner, 2008).

These many possibilities mean that there are a number of variations in the structures of logs to obtain these kinds of information. We'll illustrate the more common types, but urge you to be creative in constructing logs that meet the needs of your clients and you. But be careful: the more complex the log, the less likely it will be to be completed as desired. So, be judicious in the information you absolutely *need*, in contrast to "going on a fishing expedition" or "throwing the kitchen sink" at a client to explore information you might *wish* to have.

In Figure 6.1, we present a general format of a structured client log. You would ordinarily work with the client in setting up a log that specifies what to record as soon after the incident as possible, while the memory is still fresh. Because logs may be kept over time, it is important to identify the exact date, who is completing the log, and some description of the context. The heart of the structured log includes some critical incident that represents an instance of the client's concerns. Where did this occur? Who was involved? What happened in the interchange? What were the consequences of this event to the people involved (especially the client)? These are some of the questions you might need to consider as you try to piece together the dynamics of the incident.

Once you get the log from the client, discuss the incident as fully as needed, with the client using the log as detailed notes. It is probably the case that even a structured log gets interpreted from the point of view (and bias) of the client, so that you might want to probe about how these

Client's name _____	Day (M, T, W, Th, F, S, Su) _____		Date (mmddyr) _____		Practitioner _____		
Important Event(s) (Target of intervention)	Who was present?	Did what?	To whom?	With what effects?	Time/Place	Others	Rating scales
1. _____							
2. _____							
3. _____							
4. _____							
Notes on any of the above:							

FIGURE 6.1   General format for a structured log; Adapt size, spacing, and questions to fit your needs

events could have looked from other perspectives. For example, if a husband had been writing the log, he might have indicated that his wife always nags him to do things, and in defense, the husband withdraws to avoid the blaming behavior, which makes the wife advance even more. However, from the point of view of the wife, the husband always tries to avoid responsibility, so she has to try to make him recognize what is happening very forcefully so as to get him to fulfill his obligations. They both recognize the same pattern of behaviors (using different words to blame the other), but each starts from a different point. He starts with the nagging, and she starts with the need to get the husband to fulfill his responsibilities (cf., Satir, 1964).

There are a variety of specialized logs, which might give you some ideas for other ways to structure the logs you may use:

A *target log* emphasizes the target of your intervention, and it presents as much information as possible about events that happened before, during, and after the target event occurred.

An *interaction log* emphasizes the people involved in some event. What did he (or she) say or do? What did you say or do? Then what did he (or she) say or do in response? And then what did you say (or do) after that? Recall the example of the "nagging" wife and the "withdrawing" husband; all interactions have a history, and no one incident starts totally anew.

A *time log* emphasizes the units of time and who is doing what within that time period. For example, the hour just before dinner may be filled with tensions and exhaustion, forming a critical mass of possible problems. Is this true for your clients, and how are they able (on occasion) to avoid problems?

There are *critical incident logs* that focus on salient episodes for the client. Whenever an identified critical incident occurs, then the log keeper describes the incident, who was involved, consequences that followed, and how the client responded.

When the nature and extent of the presenting problem are not clear, it might be worthwhile to explore certain tension points in a day and see what is occurring, to whom, with what effects. *Exploratory logs* enable the clients to see somewhat objectively (because of the structure of the log's questions) what is going on in situations that bother them. Then, if needed, other types of structured logs may be used to zero in on the concern.

It is also possible to combine other types of measures with logs to strengthen the information they provide. For example, if your client has problems with anger, then he or she can record a situation that causes anger, who and what was involved, along with an IRS on the degree of anger at this specific time. Leave enough room on the log sheet for a reasonable-length answer— and space on the back, if needed.

When the client brings the log to the next session, read it out aloud (to make sure you can read the hand writing, if it's handwritten as opposed to printed or sent by text) and allow the client to amplify as needed. Logs are stimuli for memory and conversation; they are not usually adequate to make precise numerical calculations on graphs. Logs will likely lead into the discussion of the nature of client concerns, the relevant targets, and some possible causal ideas that may lead to a plan of action. Sometimes if members of a couple keep separate structured logs, they can compare answers when they are with the professional who could help them interpret what any differences may mean. Keep logs relatively simple and short so as to retain client interest in completing them; however, logs may be made as complex and as long as needed in order to obtain critical information. In sum, adapt simplicity or complexity and length to the client situation.

Will logs be the perfect answer to your information needs? Definitely not, as there are many points where errors can occur, as well as potential for exaggerations (e.g., to please you or to bolster a weak ego) and omissions (e.g., due to embarrassment, forgetting, or maybe lying). Even with your most careful efforts in constructing logs, you may not be getting at the right information in the best way. How can you tell if logs are valid (i.e., truthful) and reliable (i.e., consistent) reports? The best approach is to gain your client's trust and confidence that logs and other measures are intended to help, for which accurate information is needed. If possible, get independent reports of the same incidents—although this is more likely possible in institutional settings than in community settings.

Case Study

Mr. and Mrs. Angus Ferguson and the Issue of Continuing Care Retirement Communities

Let's say that you are a community worker at a senior center where you do a million different things, including counseling center members on housing and relocation issues. Mr. and Mrs. Ferguson, both aged 83 years, come in to talk about relocation to some continuing care retirement community (CCRC) because he is in poor health, and she hasn't been able to deal with all of the nuances of caregiving. Mr. Ferguson heard about places that had a continuum of care for couples, as needed, from independent living, to assisted living, to nursing home-like environments for the very ill and disabled. He was concerned about what would happen to his wife if he should die. She refused to discuss the relocation issue because even thinking about leaving their home of the past 45 years made her very nervous and depressed.

At the first interview, you hear his and her points of view: Mr. Ferguson has prostate cancer and has decided, on the advice of his physician, to do nothing for this slow-growing cancer because he is likely to die of other causes before the prostate cancer would prove fatal. Mrs. Ferguson is petrified at this state of affairs and insists that he deal with the cancer as soon as possible. He thinks that relocation to the right continuing care community would be the best compromise, where medical assistance would be close at hand, but so too would be a supportive ongoing community, should his wife need this assistance. She bursts into tears at the mere mention of these circumstances.

You realize that you may not get much more information from the Fergusons by talking about these issues, and so you ask if they would be willing to record information in a structured log for next week (when you will meet again) about how each of them independently views some ordinary events in their daily lives and how problematic these events are to each of them. They are a bit apprehensive until you work with them on the nature of this structured log. (See Figure 6.2.)

You construct the log from incidents they have provided, but you also add an evaluation scale (just as you would in an IRS) to get a sense of the importance of each incident. Figure 6.2 presents the information that Mrs. Ferguson brought in to the session. We are using this Figure to illustrate one kind of variation in structured logs, and also, how it is possible to build in other forms of measurement as well, such as the IRS.

Log book for _____   Date today _____

What was the most pleasant experience you had today?
Who was involved? What led up to the experience?
What happened as a result?

_____
_____
_____
_____

What was the most unpleasant experience you had today?
Who was involved? What led up to the experience?
What happened as a result?

_____
_____
_____
_____

On a five-point scale, how difficult were the following events today? Circle one point.
[1 = No problem   2 = Slightly difficult   3 = Difficult   4 = Very difficult   5 = Impossible to do without help   NR = Not relevant today]

Preparing 3 meals	1	2	3	4	5	NR
Cleaning up after meals	1	2	3	4	5	NR
Giving Mr. F his medicines	1	2	3	4	5	NR
Helping Mr. F to shower	1	2	3	4	5	NR
_____	1	2	3	4	5	NR
_____	1	2	3	4	5	NR

FIGURE 6.2   One variation on a structured log with individual rating scales included (with reference to the Ferguson case in text)

(*continued*)

It would be possible to discuss the two structured logs, written independently of one another. For instance, Mrs. Ferguson might have meditated on going to an institution in order to get the sort of help that Mr. Ferguson needed and that she was not able to provide. (Note the annotation in the log that there was one point when Mr. Ferguson fell in the shower, and Mrs. Ferguson was not able to get him to bed without a neighbor's assistance.) However, she also noted that once they got to such an institution, she thought it would be a place where Mr. Ferguson would die eventually, and she could not deal with this.

Mr. Ferguson also commented on his fall and that he was glad to have gotten back to bed in one piece. He heard his wife's statements and reached over to hold her hand, saying that he hadn't realized that she felt this way. You wondered out loud whether it was a case of Mrs. Ferguson seeing the same glass half empty, focusing on death and dying at the institution, while Mr. Ferguson was seeing it as a glass half full, focusing on all of the wonderful activities they might be involved with at the continuing care community. Both could be eventualities, were they to move; the relocation would be as much to live as best they could for whatever time remains to them, as well as a place, like a Hospice, where death might come with as much comfort and resolution as possible.

Chapter Summary

In some instances, writing out some kind of structured log, including—when possible—some individualized rating scales, might provide insight into the dynamics of a situation, which could provide the helping professional a suggested direction to resolve the clients' dilemmas. We get an insider's picture to a complex set of events that troubles him or her, as well as what strengths they may bring to the situation. This is a unique way of stirring ideas about problems, causes, and possible solutions, when none of these seems to emerge in the ordinary course of events in a case situation.

Behavioral Observations

THE NATURE OF BEHAVIORS

There is a wonderful scene in Bertolt Brecht's drama *Galileo* that will get us into the mind-set for a discussion of ***behavior***. As you may recall, Galileo, the seventeenth-century physicist-mathematician, was at the tangent between two incompatible world views, the religious versus the scientific, on the nature of the universe. The centuries-old religious view determined that the Earth was the center, around which the sun and moon move. (And, by the way, this view accurately predicted many astronomic events.) At the pinnacle of this worldview was Man, God's greatest creation. As the son of Galileo's housekeeper, Andrea, says:

> I can see it with my own eyes that the sun comes up in one place
>
> in the morning and goes down in a different place in the evening.
>
> It doesn't stand still. I can see it move. (Gassner & Dukore, 1970, p. 873)

Opposed to this long-held religious view are the opinions of a handful of seventeenth-century scientists who, using only the available crude telescopes, some simple mathematical formulas, and the slow accumulation of evidence, disputed the obvious. The implications of this scientific view are heretical; Giordano Bruno had been recently burned at the stake for his astronomical views.

Cautiously, a few scientists, including Galileo, persevere. In the play, he seats Andrea on a chair to the left of an iron washstand in the middle of the room. Then he picks up the boy and the chair, and swings them around the washstand, representing the sun, which is now on the boy's right. The youth, seated "on earth" sees the immobile sun "move," whereas in fact, it is the boy-on-earth who has moved. The appearance of a mobile sun is maintained; a totally new explanation provides the key to understanding that the sun is immobile; it is we who (on our tiny planet Earth) move around the sun. Later in the play, Andrea, who has become Galileo's assistant now says:

> The earth moves, spinning about the sun. And he (Galileo) showed us.
>
> You can't make a man unsee what he has seen. (p. 891)

So, sometimes seeing things move or behave is a lot more complicated than it is cracked up to be. Let us give you a few other examples.

1. You're standing in the hall of a large mental institution apparently looking at a picture on the wall, but actually you are peeking at an inmate who approaches the linen closet, looks around surreptitiously; and then grabs a handful of towels, putting them under her bathrobe, and casually walks toward her room. Then she goes out again, and you go look at some artwork on the wall just across from her room, which is filled with towels—on table tops, on the chair, on the floor, and so on. Staff had mentioned this woman, but now you have seen the whole thing with your own eyes.

2. It's playtime at a preschool where you are interning. A dispute seems to have arisen over a toy. One 4-year-old child is hitting another 4-year-old playmate over the head with a plastic toy train. The other child puts up a perfunctory howl, although, looking at him, he does not appear to be physically injured. They go on playing together as if nothing had happened.

3. Joe, age 13, is in his bedroom. It is nighttime, and the house is quiet. His parents have gone to bed, and the family dog is sleeping on the floor by his door. Joe listens intently to the quiet and then starts a nightly routine of masturbation. No one knows about this except Joe, and he is not going to tell anyone.

4. A couple of 17-year-olds are having sex. They enjoy it thoroughly, and are uninhibited enough to tell you about it. Oh, we forgot to mention that these adolescents are married. Does this change your view of the behaviors involved?

5. A middle-aged woman is sobbing uncontrollably in the dining room of her home. Her friend, sitting nearby with a cup of tea in hand, does not know what to do.

6. An older man is sitting at his desk, and he is lost in thought. His wife has been talking to him for several minutes, but she realizes he hasn't heard of word of it. She sighs, gets up, and leaves the room. He is still sitting there aware of none of this.

Let us raise some questions about each of these behaviors which someone has seen "with their own eyes."

Re 1. Yes, we see the woman's behavior, taking the towels and storing them in her room. We heard the label "hoarding" placed on this behavior by the staff of the mental institution. But this is weird behavior, and we don't understand why people do irrational actions. We see this woman "move," just as Andrea said the sun moved across the heavens, but we really don't understand it, until a Galileo comes along to explain what is happening and why.

Re 2. We can see the hitting behavior and hear the howl. But we don't understand how come these children can be playing together after this, as if it never happened to them. We saw it happen; we know it occurred. But we don't really understand it.

Re 3. We've read the statistics that most people masturbate at some point in their lives. So, Joe joins a long line of people with secrets. Joe will not have hair growing on his palms (as myth suggests). Perhaps Joe will alter his practice when he becomes involved with a girl (or boy). If no one other than Joe knows about his masturbation, and it has no lasting effects on anyone, is this "behavior"?

Re 4. The young married couple report that they are having sex. There should be no surprise there, as that is a key component of the institution of marriage. So, as long as you are willing to accept their report, we are all in agreement that this is behavior. But what if we get different reports on the frequency of the same behavior, which only the participants have seen?

Re 5. The sobbing woman is clearly crying, and her friend feels all sorts of empathy for her but is at a loss to explain the behavior of her ordinarily quite normal friend. We probably have to wait for an explanation from the woman in order to make sense of this aberration in her normal behavior.

Re 6. The older man lost in thought—that is rather close to home, as I (MB) do that a lot of times when I am concentrating on something like writing. [I (PAB) am not quite as old, but I get called out for this as well by my family members.] Is being lost in thought a behavior? It is like a shadow where a behavior should be.

So you see that some behavior can be overt (you can see it—like the woman who is hoarding towels) or covert (only the person doing the behaving is aware of it, as in the case of Joe). Sometimes these covert behaviors are actual physical actions (like Joe, again), but they can be thoughts (the older man thinking) and feelings (is the woman's crying a marker of some hidden feelings?) as well. Sometimes the person who is doing the thinking or feeling is probably aware of the cause of those thoughts or feelings (we hope this is true of the weeping woman, for instance), but there are others who may not be aware (the hoarding woman, for example).

What is to be learned from these examples? Seeing "behavior" alone is not enough to understand behavior. This is especially true of those covert behaviors, thoughts, and feelings. We need to have a context of knowledge to have behaviors make sense to us because we are inevitably on the outside of the behaving client, trying to look "in."

Behavioral observation is uniquely capable of providing information on the manifest behavior and the context of that behavior, and it represents a touchstone of reality when both are present. (Andrea, who saw the sun move around the earth, had, at first, only his observations; and later, he had knowledge of the context of his observations, which completely changes the way he saw things.)

What is this "context" of a behavior? It is the dominant *theory* we employ to understand how this piece of information fits together with all the other relevant pieces. As we learn more, we see things move or behave in very different ways, as did Andrea.

Remember that theories are neither right nor wrong; they serve to help us generate testable hypotheses. Let us swing you around in a chair and see if we can convince you of something perhaps very unexpected about that woman who hoarded towels. Imagine yourself interning in a state mental hospital filled with several thousand psychiatric patients, many of whom were committed for a long duration (Ayllon, 1963). Such was the case with an elderly woman who had been hospitalized for nine years when this story began. She was labeled a hoarder. If you peaked into her room, you would see large numbers of towels stored on shelves, in closets, on the floor, everywhere possible. This behavioral observation is undeniable. In fact, hospital staff went into her room when she wasn't there and counted the number of towels. There were hundreds of towels, stacked up—probably so that she could make her way through the piles to get to her bed. (There are pictures of this in the Ayllon article.) OK, she took towels from the linen storage area of this large mental hospital—she was frequently seen to be doing this—and brought them back to her room. Now, what are we to do with this behavioral observation?

The psychological or psychiatric climate of the times read this hoarding behavior as reflecting an unconscious need for love and security. Having interned at a hospital for the mentally disordered when I (MB) was a young student, I might have wondered if she were trying to soundproof her room against her noisy neighbors. Or to draw attention to herself among the thousands of others seeking care and attention to their own personal ghosts. Lots of explanations, lots of theories, all of which seem to fit the observable behaviors. We wonder if anyone ever asked her why she was doing this? Probably not, because everyone in that *milieu* "saw" that the reason was an unconscious need, and therefore, she would not be able to tell us.

Actually, not everyone. Ayllon came to this institution with a different theoretical orientation that suggested that unusual behaviors like hoarding without need to hoard were simply a matter of unusual reinforcements of that behavior. Moreover, what was learned could be unlearned. We suspect that the people of that psychiatric perspective thought this was nonsense, but they let Ayllon do his thing anyway. What he did was to instruct the staff to give towels to this patient; they did this, giving out between 7 and 60 towels a day.

Over the next several weeks, the number of towels hoarded in her room increased greatly, until it totaled 625. At that point in the ***intervention*** period, she herself started to take towels out of her room. And at this same point, the staff were instructed to stop giving her more towels, and the data showed that she went from 625 towels to having an average of 1.5 towels in her room per week. Moreover, this rate was maintained during a year of ***follow-up*** observations, contrary to the predictions from the psychiatric staff at the hospital.

Here's the point for us regarding behavioral observations. We are looking at behaviors and in particular, the "cause" of some mental illness. The two theoretical knowledge contexts squarely predicted different outcomes: (1) giving or removing towels did not affect the core problem of unconscious loss of love, and so on (psychodynamic perspective); (2) saturating the room with towels would eventually lead to the client removing towels down to a conventional level (behavioral perspective). Evaluation of the results clearly supported the behavioral interpretation (and method of "cure").

We want to emphasize the point that evaluation is at the crux of behavioral observations using some knowledge context (theory). Researchers test out ideas to approximate the truth of a situation. When evidence begins to pile up in favor of one theory over another, then practitioners had better know this—this is one instance of evidence-based general practice—and use as guiding principles those models that have proven fruitful guides. Equally important for behavioral evidence is what we learn from our clients themselves in the course of our evaluation. This is evaluation-informed specific practice. Both are needed.

In another study that I (MB) participated in, we were observing for "pro-social behaviors" in preschoolers (Chesebrough, King, Gullotta, & Bloom, 2004). And what are pro-social behaviors? We defined them as "a repertoire of skills that facilitate social interaction and social competence" (p. 178). We searched the literature and found half a dozen or so behaviors were frequently discussed by various researchers and practitioners, and we provided an ***operational definition*** of each of these behaviors so that observers could agree of what they saw behaviorally fit within one or another category.

Let's look at one of these pro-social behaviors: kindness, defined as the ability to give and receive attention, approval, affection, and support. This includes demonstrating altruistic behaviors, such as helping others and sharing. Imagine yourself in the preschool setting, with lots of small tables and chairs, a big fluffy rug, walls lined with cabinets of toys and books, other tables with rocks and flowers and junk (my interpretation of what I saw). By random selection, you are to observe one child for 10 minutes, and record what behaviors you see using pro-social categories. Your scoring sheet has brief definitions of those behaviors to remind you.

You are watching Chelsea from a short distance across the room, and because you've been there frequently, she is not paying any attention to you. Chelsea and Jed are playing with some toy trains and cars on the rug with a set of tracks. They play happily for a while until Jed tries to take the train away from Chelsea so that he can pull his other cars loaded with pencils and erasers. Chelsea hits him over the head with the toy train. Jed howls. The teacher, who has been supervising the play of several other children across the room, looks up and watches for a moment. Jed retreats a bit, and Chelsea continues to play with the train. He starts pulling his toy cars by hand over the track, holding onto their load of pencils as he goes. They appear to be playing contentedly as if nothing had happened.

Had something happened? As Freud famously said, sometimes a cigar is just a cigar (and not a phallic symbol). A hit over the head is a hit over the head, and it gets scored as a hitting behavior during that time segment, but so do the playing together and sharing the same space—under kindness. It is a good thing that we will combine these observations to see a pattern of positives and negatives that best reflect this complex thing called child's play.

Next, let's consider the cases of Joe and the Washington couple (Ben and Kat, from Chapters 2 and 3). We really don't know in the sense of a behavioral observation that Joe is engaging in sexual self-stimulation, and we even don't know if the Washingtons are having sex except by their (uninhibited) report. In the first case, we have impersonal social surveys on which to base our thinking; most adolescent boys masturbate. In the latter case, we have to accept their word at face value. These are two different kinds of behavioral evidence, neither of which we have personally observed. As a general rule, we would suggest accepting these kinds of evidence, but not to depend on them for any evaluation that requires repeated reports. There are other things to observe that are more visible and less intrusive.

Finally, let's consider the woman sobbing and the man lost in thought. These people can be "observed" but the observations do not tell us as much as we need to know to make repeated observations needed in evaluation. A practitioner would probably ask the woman how often she has these episodes of uncontrollable sobbing. And for the man lost in thought, we might ask his spouse how often these episodes occur. In short, feelings and thoughts are private events, whether or not the person can explain why these feelings and thoughts (and actions or inactions) are occurring at this time. We might have to settle for a less-direct observation, such as the older man telling us that he continually misplaces his watch and keys, which also pertain to his state of mind.

Case Study

Evaluating the Prevention of Unwanted Teenage Pregnancy at a School Health Clinic Using Behavioral Observations

The clinic was a busy place throughout the school day, what with physical exams for the sports teams, checking sniffles and fevers, putting bandages on cuts, handing out aspirin, and a lot of TLC. But even Ms. Erin, a nursing student, was surprised when Georgia walked in to ask how she would know if she were pregnant or not.

The clinic was located in a grade school in a changing neighborhood. It had been a lovely old building, but it was showing signs of its age. This pregnancy question brought home to Ms. Erin that she may have been not keeping up with the times either, and so she gently discussed how this question arose, and got an earful about modern sixth grader behavior. She checked further, recognized that Georgia was not pregnant, and sent her on her way.

(continued)

That night, Ms. Erin was thinking about this situation and realized that Georgia probably was not alone in having sex with boys from the junior high school, which was only a short way from her school. The next day she talked with the district social worker, a health teacher, the principal, and the school psychologist. Among them, they decided to expand their sex education classes to meet the needs of their students. They discussed how to bring the parents into this discussion (expanding on the existing sex ed classes that had parental support). They agreed that they needed to evaluate their efforts to see if these plans were making a difference.

Ms. Erin was at the clinic as a field placement, and it was soon agreed by all that this would be a perfect service-learning task for her to evaluate the program. Let's imagine that you are in her position with regard to evaluation. Let's think through what you might propose. We hope this would include doing some *single-system design* evaluation. Let's say that you are in a discussion of this project with your research instructor back at school. You and she talked about possibilities with selected students—perhaps with students thought to be at risk (like Georgia) and others not at risk. What should we measure? You thought the behavioral observations you were studying that week in class would be just the thing.

"What are you thinking about, when you say behavioral observations?" your instructor asked.

"I suppose we should look at the bottom line, whether any girl becomes pregnant and has the child. We would likely know this at the clinic," you suggest.

"Probably so, although girls might go off to have their child in secrecy," the teacher replies, recognizing that this isn't nearly as common as in the past. "But this is a good behavioral observation or report. Anything else? How about pregnancies that are terminated?"

You give some thought as to whether pregnancies, births, and miscarriages and intentional abortions can be determined by girls' self-reports or by *archival records* like official clinic records or girls' self-reports. You decide to consult with others about what you need to know to inform your sex ed program before making a final decision.

"How about asking test questions in the health class on such topics as how contraceptives work—being ignorant of these things puts a girl in danger." You suggest. "That would be a cognition, an inner behavior of thinking as one basis for action."

"Right on," your teacher says. "What about feelings?"

"Well, we were talking in another class about how actions, like acting out and having sex at a very young age, may reflect a very unhappy girl. I wonder if the girls would cooperate in answering questions on what is bothering them at school or at home, and how they are handling these problems?"

"Be careful about exploring too deeply; these are very personal topic areas, and you are only looking for behavioral signs that are predictive of girls who might need information on preventing unwanted pregnancies," the teacher explained.

You begin to think about all of the ways that you can "see" the problem that arose with Georgia, and remember that there is one group, almost a gang really, of kids who are in trouble much of the time. You wonder if Georgia is hanging out with this group, another indicator of problematic conditions that might need changing.

The school psychologist had mentioned that he had contact with Georgia a few months ago, after one bad episode at school, and she had some serious problems with her parents. They didn't like what she was doing or how she was doing in school, and had grounded her. She was very angry at them, but felt she could not leave home (yet) as she had no means of support. These angry feelings were simmering below the surface, and were breaking out in small skirmishes. She was wearing "outlandish" clothing and accessories—but so were many of her classmates. It may have been more offensive to her parents who were quite conventional and conservative in many respects.

Altogether you and your colleagues have a number of potential behavioral observations, and you were assigned to sketch out how you might implement them. Let's think about these possibilities:

Direct behavioral observations: You could observe and record her type of clothing and jewelry at your weekly meetings. You could also observe whom she was associating with at lunch hours at school—knowing by sight the various cliques, especially the conspicuously trouble-making group. You want to get some sense of peer norms, as they are predictive of teens' sexual behaviors. You also might hear her language, maybe for marker terms, like how many times she uses the word "f - - -" (for its shock value) in her conversations with you. You could ask questions about effective contraceptives—what she knew, where she might get them (if needed), and so on. Each of these would be susceptible to relatively simple observation and recording over time (before and during the intervention period).

Indirect observations: Feelings are more complex to observe because all we have to go on is what the person chooses to reveal, together with some external symbols (like crying or aggressive outbursts). What about a standard global question each week about how Georgina is getting along with her parents in the past week? Or with her boyfriend (if she is in a relationship)? These would reveal a feeling tone that might (or might not) reflect her true feelings or the depth of these feelings. But even the superficial weekly questions and the observer's characterizations of the client's feelings might be useful over time.

Your task is to assess each of these possibilities and decide which would be most feasible to collect and use to assess progress on various *targets* that represent intermediary steps toward the *goal*—preventing unwanted teen pregnancy. How near or distant are these various target observations to the goal? How easy or difficult are they to obtain, and how valid and reliable are your observations? (See Chapter 3.)

METHODS OF OBSERVING BEHAVIOR IN OTHERS: PRINCIPLES OF SEEING

First, know what you are observing for by looking at the situation itself, like a woman taking lots of towels to her room. What is it about towels that is important to your helping these clients? You could count the number of towels, their sizes, their colors, and so on, but what is your purpose in these alternative ways of counting? Have a purpose in mind as you choose what to observe.

Second, think about targets as those measurable events that you want to affect in your intervention. You might wish to reduce the number of towels that the lady was taking, in which case the number of towels seems like the most appropriate target. Graphing a large range of numbers can be complicated, but in this situation, what you need are some small numbers—0, 1, 2, 3, 4, 5—and then some larger categories where the precise number is less important than the scale itself because more detailed large numbers may not add more information. Here is one way to plot data in this situation with the towel hoarding example:

A score of	7	100 or more towels
	6	6 to 99 towels
	5	5 towels
	4	4 towels
	3	3 towels
	2	2 towels
	1	1 towel
	0	0 towels

Alternatively, the evaluator could annotate the graph each week with an exact number, while estimating where each point fell on the vertical axis (see Figure 7.1).

Third, consider how many target behaviors you want or need to collect. For example, you can count surreptitious thefts of towels, open taking of towels, time of day the taking of towels occurs, and so on. Some of these may be useful in your thinking about the whole situation; others may be less so. Just remember: Collecting information about clients is difficult and time consuming. Make sure to plan exactly for evaluation, and collect nothing more than what you

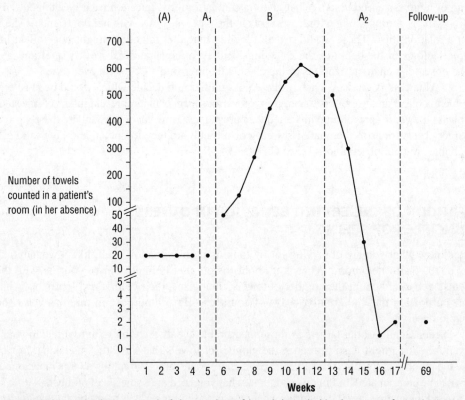

FIGURE 7.1 Cumulative record of the number of towels hoarded in the room of a patient at X State Mental Hospital.
Source: Based on Ayllon, T. (1963). Intensive treatment of psychotic behavior by stimulus satiation and food reinforcement. Behavior Research and Therapy, 1, 53–61.

need. Observing one or two behaviors at most is usually enough for one data collector. Define that target behavior clearly for all observers. Do some *reliability* checks, as we did in that pro-social behavior study, by having two observers watch the same child at the same time on occasion in order to compare results (see discussion on reliability and *validity* in Chapter 3).

Fourth, who is to collect these data, when, where, and under what conditions? These kinds of questions will influence the type of behavioral measure you choose. Clients, yourself, some relevant other person, or some independent observer are possibilities, each with advantages and disadvantages. Even when the client is the only one privy to his or her own thinking and feeling, there are the important questions of when and where and how such data are to be collected. Have the client collect such data at the same time and place each day, if possible, to cut down on other sources of influence.

Fifth, observation forms can prove to be very helpful in getting the observations made and performed in highly similar ways each time. This is very important, as is training the observer to use these forms correctly. Take the time to do this right; otherwise, your data may be filled with unintended observations.

Sixth, sometimes you may not have the time to observe every client behavior, in which case you could sample when and where that behavior is most prevalent. We've discussed some similar ideas in Chapter 5, on *structured logs*; we would add that you could pick out some high-risk times (like just before dinner when children are often most fussy) and make structured behavioral observations then. We used a time sample of behavioral observations with the Chelsea and Jed situation. There are many ways to sample behaviors (see Bloom, Fischer, & Orme, 2009; Gliner & Morgan, 2000; Greenstein, 2006). Remember to have the observer placed as inconspicuously as possible, but—equally important—placed in a good vantage point to see what is to be observed without moving around too much.

Chapter Summary

If you learn nothing else in this chapter, we hope that you recognize how important behavioral observations are, and how difficult it is to be sure that you "see" what is to be seen, and not simply what you imagine to be present before you. Both a boldness in looking actively at the target behavior and a humility in what you are seeing are called for in making behavioral observations.

Keep in mind the exercise the helping practitioner went through to evaluate the prevention of unwanted pregnancy. There are many forms of behavioral observation, overt actions to covert feelings and thoughts, public and private actions, where the client may or may not know he or she is doing them or why.

Remember to observe the physical environment and time in which these events occur, as supplying controlling or intensifying conditions. If Chelsea and Jed were at home with a parent busy preparing dinner, rather than at preschool, how might this situation evolve?

CHAPTER

8

Standardized Rating Scales

Case Study

Mrs. Cornelia Vanderveen, an Older Woman in Need of Protective Care

One cool autumn day, many years ago, I (MB) went to the door of a small house in a working class neighborhood in Cleveland. A factory was nearby; I heard the noises and smelled the fumes. Some of the houses and lawns on the block were well-tended while others needed re-furbishing. I rang the bell on this white clapboard cottage, yellowed with age. I stepped back from the door (so as not to frighten the occupant) and waited. Several minutes.

I looked around as I waited. Beautiful day, cool, and leaves were turning color. I was a research interviewer in a federally funded study of older people in need of protective care because, in the opinion of friends, neighbors, relatives, or some professional person, they were unable to care for themselves or their property without significant help from others. Mrs. Cornelia Vanderveen was one such person identified by the Visiting Nurses Association; they felt unable to assist her properly because her son, George, aged 66, threatened them with a gun, after returning from a stay at the state mental institution. I don't recall being taught anything at school about how to interview someone whose son wielded a gun, but I tried not to think about that as I waited at the door.

I could hear Mrs. Vanderveen shuffling to the door. She opened it, smiled broadly at an unknown visitor, invited me in without waiting to hear my canned opening lines: "I'm Martin Bloom from Associates in Gerontology. We are conducting a study of the attitudes and activities of older people in the greater Cleveland area. We are interested in learning how people are getting along in everyday matters, what are some of the problems they are facing, and what are some of the things that are making them happy nowadays." She didn't even look at the large-type brochure we had made explaining our purpose and our "agency"—in fact, a

(continued)

subsidiary of a well-known but unnamed agency working with the aging in Cleveland for a half century.

"Come in, dearie. The neighbors are rubbernecking." She pulled me into the house, half holding onto me for support, and half directing me to the kitchen, which was the warmest part of the house. She walked slowed and unsteadily in her floppy house slippers. She wore an old wrinkled skirt, but a bright blue sweater that appeared new (and too large for her). Her white hair was going in several directions but appeared clean. She talked volubly and nonstop. She sat down on a kitchen chair and then got up again to go to the couch in another room to lie down. "I feel sick, miserable," she moaned.

This was a natural lead into my interview questionnaire, although it did not fit into the order of the questions as written. But by my own rules (I was the interviewing supervisor, as well, and I was testing out the questionnaire in person), the interviewer was to take any lead by the client to explore some set of questions. What follows are selections from a transcript and annotations from that interview (Bloom, 1986). The actual questions and instructions are presented here in italics:

MB: I'm sorry that you are not feeling well. I'd like to ask you some questions about your health. (#14) *In general, would you say that your health is now good, fair, or poor? (Probe for degree)* Mrs. Vanderveen replied that her health was very poor. (No need to probe; she supplied the degree.)

MB: (#15) *During the past month, did any health problems, sickness, or ailment keep you from carrying on the things you usually do around the house?* Mrs. Vanderveen answered yes and proceeded to give several illustrations, such as being too tired to take in the plants before an early frost killed them. She would have happily supplied many other examples, but I took advantage of her pause to breathe to go onto the next question, because any one answer was sufficient to make the point, and the questionnaire was long.

MB: (#16) *Were you in bed most of the time for a day or more during the past month because of a health problem?* She thought a moment and replied no. Had she said yes, I would have asked about the number of days in bed.

MB: (#18) *Were you kept in the house but in a chair most of the time?* No.

MB: (#19) *Were you kept in the house but still able to get around?* Mrs. Vanderveen responded vigorously "yes" and proceeded to talk about what she was not able to do any more, such as *getting outside, climbing stairs, walking a long distance, doing ordinary housework, and doing heavy housework*—all questions on a physical functioning scale we had constructed. Because she had responded to these items in replying to #19, I just circled the correct answers in another part of the questionnaire and noted what I had done.

I later asked another set of questions. MB: (#42) *Do you need any help in matters of health, like help in reminding you when to take medicine drops or pills, or giving you injections, or making doctor's appointments?* Mrs. Vanderveen thought she could use help in these matters.

MB: (#43) *Who would you turn to for help in an emergency? Do you have someone's name and telephone number by the phone (or in your purse)?* Mrs. Vanderveen thought a moment and said that she could "ask school children passing by for help." (This item is part of a Concrete Assistance scale we developed. As you might infer, this is not a positive answer to this item.)

And later: MB: (#63): *Is there anyone who gets in touch with you if they don't see or hear from you as often as usual? Who is that?* Mrs. Vanderveen mentioned a Mrs. Young next door who was pretty nice to her, helped her with shopping sometimes, and came over to chat on occasion. This comment gave the interviewer an opportunity to go back to the opening questions he had skipped in order to follow Mrs. Vanderveen's lead:

MB: (#1) *Have you lived in the Cleveland area for a long time?* She replied "Yes, all my life."

MB: (#3) *How old are you?* She wasn't too sure. "Eighty-three or maybe eighty-seven. It was a long time ago, dearie." (These questions were part of a Mental Status Questionnaire.)

Another part of the questionnaire was for the interviewer to make observations about the living space, furnishings, stairs, rugs on floors, and so on. These and other observations would be entered in a physical environment measure. No specific questions were asked.

Other questions involved items related to actual assistance from others. MB: (#118) *Has there been any change lately in the way you get along with neighbors or friends or relatives, or the way they act toward you?* This question prompted a long monologue by Mrs. Vanderveen on how the neighbors were all nasty to her. Well, not Mrs. Young who helped her shopping and such.

This led to the next item: MB: (#119) (This item asks about family relations, but I changed it because I wanted to focus on her son.) *How do you get along with your son who is living with you? Do you get along well or not so well, or what?* With this question, Mrs Vanderveen burst into tears. In between sobs, she reported how her son was treating her against her will, such as pouring burning substances down her throat to cure her cough. Mrs. Vanderveen begged the interviewer to help her escape. Her son, George, was let out of the insane asylum but was still crazy.

Just then, we heard a car door slam. "It's him," she announced, and blew her nose on a tissue as she tried to disguise the fact that she had been crying.

George wandered in. He was a small man, wearing soiled work clothes. He was suspicious of the interviewer, and he asked many questions. He told his mother that he didn't like people prying around into their business. She replied that it was just like visiting with the neighbors, not much of importance was said, but she was enjoying the visit and wanted me to stay. George was wavering about throwing me out or leaving himself. And for no apparent reason, he walked out and left the house.

I vividly remember what went through my mind at that moment, besides relief. Was his mother in immediate danger because of her son's unusual ***behavior?*** By the rules I had established as interviewing supervisor, I thought it was best to let nature take its course in a case, unless there was some overt crisis. I had not seen a gun. I did not see the son threaten the

(continued)

mother. And so I decided this was not a life-threatening crisis as such, and went on with the interview. Finally, I came to the end:

MB: (#181) *On the whole, how satisfied are you with your way of life today?* With a deep sigh, Mrs. Vanderveen said she was very unsatisfied. (This was a contentment scale item, of which more will be said.)

MB: (#183) *I thank you for your cooperation (in this interview).* I then made some small talk about the weather, and the like, and as I was leaving, I asked: *Can you tell me how to get to*—(I name the nearest main cross-street)? She was able to give me the name of a large street a block from her home. (This is our substitute for the final item in the Mental Status Questionnaire that is usually used in institutional settings.)

As you can infer, every item was asked not only for its own sake but also because it was part of a set of items we had constructed for various scales, on mental status, on physical status, on concrete assistance available—in contrast to interested parties who were not providing concrete assistance (like a minister who came around once and was flummoxed by the situation, and never returned). We also developed a contentment scale, which turns out to be critical to the outcome of this study.

MY (MB) EXPERIENCES IN DEVELOPING AND TESTING A STANDARDIZED RATING SCALE: THE BENJAMIN ROSE INSTITUTE PROTECTIVE CARE STUDY

It's one thing to read in a textbook about **standardized rating scales**—a measure that involves presenting the same items to different people using the same administrating and scoring procedures so as to be able to compare one person's scores in reference to the scores of other people with known conditions. It is another thing to have lived through developing and testing such a device. I wrote a whole book about my experience with research on a single project (Bloom, 1986), but will spare you nearly 400 pages of exciting details to focus on one standardized rating scale that I helped construct for the study: the Contentment Index (CI).

Background: Back in the early 1960s, I was a recent PhD from a good university with my head filled with social psychology *theory* and research. I was looking for a job when academic positions were few, and so I happily took a research associate position at a social agency dealing with the aged, and in particular, with a new project dealing with *protective care clients*—older people living in the community who were not able to care for themselves adequately and safely, and had no friend or relative willing and able to assist them. My boss, Dr. Margaret Blenkner, a major social work researcher, had come from a study of protective care cases in New York City to continue her research in Cleveland. It was a terrific learning experience for me.

At a time when most social workers were not well informed about research, Dr. Blenkner was constructing large-scale experimental/control group designs in community settings, employing highly trained social workers to perform a planned *intervention*, and using advanced statistics to analyze her data. The focus of the Protective Care Study was to see whether well-trained social workers could assist an experimental group of protective care cases better than what occurred to these same kind of people in the community at large (the control group) where there was little formal aid available. We developed a long list of *concepts* relevant to this project; ultimately, success was defined in terms of two outcomes: the greater survival rate of people in the experimental group compared to the control group; and whether the experimental group showed a higher level of contentment, compared to the control group. My job was to construct that Contentment Scale (CI).

Every standardized rating scale probably begins in the same way, a mad scramble to find relevant questions (or items), and then to try them out on some known samples of people, winnow the questions down to a manageable number, and then figure out how to ask them in a questionnaire addressed to people who did not like strangers, did not answer personal questions, and who tried to hide from everyone because these strangers might institutionalize them for being incapable of living in the community. I will skip over the details, but we eventually generated empirically 10 items that constituted our CI (see Figure 8.1). Contented community folks answered these questions easily; people who lived in nursing homes rated their contentment more poorly because of substantial psychological or physical problems.

There are 10 items in the long form. We even had a short form of five items that we used in desperation when we thought our client's patience was about to be exceeded; these are listed first in the figure that follows. (Remember: these were frail older people, not college sophomores on

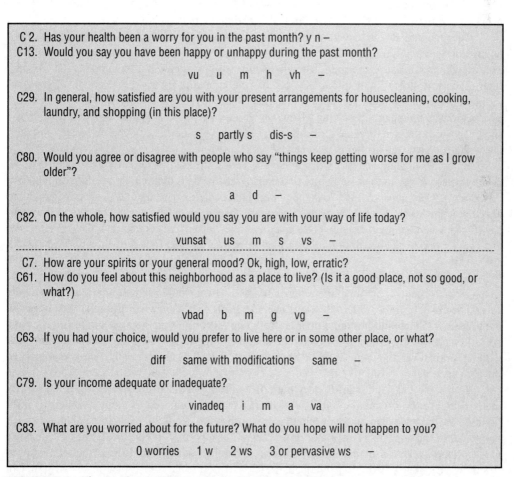

    C 2. Has your health been a worry for you in the past month? y n –
    C13. Would you say you have been happy or unhappy during the past month?

                        vu   u   m   h   vh   –

    C29. In general, how satisfied are you with your present arrangements for housecleaning, cooking,
         laundry, and shopping (in this place)?

                        s   partly s   dis-s   –

    C80. Would you agree or disagree with people who say "things keep getting worse for me as I grow
         older"?

                            a   d   –

    C82. On the whole, how satisfied would you say you are with your way of life today?

                        vunsat   us   m   s   vs   –

    C7. How are your spirits or your general mood? Ok, high, low, erratic?
    C61. How do you feel about this neighborhood as a place to live? (Is it a good place, not so good, or
         what?)

                        vbad   b   m   g   vg   –

    C63. If you had your choice, would you prefer to live here or in some other place, or what?

                    diff   same with modifications   same   –

    C79. Is your income adequate or inadequate?

                        vinadeq   i   m   a   va

    C83. What are you worried about for the future? What do you hope will not happen to you?

                    0 worries   1 w   2 ws   3 or pervasive ws   –

FIGURE 8.1 The Benjamin Rose Institute Contentment Scale.
Source: The Benjamin Rose Institute Contentment Scale (Bloom, 1986).

whom many standardized scales are tested.) The numbers in front of the item mean that is where they were placed in the long form of the questionnaire that four interviewers were trained to use. The letters and dashes after the item represent possible answers, y = yes, n = no, – = did not ask question, m = mixed response, and so on. We eventually put the short form of all of our variables on one sheet of paper because we had to use them so frequently with this group of people.

Assuming all 10 items were used, and the responses were recorded to mean contented or discontented answers, then a respondent could receive a total score from 0 (no contented answers) to 10 (all contented answers). Vague responses (for which the interviewer could not easily pin down the respondent to one answer) were coded as indicating discontent. For example, one elderly gentleman responded to every question I asked in the same way: "That's a damn fool question."

As you can guess from the numbering, we embedded the items in the questionnaire where they "logically" fit. For example, on my first visit to one client, she took one look at me and slammed the door in my face. In the second try a few days later, I used a contentment item (#2 on our questionnaire) in a desperate attempt to get her to stay and talk. I quickly asked: "Has your health been a worry for you in the past month?" That question turns out to open a floodgate of worries, comments, observations—some of which were indeed answers to later and, therefore, unasked questions. We talked for over an hour standing by the open door.

Then, about a dozen questions later, I asked: "Would you say you have been happy or unhappy during the past month?" This second item in the Contentment Scale also seemed to strike a chord with her, because she again listed her sources of unhappiness, and I nodded in sympathy (and made tiny notes inconspicuously on the questionnaire on my clip board). And so on, throughout the questionnaire that dealt with many variables relevant to our study: What concrete assistance was the person receiving? How was his or her physical functioning? Did he or she show signs of affective or behavioral disorder? Did this person have people interested in his or her welfare? What was his/her mental status?

By doing an item analysis, we were able to code each kind of response as belonging to the healthy person living in the community or the distressed persons living in an institution group. So, for example, "very unhappy" and "unhappy" were both coded as typical of the distressed institutionalized group, whereas "mixed happy and unhappy," "happy," and "very happy" were coded as typical of the health community group. (That middle score, "mixed," might end up typical of either the distressed group or the healthy group on some other item, as determined by an empirical content analysis.)

Interviewers would see their clients four times during that year; they were blind as to the status of each client, experimental or control. Each time we would ask the same questions on the several scales, plus other filler questions to make each visit somewhat different. (Many times, the protective clients did not remember us from one meeting to the next.) Then, changing hats, I would return to the office to become data analyst, trying to see what happened over the year with our critical variables, survival and contentment, as well as the others that were secondary to the core variables.

To make a long and painful story mercifully brief, we discovered that indeed the experimental intervention was associated with higher contentment scores—but not significantly higher. However, we also discovered that a greater proportion of the experimental clients died, compared to the controls. This is not how research is supposed to come out, but Dr. Blenkner was an honest and conscientious social work researcher and reported these findings without flinching (Blenkner, Bloom, & Nielsen, 1971). All hell broke loose (see pages 273–307 in Bloom, 1986).

Our reading of these data suggested that our very capable and sensitive social workers, fearing the worst for their fragile clients, institutionalized them (often against their will) into nice healthful surroundings, filled with staff who showed tender loving care, wherein the protective care people inexplicably died for no good medical reason. I have to report that traditional social workers and nursing home personnel were not as happy with our findings or interpretations as we hoped they would be.

Actually, the story has a happy ending, where we did further research on helping medically frail older people, not with highly trained social workers, but with home aides, paraprofessionals working in client home situations. This was one of the beginning points for what became a national phenomenon—in-home services, with supervised paraprofessionals.

Now, back to the standardized rating scale: We winnowed down the scale to 10 items that distinguished between distressed institutionalized and healthy community people. We asked (or tried to ask) these questions of both the experimental and control groups over four time points, and then compared the average score of experimentals against those of controls (making certain statistical corrections for differences between the two groups). We grouped our results by experimental and control *groups* because this was a research study. If we had been evaluating the practice with individual clients, we could still have used the CI for some very good reasons. (See Figure 8.2.)

First, it attempted to measure complex feelings, thoughts, and actions in a standard way so we could compare a client about whom we knew little with known groups of others who had answered the same questions. (Our development of this CI was in fact a pale version of the huge projects to develop such standardized scales as the MMPI and the like. But ours was a do-it-yourself standardized scale when no other one like it existed. We spent more than a year working on this and other instruments.)

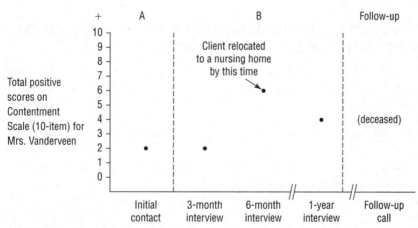

FIGURE 8.2 Illustration of a standardized scale employed within a larger community project (Bloom, 1986)

Note: Each point on the graph represents the total number of positive interpretations made on the client's answers to 10 standardized contentment questions. However, at different times, she responded in different ways, so that a given item would appear as negative one time, and positive at another time.

We justify using the standardized scale on this single-system evaluation because each point represents a cluster of 10 answers. We did not connect the three intervention data points because the time differences were too great. The data are, therefore, illustrative of only the trends.

Second, the CI was repeatable, which was important for any time series studies. We did a rudimentary check for *reliability* and *validity*, within the limits of our funding at that time, and found this scale to be reasonable—not perfect by any means. And so we used it, when no other scale was available that fit our client group. There are now many more standardized instruments, and source books to locate them (such as Fischer & Corcoran, 2007).

Third, the structure of the standardized rating scale means that many practitioners have an economical way to obtain important information related to a *target* of their intervention, relative to some normative population (the known status of people from the rating scale development stage). Commercial or experimental scales abound these days, usually for a nominal fee, and they take only a short time to be put into use (compared to our year of development).

However, don't be too complacent about using standardized rating scales because the label "contentment" may mean one thing to the scale developer and another thing to practitioner. For example, a "contentment" scale developed by Hudson and Faul (1998) is, in fact, a scale intended to be used as a disguised depression scale. So, read the items making up the scale, rather than merely the title. Standardized rating scales are like ready-to-wear items compared to the custom-made fashions that usually fit better. Remember to consider *Individualized Rating Scales* (Chapter 6) to complement standardized ones.

Do not be tempted to change an item on a standardized scale because you think it fits your client better. If you do make a change, you have an entirely new scale, and it is not standardized. Being scientific is not for the faint of heart.

With luck, you will never have to construct and test a standardized scale; this is what keeps some psychologists and psychometricians in business. But it is important that you understand how it is done, and especially where the ivory tower of test construction meets the brick wall in the community. It's rough out there; don't assume your client has read your textbooks. As Samuel Johnson once said of second marriages, it is a triumph of hope over experience.

SELECTING, ADMINISTERING, AND SCORING A STANDARDIZED RATING SCALE FOR YOUR SPECIFIC PURPOSES

There are many standardized scales of various types, but very few are relevant to most situations involving a practitioner with a specific client who is to be seen over a period of weeks of service. Such a standardized scale has to be relatively brief and its delivery has to be adaptable to situations in which an observer finds himself or herself. Yet it has to undergo rigorous construction so that it is acceptably valid and reliable. The more structured a scale is in order to serve a particular purpose, say, measuring a child's fear of monsters, the less flexible it is to reflect the range of possible ways children may be anxious. So, select a standardized scale with care and be willing to accept the limitations it imposes on a user by its very nature to measure one specific thing in one specific way.

One very useful place to look for such standardized measures is in Fischer and Corcoran's (2007) *Measures for clinical practice and research: A sourcebook*, which has grown so large that they had to divide the scales into two volumes, one for adult measures and one for couple, family, and child measures. For example, one measure for children is the Rosenberg Self-Esteem Scale (RSE; Rosenberg, 1965), a 10-item measure divided randomly into 5 positive statements (like "On the whole, I am satisfied with myself.") and five negatives (such as "At times, I think I am no good at all."). Children can respond on a four-point scale, strongly agree (= 1) to strongly disagree (= 4) (see Figure 8.3). This scale has nice properties that test constructors love, on reliability and validity, along with norms on 5,000 high school students of different ethnic backgrounds (see Fischer & Corcoran, 2007).

Instructions: Below is a list of statements dealing with your general feelings about yourself. If you strongly agree, circle SA. If you agree with the statement, circle A. If you disagree, circle D. If you strongly disagree, circle SD.

1. On the whole, I am satisfied with myself.	SA	A	D	SD
2. At times, I think I am no good at all.	SA	A	D	SD
3. I feel that I have a number of good qualities.	SA	A	D	SD
4. I am able to do things as well as most other people.	SA	A	D	SD
5. I feel I do not have much to be proud of.	SA	A	D	SD
6. I certainly feel useless at times.	SA	A	D	SD
7. I feel that I'm a person of worth, at least on an equal plane with others.	SA	A	D	SD
8. I wish I could have more respect for myself.	SA	A	D	SD
9. All in all, I am inclined to feel that I am a failure.	SA	A	D	SD
10. I take a positive attitude toward myself.	SA	A	D	SD

FIGURE 8.3   Rosenberg Self-Esteem Scale

Another standardized scale by Alpert and Britner (2009) was recently developed for a specific audience (parents of children in foster care, a relatively neglected group) using all of the traditional steps for constructing a meaningful standardized measure. These steps include constructing a scale that stems from an hypothesis emerging in the literature, namely, that parents who have had children removed from their home but show engagement in the process to regain them (presumably because their caseworkers are working to engage them, *and* the parents are making an effort as well) will be more successful in this endeavor than parents who do not exhibit engagement. Alpert and Britner constructed a 31-item "parent engagement" scale, tested the items with 46 parents of children in foster care, and did item analyses to reduce the scale to its final size of 22 items. Items on the scale tap clients' views about whether they "feel respected as a parent by my caseworkers" and the extent to which they "have a say in creating the goals in my service plan." Several important results emerged: first, parent engagement was significantly but negatively related to the distance from the parent's home to the child welfare agency, and to the length of time the parent spent working with his or her longest running caseworker.

Modified versions of the Alpert and Britner (2009) scale have recently been used in studies of client engagement with different populations, including: (1) parents with mental health and/or substance use needs who are at risk for having their children removed from the home (i.e., family preservation cases); (2) professional (long-term) foster parents; and (3) first-time parents receiving preventive home visitation services (including child abuse prevention modules). Consistent with our focus in this book on *client validity*, the measure asks clients to report on the extent to which they feel empowered, supported, respected, and understood by their caseworkers. Specifically, for *single-system evaluation*, repeated measures using this instrument may indicate shifts in engagement (or disengagement), indicating what efforts the helping professional should exert to obtain a successful goal.

Should you find yourself in need of administering such a standardized scale, you would do well to read suggestions on how to do this; Fischer and Corcoran (2007) recommend being well-informed about the chosen measure and choosing an appropriate setting and time for giving the questionnaire to a client—by you or some other staff person, before or during an interview. Be careful about administering the standardized scale too often, as the client will begin to remember prior answers. As a rough indicator, consider once a week when you need continuous information. Make it as least aversive as possible. Be aware of ethnic differences in delivering the test; be sensitive to the needs of all clients as you consider the words you use and the clients' understanding of those words.

Scoring a standardized scale is usually included in the scale instructions. Pay careful attention to directions, such as reverse scoring of negative items so that they match positive items. Remember that these are complex measures, and it will take time to comprehend the scores, and more time to explain the scores to clients and relevant others.

Chapter Summary

Standardized scales give you the opportunity to "stand on the shoulders of giants" in that you make use of enormous research efforts of others. However, they were constructed with some purposes in mind, and you have to decide whether knowing that kind of normative information will be useful in working with your client. Practically every topic under the sun has been the subject of some standardized scale, but you may find that no standardized scale fits your client exactly. It's your choice. How close do you have to come to your client's situation before you accept a standardized scale that doesn't fit your client in all particulars? We would suggest that you use the standardized scale as is, and also add new items to the questionnaire to individualize the questions. Of course, keep separate the scoring for the standardized scale and the few items you added on your own.

Qualitative Data in Single-System Designs: Self-Monitoring

THE PLACE OF QUALITATIVE INFORMATION IN A QUANTITATIVE WORLD: SELF-MONITORING

The methods of measurement discussed in Chapters 6 to 8 are used to obtain quantities: How many of these? How much of that? Such quantitative information produces the kinds of data that can be easily graphed and which make precise pictures. Unfortunately, not everything in life, especially with clients, is as neat as this, and we have to use what is called qualitative information to get at the messy details of complicated lives. We want to understand the whole experience through the eyes of the client, not simply tiny fragments of information through the eyes of a scientist who constructed some scale. We want dynamic stories of who was there, doing what to whom with what reactions, not static numbers generated by a computer. In a word, we want to know about the qualities people possess, and the quality of their lives; these are the qualities that we hope to influence positively.

In fact, this is the kind of information that practitioners want as they assess the clients in their unique situations. Both practitioners and evaluators want to use the information not only to understand the client but also to assess whether the client is achieving her or his goals. Doing both is challenging. Let us provide some background to make this chapter understandable.

First, let's discuss *self-monitoring*, a general term that means the client takes some part in observing and measuring some aspects about himself or herself. With this definition, the discussion of *structured logs* (in Chapter 6) would involve self-monitoring (even though it is structured by the practitioner who designs the log). Also, when the client records his or her own information on *individualized rating scales* (in Chapter 6), it could represent self-monitoring (although the practitioner still constructs these IRSs). There is very little self-monitoring in most behavioral observation or in the use of *standardized rating scales*.

Let's push self-monitoring to its limit. Say we are in a situation in which the client defines the *goals* of service; participates in constructing *targets* of *intervention*; introduces not only the problems he or she is facing but also the strengths and resources needed to resolve them—these strengths and resources are used by the practitioner to design an effective intervention, based on evidence from the literature; is involved in much of the data collection; participates in interpretation of graphs; and tells the practitioner when the results have attained the his or her goal.

That is one very involved client! (And that is exactly what client-centered evaluation of practice seeks to attain as well.) We will illustrate self-monitoring as a highly developed form of qualitative information, quite unlike anything that has come before. To do this, we will combine three major ingredients: (1) information about narrative approaches to helping; (2) ideas from the movement called positive psychology or the strengths perspective in social work; and (3) a new idea in *single-system* evaluation: global assessment, which we will introduce in the next section.

The Narrative Approach

The *narrative approach* (NA; White & Epston, 1990) is a therapeutic tool based on the rationale that clients come to practitioners with their *story* in mind usually consisting of difficult problems or concerns. NA practitioners see this as the client's *dominant story*, but there are also other possible ways to interpret the client's situation, some involving positive factors and unused resources. After all, the clients have survived these terrible burdens into the present time, so they must have had something going for them to achieve this. The method is to get clients to explore in writing what these positive factors might be. Then, it is the task of the practitioner to help the client use these positive ideas and resources to resolve present concerns and address the future.

Positive Psychology and the Strengths Perspective

The movement in the social sciences and the helping professions called *positive psychology* (Seligman, Steen, Park, & Peterson, 2005) or the *strengths perspective* (Saleebey, 1996) is based on the rationale that clients may have some problems in living, but they also possess many strengths that can be mobilized in advancing their lives as well as dealing with problems. Whereas many thoughtful people have recognized this truism, earlier generations of practitioners focused on problems or pathology, and—no surprise—found problems and pathology at every turn. Now the question is how to stimulate clients to think about their own strengths and available social resources in order to address their concerns. Many people throughout history have made lists of virtues, personal strengths, or resources, but none are exactly relevant for our purposes. Thus, we will select from among these lists those strengths and resources that appear to be useful in achieving the goals of our clients.

Benjamin Franklin's (1793) autobiography contains a marvelous section on his determination to be virtuous in 13 specific ways. Among these he listed temperance (**operationally defined** as not eating to fullness and not drinking to elevation), orderliness (a place for everything and everything in its place), and humility (which must have been quite a stretch for this public intellectual and celebrity). More to the point of this book, Franklin practiced a form of self-monitoring for several years, and he devised his own system of data tabulation as well. Had he not been so deeply involved in America's war of independence, he might have written a book like the one you are now reading! Erik Erikson (1950) formulated a neo-Freudian theory of eight psychosocial stages, each one with a dominant character strength relevant to the developing individual's world, like infants coming to trusting that their caregivers will nurture them or adolescents settling on an identity. Abraham Maslow's (1943) hierarchy of needs hypothesized a different kind of progression, from basic physical and psychological safety needs, to attachment needs so as to love and be loved, to a high need for self-actualization, or becoming and being all that one can be; at the very highest step of the pyramid comes a need for transcendence, a search for meaning in the universe, or what might be termed *spirituality*.

More recently, Peterson and Seligman (2004) listed elements of psychological well-being, along with thorough review of the values literature, and generated a work comparable to the *Diagnostic and statistical manual of mental disorders* (*DSM-IV-TR*; American Psychiatric Association, 2000)—the psychiatric "bible" of psychosocial pathology. It is too soon to tell if this is the wellness bible we are seeking, and it already has its critics (e.g., Ehrenreich, 2009). However, all of these authors will serve helping professionals as a starting point to suggest to clients strengths and resources that they had not used fully in dealing with their problems.

First, let's define values as a statement of preference about some topic that is firmly held, and which organizes the direction for that person's actions (Bloom, 1986). We know a person's values in part by the way he or she persistently acts toward some object, human or otherwise. Therefore, every persistent personal or social action involves a person's values. As helping professionals come to know the values of the clients, these practitioners can predict how the client will act in certain situations, at least on a probabilistic basis (because there are so many influencing factors in any situation).

Let us distinguish positive values, that subset of a client's entire set of values, because these are the ones helping professionals want to mobilize in helping the client resolve his or her own concerns. There are various kinds of cognitive, affective, physical, and social strengths or virtues that, for one reason or another, clients are not using fully or effectively in resolving their own concerns. Part of the helping professional's task is to encourage clients to make use of these persistent preferences, for example, for learning new things; for being persistent and creative in problem solving; for having friends and being part of a community of people, so as to exchange friendly support to one another; having a sense of purpose or meaning in life (spiritual or otherwise); among many other possible ways to define values or virtues or character strengths—to be employed in resolving client concerns.

The importance of these values for our present concerns is that they point to assets within our clients that might be employed to address problems (or, in the future, prevent them) and advance positive goals in life. Various authors have offered evidence of the usefulness of their lists of values, but we want to call attention to Seligman and colleagues' (2005) study because their suggestions are related to our notion of the structured log. Three happiness interventions (described later) produced lasting increases in happiness and decreases in depressive symptoms. What is interesting for our present purposes are the tasks that Seligman et al.'s (2005) participants were asked to perform. The "Gratitude Visit" exercise asked experimental participants to *write* and deliver a letter of gratitude in person to someone who had been especially nice to them. The "Three Good Things in Life" exercise asked them to *write* down three things that went well each day (and their cause) every night for a week. The "You at Your Best" exercise asked participants to *write* about, and reflect on, a time when they were displaying personal strengths, every day for a week. In fact, after the study was completed, the researchers went back to see if the participants were continuing these methods on their own. (The control group in this study had none of these practical assignments.) They found the strongest effects on happiness for those participants who continued using these methods on their own (Seligman et al., 2005, p. 419). (We will discuss some parallel ideas with regard to the *maintenance phase* in evaluation designs in Chapters 12 and 13.)

We see these writing exercises as forms of the narrative approach! That is, the writing task is something practitioners might assign to help clients move away from their dominant story of problems and limitations toward some other directions that involve their strengths and resources so as to be more fruitful in addressing the immediate problems and taking control for future directions, if at all possible. Note that we are not using the therapeutic ideas of the narrative approach, nor the categorical perspective of the Peterson and Seligman (2004) approach, as such—only ideas stemming from them. Let's see what we can make of these ideas for client-centered evaluation of practice.

A NEW IDEA IN SINGLE-SYSTEM EVALUATION: GLOBAL ASSESSMENT

How should the practitioner make use of a client's narrative material describing positive aspects of the client's life? We think the answer is to make a holistic judgment on how well all of the aspects of this complex life are moving in a desired direction. The first step is to grasp this holistic idea, and then plot it in graphs as usual. As client and practitioner discuss the client's writings about positives and strengths in the client's life—even amid problems that the client came with—a sense of the whole situation may emerge—at least to the extent that the client can answer this "big picture" question:

"Where are you today along the path of attaining your desired goals, given all of the things (problems, strengths, resources) that are going on in your life situation?" Various scales may be used, depending on the sophistication of the client, such as this one:

As of today, all things considered, this is the degree to which I have attained my goals:

1 = To a Great Extent

2 = To Some Extent

3 = Mixed—Some Things Attained, Some Not Attained

4 = To a Small Extent

5 = To a Very Small Extent, if at All

What this *global assessment* reflects is the person's analysis of the whole of his or her life situation at this time. We think of this holistic measure as a kind of center of psychosocial gravity in the client's life, and how it shifts (in positive directions, we hope) during intervention. No one measure can describe such a complex package, but this does not make it less meaningful to the client who always lives with the entirety of her or his life situation, and has some ongoing sense of the whole.

Thus, what began as a narrative of problems and continued in the discussion of positive strengths and available social resources, proceeds with the application of these positives in the client's life, and ends as the client *takes charge* of her or his life using these skills and resources. The single-system evaluation format we are proposing in later chapters reflects this complex movement. First, the global assessment reveals the client's sense of the whole situation, using self-monitoring. Second, specific targeted events, each with their own baseline and intervention period changes, are measured using techniques we discussed in previous chapters. There should be some meshing of these two types of targets, such that positive changes in specific targets begin to have some effect on the client's general sense of the whole situation.

Case Study

Problems for Professor Ahmed V., a Religious Man in a Foreign Culture

Let's consider a case study and see how these ideas may lead to a qualitative view of the situation.

You receive a rather mysterious phone call from a man with a foreign accent. "Hello, this is ____. I am a social work intern at this agency. How can I help you?" He tells you in a soft and hesitant way, as if he is afraid of being observed, that he has some . . . (pause) . . . problems he wants to discuss with you, but not at your office where he can be seen. You reply that agency rules require him to come to the agency, and he reluctantly agrees. At the appointed time, a slightly built man in his early 40s comes into your office, closes the door, and sits down in a chair in front of your desk. He is neatly dressed, but he slumps in his chair. He hands you his business card, Ahmed V., PhD, associate professor of X at University Y, and accepts yours. (Better be formal, you tell yourself.) You lean forward, and with a friendly but confidential tone ask if he can tell you what brought him here today. He looks down and does not speak. You wait. He looks up and then down again. Then he begins to talk, without looking at you.

"Is what we talk about confidential?" he asks

"Yes, within the limits of the law on protecting innocent people from violence," you reply. He nods, in understanding. (Pause)

"I am very ashamed of myself, an educated man, having to come here for help." (Pause.)

"It is often difficult to ask for help, but life is complex, and it really is a very good thing to seek help when you are unable to resolve a concern by yourself," you say. "It may be the first step in lightening these burdens. Can you tell me more about yourself and your concerns?"

Slowly, the story of his problems unfolds. "I am 44 years old. I am unmarried. I . . . I have never had a relationship with a female. I am not a homosexual, but I have never . . . known a woman. I am getting to be an old man. I am an associate professor at University Y, and I work all the time on my teaching and my research. I am a Muslim, a religious man. I pray five times a day; I give to charity; I fast during Ramadan, and in all ways, I try to be a good man. I want to be successful in my career. But I also want pleasure. But I cannot find it. I respect women, as the *Koran* instructs us to do. But I cannot talk with them about ordinary things. I am afraid to go back home to my family as a failure. I am so lonely, and this loneliness brought me to your agency." (Your class in comparative religions of several years ago suddenly becomes very important.)

You explore what Prof. V. has done to meet people, especially women, and his answer indicates that he has done almost nothing because he doesn't understand this country's mores regarding meeting women—"women here do not dress modestly"—and he feels inadequate. Or perhaps embarrassed. You ask whether your being a non-Muslim makes it more difficult for him to discuss this, and he replies that it does, but he doesn't want any Muslims to see him in such a weakened state, and so he came to this agency, rather than some Islamic counseling system.

You explore what contacts he has with Muslims in mosques or in other associations, and he confesses very little. He is a member of a mosque, yet he generally prays alone. The young members of the mosque seem so Americanized, and he is very much a traditionalist.

The session is drawing to a close, and you summarize what you have learned, that he wants to meet women, but feels socially inadequate and culturally unaware of how to do so. You also mention positive factors he has not emphasized, such as being a tenured associate professor and a productive scholar, suggesting that he has considerable gifts and talents that he may not be bringing to bear on the problem. You wonder out loud what other talents or strengths he could bring to this situation. Mustering up some courage, you (a student intern) suggest that this professor do some "homework" until you meet again next week. "Clients know themselves far better than the practitioner ever can. The role of the practitioner is essentially to bring out other positive alternatives for the client to use in resolving the presenting problem and move ahead in life goals."

You suggest that he write a short narrative or log about alternative ways of thinking about this presenting problem, looking specifically for the strengths that brought him to this

(continued)

situation, the dreams he has for himself, the values he holds, the skills he possesses that might be relevant in this situation. Consider these statements, translated from common persistent values:

Do you enjoy learning new things? (because what we discuss here may involve your learning some new ways of dealing with ordinary situations)

You clearly are able to create new and socially useful ideas in your professional work; do you think you would be able to apply these same creative efforts in your personal life?

You feel part of your Muslim community, and I suspect you have contributed to making it a vital aspect in the lives of others. Can you see yourself as becoming a more active part of that community, and receiving as well as giving help and comfort?

I think you have defined your immediate purpose in life as being related to your professional career. Yet, as a teacher, you have most likely helped many students over time, and indeed, have probably supported many others in your home country. Have you considered working with others here to help students in need of counsel and guidance?

Looking at this sample of possible writing topics, we can see some values that might be very useful in communicating with others. The point is to get Prof. V. to see these values in himself and to begin using them. As he writes his answers, and builds upon earlier ones, he may come to see himself in a more positive light and be able to tap these resources and characteristics when he meets suitable women in appropriate settings. He is self-monitoring by looking inward at himself and his situation. He is being prompted to find assets that will eventually be employed to help himself. It is quite possible that he may not previously have considered these positive aspects as the bases for meeting people. As Professor V. rises to leave, he mentions that he could invite his brother's college-age son to study at his university, and thereby get involved with guiding this young man into a positive educational and social experience—one that he, too, might share. You comment that this is very good thinking; why doesn't he consider it further for the next session.

There are two ways we can move with a situation like this. First, we can ask the client to do something that we cannot do well, that is, make a global assessment of these factors in his or her situation. For instance, you might ask Professor V. the following question each week: "Can you give me a global assessment of how the pieces of your life situation (good features and poor) are being resolved this week?" He might provide a scale like:

1 = Most Issues Are Being Resolved Positively.
2 = Many Issues Are Being Resolved Positively.
3 = Some Issues Are Being Resolved; Others Are Not.
4 = Many Issues Remain Unresolved.
5 = Few, if Any, Issues Have Been Resolved.

A series of weekly answers to this question could show a moving picture of this client's global center of psychosocial gravity, and probably represent the largest single picture we can record in the client's presenting situation.

The second way to use these self-monitoring narratives is to measure change in his characterization of his positive abilities. Does he indicate a development in whatever values you felt best defines his potential to help himself? For example, you could ask Prof. V. to assess himself on whether he has moved on "working with others" (and the other questions) using a five-point scale. It would be wise to work together to create the form he is to use for the various tasks, so that these ideas are clear to him throughout the week (see Figure 9.1).

The purpose of this form is to identify and use your personal strengths and social resources ("assets"), which may have been previously underutilized, to attain your goals. First, you are asked to describe briefly these assets, and then rate changes on each using a five-point scale.

> 1 = Great Positive Change
>
> 2 = Some Positive Change
>
> 3 = Mixed Changes, Some Positive, Some Not; or No Change
>
> 4 = Some Negative Change (Things Got Worse)
>
> 5 = Great Negative Change

A) Your Ability to Produce Novel Ideas or Products Making a Contribution to Yourself or Others.
Day 1 =

_____

Day 2 =

_____

Day 3 =

_____

Day 4 =

_____

Day 5 =

_____

Day 6 =

_____

Day 7 =

_____

B) Your Ability to Be Persistent, Doing What Has to Be Done in the Face of a Challenge
Day 1 =

_____

And so on, for the other days and with the other specific assets that the client was asked to write about during the intervention week, including the abilities to be fair to all without prejudice, humble without self-deprecation; hopeful; and work with others toward a common goal.

Global Assessment:

Looking at your whole situation (problems, strengths, social resources), what overall judgment would you make about changes in this "complex whole" during the past day? What do you see?

> 1 = Great Overall Improvement
>
> 2 = Some Improvement
>
> 3 = About the Same as (the Day) Before
>
> 4 = Some Deterioration
>
> 5 = Great Deterioration

FIGURE 9.1   Illustrative form for gathering self-monitored qualitative information including a global assessment

(continued)

> You suggest he re-read what he had written in the prior days and build on this narrative each day. Then, he should return for another appointment at which time he and you can discuss how to put these strengths to work in achieving specific objectives. Professor V. looks down for a long time while he digests these suggestions. He slowly brings his head up and looks you in the face for the first time and says, quietly, "Yes, I can do that. Yes, I will do that." He is sitting upright now, and you believe that you see a hint of a smile on his face, for the first time. You and he sketch a form that will summarize these ideas (and help him gather some data as well).

In the week that followed, you contacted your Muslim friends for some ideas about helping your (unnamed, unidentified, so as to maintain his confidentiality) client, and received several good leads that you planned to introduce into the discussions during the coming weeks as your intervention, such as joining green organizations, interfaith groups, or outdoor clubs, each of which might offer opportunities to meet other women and men in the context of doing things together.

Chapter Summary

If you want to collect qualitative information about the richness of a client's life, both the problematic and the positive, then probably the best approach is to involve the client directly in some form of qualitative data collection. We have proposed several mechanisms, starting with the idea of written self-monitoring. The act of writing about strengths and supports may help to reinforce or even identify such positive resources; one idea may lead to another, as if the client is putting additional arrows into her or his quiver. The client is uniquely situated to give global assessments about her or his life situation, and we propose ways to put these assessments into a moving and measurable form (on graphs).

It may also be possible to observe how an identified list of character strengths and social resources become called up during the intervention period, a measurable period that also permits graphing. Again, these are subjective and complex factors, and the client is probably the only one who can provide this information. Choose these values and characteristics wisely, as these qualities become the dimensions of a qualitative life. (Of course, other quantitative measures might also be suitable and provide quite different information on which to base your plans of action and decision making.)

Change in the specific characteristics discussed above should, over time, be reflected in the overall movement—what we call the client's psychosocial center of gravity.

CHAPTER

10

Measurement Cautions

Case Study

Measuring Outcomes in a Women's Support Group

Every Thursday night, a group of women met in the basement of a Quaker meetinghouse. The room was brightly lit, even if sparsely furnished, just a ring of folding chairs in the middle, with some tables off at the sides. One table had some bowls of fruit, cookies or cakes baked by one or another of the participants, some fruit punch from a large plastic bottle, with plastic cups. On the walls were some prints of art depicting love among fellow human beings. This was a meeting room for any community group without discrimination.

As the women came in, they hung their coats on the rack at the far wall and greeted one another as old friends, or comrades in the combat against homophobia and discrimination. They pushed a dollar bill into the large jar that paid for some food and whatever else the group needed. It was a low-budget operation with a high value for the participants. As one of the women said, the ring of people sitting here was her life preserver.

Debra is a 30-year-old single African American woman who works at one of the branch post offices in town. She uses a quad cane for support, due to some congenital problem that led to difficulties in walking or standing for long periods of time. Her colleagues make fun of her for "sitting down on the job" all the time she is dealing with customers, even though the manager of the office said she does as well as the other clerks (mostly white men). She's been there for some years, and wonders if she has been getting the same level of raises as her male colleagues. She is afraid to confront the manager, because she thinks he disregards anything she says anyway.

Jean is in her 50s, an overweight white woman who does not dress in any recognizable style, and perhaps drinks too much. (She sometimes came to the meetings in a less-than-sober state.) She has clerked in a large chain home supply store for many years, and has few friends to show for it. She leads a life of quiet desperation, and was the one who coined the

(continued)

life preserver phrase. She reads all of the time and is well informed about current events and literature, on which she has pronounced views.

Marybeth is one of a set of twins. She is white, of indeterminate age, maybe 35 to 40, and very angry. She is angry at her family, especially her twin sister, who has rejected her because she is a lesbian. She had a wonderful partner, who had to move across country when her company relocated, and the partnership sort of faded. She is angry at society for its homophobic orientation, and rages against politicians and lawyers who are holding back the floodgates of humanity, as she expresses it. She is terribly lonely, now that her partner has gone. She works at a glasses-fitting optometry store all day, and she goes home and watches TV all night.

There are several others in the group, but these three are the core participants. We'll introduce others later.

Measurement of *groups*—in distinction to measuring the individual people who are in the groups—calls for some additional thinking. We have to use **group measurement** tools that reflect the whole group rather than any one person's views. For example, consider the **concept** of group morale. This is a traditional concept for social psychologists and represents something about the whole group, not just individual opinions. As Jean described it, the group as a whole is a life preserver for its members. The health or strength of that life preserver is something apart from the health or weakness of its individual members. In fact, each of the women in the group may be individually limited or bothered by some problem, but when the group meets, it is as if they each give something to each other that is magnified or synergized by being in the room together. It is that something that is the group-level concept of morale or life preserver.

So, how are we going to measure it? Traditionally, scientists have looked at group behaviors, such as attendance, which represents "attraction to the group," and can be observed independently, rather than asking each individual some question. We noted above that only three people were the core attendees, which is a small group, but nevertheless a meaningful group to them. Others, like Susan or Kathleen or Leala, come in from time to time, usually after some blowup of their home or work situations, so as to let off steam and get revitalized by the group, so they say. As soon as matters calmed down, these women tended to drop out temporarily. One other woman, Zelda, came in only once so far, and said little except that she was very depressed and saw nowhere to go in life. The others were very sympathetic—putting aside their own weekly dramas—in an attempt to support her. But she moved from her apartment, and they lost track of her. Every so often, they lament this at the meetings, and say they should have tried harder to maintain contact.

Another approach to measuring group-level events is to ask members to evaluate each meeting on some relevant dimensions, such as satisfaction with responses each received to her presentations. Then, the average of these satisfactions might be interpreted as reflecting the strength of that life preserver on that given weekly meeting, that is, how much the group helped each individual that night.

Because this is a textbook, let's go along with our fictional drama (based on mixed-group meetings we have attended) and measure both group attendance (the number of people at the meeting each work) and level of satisfaction on a five-point scale collected privately at the end of each meeting, along with some other questions on outcomes of the meeting. Let's say that you have been asked by the church leaders to evaluate the effectiveness of several community groups at different times in the week. These leaders want to use their facility for the community as best they could; other groups were petitioning to get into the facility.

Observing attendance is easy, but how are you going to measure the level of satisfaction of each member privately so that one person's attitudes won't influence another member's ratings? Let's say you figure out a way to ask each one alone as she is about to leave the building. What we are going to discuss in the next two sections of this chapter apply by degree to all of the previous methods of measurement, and in general, to contact with clients.

UNOBTRUSIVE AND NON-REACTIVE MEASURES

In a classic book, Webb, Campbell, Schwartz, and Sechrest (1966) introduced what should have been obvious to any scientist: That *whatever* questions we ask of a client, and in *whatever ways we ask these questions*, are, to some degree, obtrusive into the life of that client and cause the client to react in some atypical way, maybe to give "positive" or "socially acceptable" answers— or intentionally misleading answers for their own self-defense—and not the truth of the situation. People almost never experience some stranger coming up to them, week after week of intensive group meetings, to ask: "How satisfied were you with today's group meeting, in hearing what your issues were, and helping to supply support for you?" They have every right to be suspicious and on guard.

Consider the satisfaction question. Here you are, let's say, a young Asian American woman, age 21, from a lower–middle-class background and going to a state university in the undergraduate social work program. You come to the meeting dressed professionally, in a neat skirt and blouse, with a nice sweater—something you might wear to a school meeting. What do you think these group members see in you, before you have opened your mouth?

Remember Jean, the overweight 50-year-old in beat-around-the-house sloppy clothes? She's sober tonight, but she takes one look at you and thinks, "Where did this innocent come from, and what is she doing here?" Marybeth often rages, but she thinks you look like a nice person, and she is pleasantly quiet. Debra wonders privately, but says nothing: "How on earth a person like you is going to be able to understand, let alone help, a person like me? You come from a different world."

Your task in this meeting is to evaluate the group's functioning, not to intervene as such. You promise to report your results to them as well as to the church leaders; no names will be used. You tell them about the exit interview involving several brief questions that you will tape record and transcribe later, so as not to detain participants too long.

Jean is first to leave, and she comes to your small room next to the hall where the women hold their meetings. You smile in a friendly manner and present the questionnaire to her. She takes it, looks at it a moment—you had presented these questions at the beginning of the evening—and says, "Sure, I'll answer your questions." She smiles as she responds, all very positive, and rises to leave. You thank her as she goes—and you wonder what that smile meant.

Marybeth enters, quickly does the questionnaire, and then tries to have a little private conversation, but you remind her of your pledge not to hold up the others too long. You wonder how that private conversation is reflected in her answers.

Debra comes in next, and you politely wait while she sits down with a thud and speaks laconic answers into the microphone. She hardly even looks at you, even after you thank her for her answers.

And so on, for all the people in the group that night. As you score this short questionnaire, then sum the answers on each item, and divide this sum by the number of people in the group that night to get an average satisfaction score, you wonder how good any of these answers are. The mantra your research teacher used to recite comes back to you now:

Whatever questions we ask of a client, and in whatever ways we ask these questions, are, to some degree, obtrusive into the life of that client and cause the client to react in some atypical way, maybe to give "positive" or "socially appropriate" answers, or some intentionally misleading answers for their own self-defense—and not the truth of the situation.

How can you minimize the possibly harmful ways that clients react to you (because there will be inevitable differences between you and them) so that their answers are a closer approximation of the truth? Here are some suggestions:

First, be unobtrusive as possible. Don't dress in ways that call attention to yourself as being different from the respondent. This means finding out in advance, if possible, what participants of the meeting will likely wear. If this information is not available, consider some universal uniform, a pair of ordinary jeans or pants and a plain shirt or sweater. You want to be professional but also respectful of the respondents and fit in.

Second, your presence at the meeting should be explained in advance with straightforward language as being a job the church leadership asked you to do, and who you are. The group averages will be shared with the leaders of this church; however, no individual names or opinions will be given. The members will have a chance to see the averages as well. If you are recording some other content emerging from meeting, inform the participants of this, so that there will be no surprises.

Third, make sure the language and format of your questionnaire are respectful. Be certain that the language is understandable, even by an adult who may not have had the benefit of advanced education. Check questions with members of minority groups to make sure there are no unintended meanings, for which you may be culturally naïve.

Fourth, have all of your materials (questionnaires, recording equipment, etc.) set up and ready to go when needed. Provide privacy when appropriate. Be polite and respectful of all people at the meeting. You should provide your supervisor's phone number, in case any respondent wants to inquire about your study or to comment about you as an observer.

Now, the fun part: We'll review suggestions to use unobtrusive and, therefore, nonreactive measures (Webb et al., 1966). As a group, the following measures are often indirect and, therefore, should be used as secondary information sources, unless nothing else is possible.

Archival Records

There are all kinds of public and private *archival records* that can sometimes be re-deployed as evidence in a specific case. Public school records of grades, absences, visits to the principal, and so on may be used (with clear permission from all involved parties). Many helping professionals keep their own records for their own purposes, but sometimes they may be useful for your client situation—for example, a nursing log on a patient's mental state (depression), which could be used as baseline evidence, and continued during the intervention. Private people may keep monthly calendars about social contacts; their checkbook or itemized credit card bills might record their spending that has put them into debt. It is hard to know if these are fully valid, but they can be used as indicators of outcomes of your intervention—with due caution about their limited validity.

Behavioral Products

Nervous people may smoke many cigarettes during the course of the breaks built into treatment hours, and this smoking behavior may increase or decrease, as the intervention continues. Head to the designated smoking area outside your office door, clean up after the clients have left, and count the cigarette butts. The smoking rate may be a ***behavioral product*** that you could use as an indicator of tension over the course of multiple intervention sessions. Just as your online viewing habits and purchases are tracked by the online merchants and used to suggest new products that might fit your interests, analysis of patterns of signing in and out at the gym (how often? how long? only for 20 minutes when you go alone vs. 60 minutes when you go with a training partner? when? only in the weeks leading up to spring break?) might be helpful to crafting a more effective exercise plan. Develop your own rating, or count items, and keep track over time. Make sure that the behavioral products you are observing have some conceptual linkage to the condition you intend to measure.

Unobtrusive Observations

A family comes to your agency; observe where they sit in the circle; consider how they are dressed (perhaps reflecting how they are feeling at this time); observe their expressive movements, like frowns at what the spouse is saying, turning a chair away from the spouse, and so on. All of these might be observed, and later recorded privately. While the group meeting is going on, do not make obvious recordings, but put a check mark in a defined field on you notebook to indicate some behavior or event of interest, and tabulate these check marks later on a graph. Do minority members of a group sit together, or is distribution more or less random? How many interruptions for private concerns are there in the course of a group meeting? Be imaginative in looking for ***unobtrusive measures*** of meaningful activities—that is, activities that reflect the presenting concerns.

Physical Traces

This is something like behavioral products, but they are unintended. For example, how many people actually come to a meeting for which a number of chairs suitable for the total membership have been set up, which nicely indicates the percentage of persons attending? How often does a student forget to bring pencil and paper for taking class notes? If you are working at an institution, see where the floor or rugs are most worn, indicating popularity of places or events in the institution—in front of the TV or by the front door or window looking at people passing by outside? You don't have to be Sherlock Holmes or a crime scene investigator to spot ***physical traces***. Just look around. Are things broken and unrepaired, reflecting a broken relationship or an institution just broke (financially)? How many beer/wine/liquor bottles are in the trash/recycling bins? Are there any books or magazines around the room of a literate house-bound person?

The general advice people make on these points is to try to relate whatever archival record, behavior product, unobtrusive observation, or physical trace you are considering using to the actual concept under consideration. These records, products, observations, and traces have to be repeatable, observable, and countable to be plotted on a graph.

Next, let's look at the group morale, as reflected in the average satisfaction scores. We've added an ***intervention phase***, just to make life interesting—maybe you invited the church staff member who ordinarily does the assertiveness training groups to sit in on those five sessions. Let's call this the intervention for this group, as training not to be passive, but to stick up for one's rights in a positive, not aggressive, manner. Given this intervention, what changes do you see in the group morale? (See Figure 10.1.) What argument can be made that these satisfaction scores support the claim that the women's group is providing a needed service for the community?

This graph (Figure 10.1) indicates both a ***baseline*** (4 weeks with no intervention phase) and an intervention phase (the remaining 5 weeks). The average satisfaction score of the group in baseline is 3.75 (totaling 3.5, 4.5, 3, and 4, and dividing by 4), and 4.0 (totaling 5, 4, 3, 4, and 4,

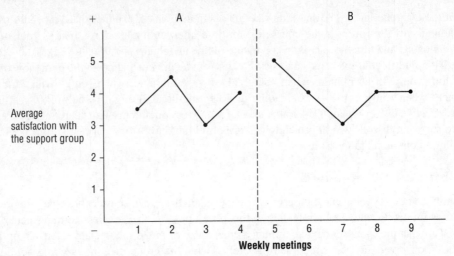

FIGURE 10.1   Hypothetical data from weekly meetings of a women's support group

and dividing by 5) in the intervention period. There is some improvement, but is it real? Or are the various personality factors emerging to disguise the group "life preserver" quality? We know that all people are different in some ways, and we have to expect different responses. The question is, do these differences cancel out each other to reflect what is a center of gravity, so to speak, for the whole group, which is not dependent on any one individual? This is the hope of people who collect measures on group members. Is it true?

Guess what our answer will be. Yes, you're right. In a client-centered approach to evaluation of practice, we could ask the clients, in this case the group members, how they understand this "group-level number." Is it meaningful to them? Do they see the group as being effective as a whole, whether or not they themselves were helped that night? Let's say that the group mostly agrees that they feel a degree of closeness and helpfulness growing, and this is satisfying to them, thanks to a practitioner's intervention. Then, after the intervention was concluded, it might be possible to arrange to have the group members take over the intervention for themselves. For example, as part of the *M phase*, the group members continue to coach each other on assertive actions in their own settings. This is a stringent test: Would the improvement in morale hold up when the group members were supporting each other's assertive actions? If the answer is yes, then we have some evidence that the group goals (providing support and encouragement to each member) were being met.

MEASURING THE IMPACT OF THE PHYSICAL ENVIRONMENT ON CLIENT CONCERNS

Helping professionals are often keenly aware how the physical environment in which the client lives affects, positively or negatively, that client's concerns. A house-bound older person faces a very different set of challenges if that house is in an isolated rural area, compared to a cheek by jowl urban setting. The youth who is questioning his sexual orientation may have few people to be open and at ease in these discussions in some places where the culture is intolerant. A visiting nurse may observe whether there are child-accessible books in the front room of the child's home, as a part of assessing whether parents are helping their child to become reading-ready at school.

Every client situation takes place in some physical environment, and the helping professional ought to consider its implications, especially when these factors stand in the way of a successful outcome for the client. In this section, we draw heavily on community psychology, public health, and some scales developed by psychologists to assess aspects of the physical environment.

Unfortunately, changes in this physical environment are rarely measured in the ***single-system design*** evaluation literature, even though they are clearly a part of every situation in which the client's case takes place. The problem is that the physical environment is sometimes less change-able than are human ***behaviors***. How are you going to reduce the isolation in some rural areas to make life more meaningful to a house-bound older person? How are you going to open up a gay-friendly youth club in an intolerant climate? How are you going to change parents' habits and get books into the house, as well as parents reading to children? Working with aspects of the physical environment requires some creativity and imagination. But so does every other aspect of professional helping, so let's dig into this question of the physical environment and client concerns.

Let's distinguish natural environments from built environments. Natural environments like isolated rural villages resist physical change, but not necessarily social change, such as introduc-ing busing for older people several times a week. (Buses are mobile built environments, if you use your imagination.) A youth exploring his sexual concerns or questions may be very isolated in a large or a small city, if the culture is not permissive. However, opening up a computer Web site in an agency might connect this youth with others as they explore their feelings. (The com-puter is a trans-environmental device that can establish electronic connections where none exist physically, if you use your imagination.) A non-book home environment, which has detrimental effects on reading-readiness, might be surmounted with a library card admitting child and parent to fun occasions involving words and books and whole new worlds for the young child. (The free public library is an extended environment beyond the home, where parents may not have the funds for books or the background to be able to read to children, if you use your imagination in making this connection work for the family.)

What we are suggesting, as part of the evaluation process, is to consider the factors inter-fering with a successful resolution of a case. If physical environmental conditions are part of the problem, then use your imagination to avoid those problems, to surmount them, or to introduce suitable changes to enable the client to achieve goals. How should we measure these things?

Take the house-bound older person before and after bus service is introduced (for her and for others equally isolated). How many times is this bus service used? (This might be a measure of cost-effectiveness in continuing the bus service.) What levels of satisfaction do bus patrons achieve? (This would be a measure of attitude change at the least, and increased connectedness as well.)

Or the youth exploring his sexual feelings, before and after he connects on the computer with others in a virtual discussion room. There could be measures of self-esteem, connectedness, or self-efficacy. "I am not alone anymore." "It's OK to be different from my friends and still be friends with them." "I don't have to rush into any decision." Can you see how these statements represent types of ***individualized rating scales***. For example, "How lonely do you feel?" Very lonely, somewhat lonely, occasionally lonely, rarely lonely.

Or the book-deprived house, before and after the local public library was introduced into the child's (and parents') life. How many books are visible in the front room (or wherever the child ordinarily spends time each day)? How often do parents report reading to their child?

In short, we employ the conventional measures described in earlier chapters as we try to assess interventions seeking to improve the impact of the environment on the lives of clients. It does take some imagination to see the environment in new ways, but the measures are old familiar friends.

ETHICAL ISSUES (SOCIO-CULTURAL, GENDER, ORIENTATION, STATUS ISSUES)

Ethical issues abound at every stage in the helping practice, including the evaluation process as well. They often come in forms for which a given practitioner may be insensitive because of his or her own life experiences with what is "natural" or "proper" in human behavior. Fortunately, we can learn about differences in cultural practices and respect these differences under the law. "All men (and women) are created equal . . . (and by law are entitled) to life, liberty, and the pursuit of happiness." We can't hide our differences from clients, but we can address them and emphasize our intention to help (and to learn from clients how best to help).

Whole courses and texts are devoted to the nuances of ethics for practitioners (e.g., Bernstein & Hartsell, 2000; Dolgoff, Loewenberg, & Harrington, 2009). Our concern here is only with those issues that affect evaluation using single-system designs. From a client-centered evaluation of practice perspective, we can reduce or eliminate a number of problems plaguing other forms of evaluation.

Clients define their own **goals**, while practitioners help to shape **targets** and find ways to measure them. Clients should understand and agree on the intervention to be used. Clients can be involved in a discussion of the evaluation designs used (see Chapter 12) as well as measures chosen; indeed, many of these measures could involve the clients themselves in their own self-study. The practitioner should plot the data collected in this process, and interpret these data for the client. However, the client reserves the right to agree or disagree that these observed changes reflect the attainment of his or her goals using the practitioner's intervention. This is part and parcel of our **concept** of **client validity**. We also assert (in Chapters 12 and 13) that it is possible for many clients to take over the intervention by themselves, as they would in life after therapy in any case, and still measuring results, to see if they can maintain these desired outcomes. In short, clients should give their assent twice, once with the practitioner's intervention, and again, when the clients conduct their own form of this intervention independent of the practitioner.

Chapter Summary

This chapter was intended to caution you about being too convinced about the power of science in the helping professions. (If you are interested in telling the difference between science and pseudoscience, we recommend that you read Massimo Pigliucci's *Nonsense on stilts: How to tell science from bunk*, 2010.) There are many places where things can go wrong—ably assisted by naive practitioners. However, don't be afraid of scientific procedures in your helping practice. They are there to help you, if you give them a fair chance. (They are often self-correcting, if you make a mistake along the way.)

You will differ from your clients, and that may make them or you a bit suspicious of each other, and damage the quality of the information you obtain in order to help them help themselves. Recognize the multiple ways observations can be intrusive and thereby affect the kinds of answers you will receive. Try the various methods suggested in this chapter to reduce this reactivity, not the least of which is to emphasize and prove that you are a team with your client, and when you both pull together, you can move obstructions that perhaps one alone could not move.

Evaluation Basics: Baselines, Designs, Analyses, and Decision Making

Much of this part of the book should sound familiar as we have mentioned many of these ideas in passing. Now, we'll go into detail, as by now you probably have the big picture.

This is a challenge for textbook writers who would like to say everything all at once, but in fact, no one can do this and still make any sense of the matter. Pieces of the puzzle have to come in some order. We'll begin in Chapter 11 with baselining, which involves clear measurement of the presenting concerns so that we know the challenge we are facing.

In Chapter 12, we present the basic single-system design for client-centered evaluation of practice. It is going to look like fireworks—the AB*M** Design—with the asterisks marking the places of new ways of performing evaluations. No mere footnotes, these asterisks will be significant to the method by which we evaluate practice.

In Chapter 13, we go on an advanced tour of designs, the kinds of designs that may provide the basis for inferring causality of your intervention. But because of the changes we made in basic single-system designs in Chapter 12, we have some surprises on these logically powerful designs that, in a few cases, turn out to have clay feet; that is, practically, in terms of client outcomes, these powerful designs are badly flawed.

In Chapter 14, we discuss analysis of data, a topic we are sure you are all looking forward to, like having a tooth extracted. But hold on: We know we will bring joy and gladness to the hearts of the statistically challenged, while still constructing an analysis of the case situation that pulls together multiple perspectives on evaluation without statistical trauma.

In Chapter 15, we come to the most important question of all these evaluation procedures: What are we going to do with these data? How should we use these ideas—concepts, empirical operations, designs for evaluation, graphs, data, measurement procedures, and numbers—into making one single meaningful decision on what to do in a particular case. In client-centered evaluation of practice, we have to discuss fruitful decision-making—or else all of the preceding efforts will go for naught.

Baselining and the Beginning of Evaluated Practice

Case Study

Bullying in the School

Your internship is at an attractive middle-size public school, in a middle-class suburban setting, where, on the surface, everything looks like sweetness and light. You are very surprised when your first clients, a father and mother, come in to complain that this school is overrun with bullying behavior, and that shy children (like their daughter, Clare, age 7) are having a hard time learning while having to put up with harassment. What can be done?

Your practice methods teachers will give you lots of information on how to zero in on the problem and situation, and what we will do here is to offer some kinds of approaches that will connect evaluation to your practice. Our experience has been that these are often the same kinds of challenges.

You might begin by asking the parents what they mean by bullying. If needed, you could also offer a definition to set some parameters in the discussion: bullying involves one or more people inappropriately threatening other persons physically, psychologically, or socially, to make them do something against their will. (Physical means touching, pushing, or hitting; psychological refers to verbal or emotional abuse; social means getting others to ignore, exclude, or laugh at the victim.)

First, you get some parental view of the situation—say, they report no physical bullying yet, just some psychological harassment (threats) to force victims to give lunch money to the bullies. And yes, there is a lot of social harassment as well, although they were vague as to its nature.

(continued)

Now you have some view of the territory as a place to begin, and you ask some other questions reflecting a systems orientation in thinking about the issue:

What forms does this bullying take, who's doing it (numbers involved), and to whom is it directed (only their daughter, or others as well)?

What are teachers and staff doing about it?

Where in the school (or outside on the playground, on the bus, at the bus stop) does the bullying occur?

Does it also occur beyond the school day (in person, or by phone or e-mail or the Internet)?

When does it occur (time of day)?

How often does bullying occur?

Are others (not otherwise involved) present when the bullying occurs?

The parents may not know all of the answers to these local questions, and you may not know what others have said in the literature about bullying in general and its resolution either. So you plan to do your information search on bullying as soon as possible. (See Chapter 5.) You invite the parents to bring in their daughter for a visit next week. And you will discuss this problem with your supervisor and the school administrators.

The important point to recognize is that these kinds of assessment questions will help you to be clear about the situation for which you must plan an intervention, *and* they may offer some perspective on ways to calculate whether your intervention reduced (or increased) the problems. They provide a reference point on where you begin, before you start any intervention. In a word, this kind of information provides the ***baseline*** for your evaluation of practice.

BASELINING: GREAT POSSIBILITIES

So far, so good. You are beginning to realize that assessment of the client's situation and the collection of baseline data are very closely aligned. *Baselining* involves the regular and consistent collection of information on targets to be addressed, so as to provide a reference pattern to compare against what will be happening during intervention. "This is what the problem looked like when I entered the case, and this is what it looks like at several times during the intervention (or at the end of the intervention)."

The ***targets*** that you choose to be measured are very important. They should be meaningful and representative of the package of concerns the clients have presented to you. For example, based on the parents' comments that money was being extorted from their young daughter, you might have selected "instances in which lunch money was extorted" and "social exclusion tactics, such as excluding Clare from playing with desired gym equipment or joining groups of children in after-school play" as representing the two key points your clients made about bullying of their child. You sketch one graph (see Figure 11.1), as follows:

CONCURRENT BASELINING: POSSIBILITY FULFILLED

Let's follow this baselining process. The graph first uses reconstructed memories of the extortion events from the parents. We'll label this reconstruction as the (A) phase, or ***reconstructed baseline***. This establishes a "ball park" in which the bullying takes place regarding the extortion problem. Then a ***concurrent baseline*** is constructed, starting from the day of the parents' first visit; this would be the *A phase*.

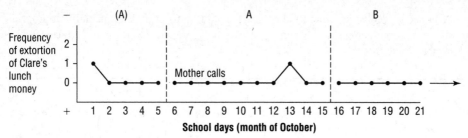

FIGURE 11.1 Extortion of lunch money

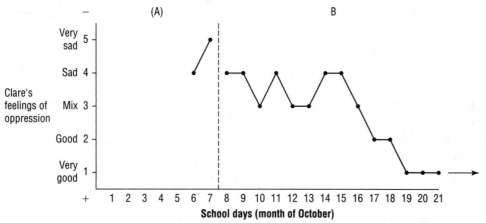

FIGURE 11.2 Clare's feelings of oppression from bullies (illustration of a delayed start of data collection)

Notice what happens next. According to the annotation in Figure 11.1, two days after their first visit, the mother calls the practitioner to say that something is not right. Even though no instance of extortion occurred in these several days, Clare has been very unhappy. You suggest a second visit later that day, after school is over, so you can meet the daughter. At this meeting, you begin to reconstruct what has been happening: Extortion of lunch money is only part of this situation. Clare feels oppressed by the possibility of extortion, and spends too much of her school day trying to avoid the bullies and thus being distracted from schooling. So you add a new graph, Figure 11.2, for Clare's response. There is no concurrent baseline phase in Figure 11.2 because you start the emergency intervention with Clare immediately.

Observe that while you are continuing to monitor extortion, you construct a new baseline on Clare's feelings of being oppressed by bullies, along with some reconstructed baseline. However, these two graphs, in Figures 11.1 and 11.2, are running on the same time frame. Put in simple terms for this child, you ask her to indicate by checking which "face" most represents her feelings of oppression that day at school.

"This is how I felt when I came home from school today:"

You need to consider what kind of scale would be most developmentally appropriate for your client. For an older child (e.g., age 9), it may be appropriate to present the faces and associated numbers, like this:

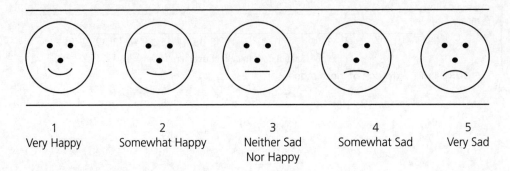

1	2	3	4	5
Very Happy	Somewhat Happy	Neither Sad Nor Happy	Somewhat Sad	Very Sad

For most teens, you could skip the faces, retain the numeric scale, and have them keep track of each day across a week.

"This is how I felt when I came home from school today: (put # in box below)"

Monday   [ ]
Tuesday   [ ]
Wednesday   [ ]
Thursday   [ ]
Friday   [ ]

The third graph, in Figure 11.3, represents various (equivalent) forms of social harassment. (You understand that social harassment will vary by content from day to day, and that it is reasonable to assume that any instance of such harassment will be troublesome for its victim.) We'll discuss soon what these graphs tell us about bullying in Clare's situation, but let us raise another question about evaluation and practice. The helping professional is busy at work trying to resolve the bullying situation with Clare (and at the school in general), while at the same time, she is collecting data for evaluation. What is the relationship between practice and evaluation at this moment (before the intervention to end social harassment has begun)?

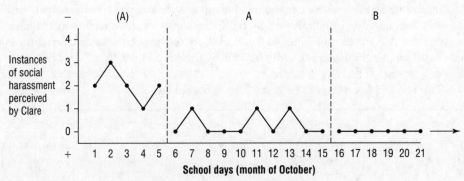

FIGURE 11.3 Social harassment experiences reported by Clare

"Wait a minute," you may be thinking, "What about all those good things I learned about core interviewing skills, active listening to the client, nodding my head to encourage him or her to go on, asking for clarification as needed, and so forth. Isn't this practice?"

No, it is just good interviewing skills, unless you are a follower of Carl Rogers (1951), who wrote that active listening *alone* was the important part of therapy, because any comments or questions we introduce shape or influence what the client thinks we want to know—rather than the real experience that only the client knows. ***Intervention***, in our point of view, is an intentional action seeking to change specific client ideas, feelings, and/or behaviors, or the social or environmental contexts in which these occur. Sometimes keeping quiet and letting the client do all the talking might be your intended method of intervention, but more of the time, we think it advisable to address specific targets with clearly constructed interventions. Thus, your assessment of the client's situation, even using good interviewing skills, is not yet your intervention, and to this extent, this assessment is very close to the evaluation process.

You should continue to use these good core interviewing skills during baseline and intervention alike, as they are non-specific goods that practitioners do, even if they do not advance the client along some specific path using intentional interventions. Interventions are ethical actions, helping the clients as best we can, but doing no harm.

RECONSTRUCTED BASELINING: THE BEST WE CAN DO UNDER THE CIRCUMSTANCES

Now let's look closely at what we have in the three graphs (Figures 11.1, 11.2, and 11.3) to illustrate the flexibility of ***single-system design*** evaluation. First, we have some reconstructed baselines that tell us about the general nature of the client's concern, as indicated by the (A) symbol. It may or may not be accurate; therefore, we try to get a concurrent baseline to the extent possible, indicated by the A symbol. There are no absolute length requirements for baselines, but we recommend a minimal length of 5 to 7 time units, or more, in order to show some clear pattern of stability in the presenting concern. If no stability emerges, then we really don't know what the presenting concern is, and we should extend the baseline period until we have a clear pattern as a reference point.

We should note that sometimes *only* a reconstructed baseline is possible to obtain before events of the case force the practitioner into immediate action. This might be described as an (A)B or (A)BA design, although we would recommend the longer but more descriptive (A)B*M** or (A)B*AM** design to reflect the client-centered approach. We will explain the use of the asterisks in Chapter 12 (but, as a sneak preview, it's an indication of the views of the client); the M, you will remember from Chapter 1, is the ***maintenance phase*** after the intervention.

Another important observation from the three graphs (Figures 11.1, 11.2, and 11.3) is the placement of baseline information relative to each of the other graphs. Recall that observation of extortion (Figure 11.1) and social harassment (Figure 11.3) began on day 6, when the parents first met with the practitioner. But the new target on feeling oppressed (Figure 11.2) began several days later, on day 8. Yet, all three graphs follow the same time line so that comparisons can be observed among them. We'll come back to this point as we analyze all three graphs together.

Sometimes it is helpful to put the days of the week on the graph, to see if there is any time cycle, such as near the end of the week when bullies are getting ready to go to the movies or such. Just put a second row of symbols on the graph like this:

1	2	3	4	5	6	7	8	9	10
m	t	w	th	f	m	t	w	th	f

PATTERNS AMONG BASELINES IN MULTIPLE GRAPHS

Something is happening at this school in regard to bullying behaviors and the reactions of victims. We are following one such victim, and we will discuss what we see in her three simultaneous graphs. You could take this one case as a marker for the whole situation, or you could follow several students (selected at random; then plot the average scores) to see if there is any pattern.

Now let's look at the graphs: In Figure 11.1, there was one instance of extortion in the (A) phase, and again, one instance in the A phase, which was about twice as long. So the parents were relatively correct about estimating the scope of this problem. In Figure 11.3 (on social harassment), the parent reconstruction of the concern was not accurate; they thought they recalled more instances than was true of the concurrent baseline phase (when nothing had been changed at the school). This is why it is a good thing to get concurrent baseline data when possible, and to use the reconstructed baseline data when nothing else is possible. According to Clare's data in Figure 11.2, the parents were relatively accurate that the child was feeling quite oppressed.

In each of these cases, the baseline gives us a beginning point (or really, a beginning pattern) that we are trying to change for the better. What happens in the intervention period? What you may be learning is not to trust overly optimistic textbook writers on case outcomes, but bear with us for this learning illustration.

There are no instances of extortion for the rest of the month (Figure 11.1), and there are no instances of social harassment as well (Figure 11.3). This is good news, although we do not know from the logic of the design whether the intervention was the likely cause of this pattern. They could have happened by chance alone. (Come back to this chapter after you have read the discussion on analysis in Chapter 14, and consider the various methods of analysis here.)

Figure 11.2 is quite interesting when we compare the (A) and B periods, where there is a marked improvement in Clare's sense of oppression. Whatever was happening at the school apparently made her feel better. She was also reporting no extortion of lunch money nor any social harassments, which might have affected her feelings of oppression. We can't say for sure with this limited design. There is not much opportunity to let Clare take over the intervention, as indicated in the AB*M** design (discussed in Chapter 12), because it was likely to have been school-wide, with teachers, aides, administrators, janitors, and children—all involved in working to change the bullying climate. So this is pretty much the end of the trail on identifying causation; we sometimes have to be content with simply the facts that the presenting concern is no long active in the lives of the clients.

A WORLD WITHOUT BASELINES: THE EMPEROR'S NEW CLOTHES

Is it ever possible to intervene without any baseline, concurrent or reconstructed? Certainly, some practitioners do it all the time. To skeptics like us, it is sort of like driving a car blindfolded; you may be going places you might rather not want to go. So we do not suggest going into practice wearing blinders. You need to have some sense of problem, some assessment of the situation, to have any idea what to do and where to do it. With reconstructed baselines, there is no reason to fail to collect some reference point data. So don't kid yourself or your clients, like a certain emperor we might name.

Chapter Summary

Here are the important points to remember:

1. *Ask yourself:* What would I need to know in order to figure out if my future intervention was working or needed changing?

2. *How am I going to collect this information on a regular and repeated basis?* Remember that you don't always have to involve clients directly in collecting baseline data; you might be the instrument of data collection at times, so as not to interfere with the flow of client–practitioner communications.

3. *Put it down on a graph.* This will aid systematic and regular data collection. Graphing is a universal language, so other practitioners at your agency can understand what has been happening and what you are doing. Annotate any special circumstance that will explain a rare event for the client directly on the graph when needed.

4. *Stable and steady:* Baseline information has to present a reasonably stable picture of the client's problems and potentials before you can make use of it. Collect enough data points and identify enough of a pattern to make those comparisons with intervention data.

5. *Share the baseline data with clients:* This can be useful in many cases, to get a confirmation that this is a typical picture of the client's problems and agreement on how to measure the problems. This is also a clear way to state the goals of service—to know when those goals have been attained. Again, it is *client validity* with which we are most concerned.

6. Share the excitement when you observe how patterns change during the intervention. It is good to know when things are going well; it is important to know when they are not.

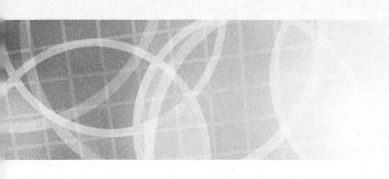

AB*M** Design

PURPOSE

The essential purpose of having a *design* in evaluating your practice is to make your evaluation logical, and not just impressionistic (and possibly biased). We will draw on the logic that has guided scientists of all sorts for hundreds of years. These designs not only provide a guideline for action in field settings but also introduce ethical issues we may have overlooked. So, on your mark, get set, and then let's go on constructing designs for client-centered evaluated of practice.

ON YOUR MARK

Some History of the Case Study

First, some ancient history: Hippocrates (*ca.* 460 BCE–*ca.* 370 BCE) reported his experiences with a large number of case studies, many of which concerned patients who died. This set the standard for reporting honestly. Unfortunately, other practitioners over history were not as scrupulous as Hippocrates; the public reaction to these snake oil therapists, ancient and modern, moved us to the present stage where practitioners are practically required to provide objective evaluation of their efforts. Or else.

Think kindly on case studies, because until objective evaluation methods became available, they were the only game in town. For example, one of my (MB) favorite stories of brilliant intuitive practitioners comes from the autobiographical writings of psychoanalyst Theodor Reik (*Listening with the third ear*, 1948) in which he was talking to a Jewish woman client in Holland about the serious disturbances that interfered with her work. These included the memory of a love affair in Germany that lasted several years, but which had now ended (as of 1935). The man was a gentile physician who had promised to divorce his wife and marry Reik's patient. But when Hitler came to power, he lost his nerve and broke off the relationship. She was in grief about this lost relationship, but was not making any progress in analysis. Then, one day, the following events occurred, as reported by Reik:

> After some polite exchanges about an uneventful day, the patient fell into silence. She assured me nothing was in her thoughts. More silence. After several minutes, she complained of a toothache, stemming from an extraction earlier that day. More silence. Then she pointed to my bookcase and said "there is a book standing on its head."

Instantly, Reik says to her: "But why did you not tell me that you had an abortion?"

Had I been the practitioner, I probably would have said, "Thank you for telling me about the book" and thereby missing what was for Reik a brilliant therapeutic insight that was key to the whole complex situation.

Reik meditates on his own insight, for which he says that he did not ". . . give a damn about logic and what I had learned in the books . . . I just said what had spoken in me despite and against all logic, and I was correct." (pp. 264–265). It turns out that the physician-lover performed a secret abortion on the woman that no one ever knew about, because such operations were punishable by death in Nazi Germany. She was still grieving about her lost lover and child. For Reik, the associations among the tooth extraction, pain, upside down book, a lover who abandoned her . . . all in the unconsciousness of the psychoanalyst, fit together symbolically and may have resolved the case (Reik does not provide any evaluation of its outcome).

Of course, we advise you to skip the part about not giving a damn about logic and what you have learned in your textbooks. But Reik had a point: Human situations are very complex, and scientific logic touches on only a portion of this complexity. So, if you believe that you have to violate everything we are trying to teach you, go ahead—just accept the consequences of your actions as well.

Moreover, if you think that our discussions about *single-system designs* are going to turn you into a brilliant Theodor Reik therapist, you have another think coming. All we can do is to address the last part of the story, the presumed but undocumented statement that the therapy had a positive outcome.

Hippocrates presented his experiences in an orderly fashion to show that there were knowable causes of states of illness and health—in contrast to the vast superstitions of his time (and ours). His orderly presentation of his bedside observations, his code of ethics, honesty, and service to the ideal of helping others—these are what have animated case studies for thousands of years. They survived because they succeeded in passing along vital information on how to practice and, generally speaking, how to evaluate that practice. For Hippocrates, evaluation was dramatic: The patient either lived or died. Today, we need to indicate some degrees of success, a topic to which we now turn.

Logical Changes to Provide Scientific Grounds of Practice

As helping professionals, we want to follow a code of ethics dating back to Hippocrates: "help if you can, but do no harm." (Veach, 1981) This means that we need to learn "what works and what doesn't," and to what degree, so that we can help our client, or at least avoid harming the client. In so doing, we may build a professional basis for helping other clients, what is known as *practice wisdom* in the literature (e.g., Klein & Bloom, 1995; O'Neil & Britner, 2009).

Let's begin this transition to modern times by putting the ancient case study method into our own symbolic notation. (This is where you just can't skip logic, even if Reik did.) The classic case study is what we call the B design, where systematic observations and interventions are combined. Reik observed the client, heard her comments, and then instantly intervened with his abortion comment. This apparently dislodged a flood of new information and presumably more psychoanalytic interventions, until a satisfactory resolution was reached—whatever that means in such sticky personal and destructive social situations.

You don't have it that easy. You may think your client is feeling better about himself, and you may think he is looking less depressed, but that won't cut it these days. You need stronger evidence—which is where we leave the old case study and move to the new scientific case evaluation that may be labeled the AB design.

GET SET

AB Designs

You have heard much about AB designs in prior chapters. Here, we'll bring all the information together in one place for your convenience, including steps to generate such an evaluation design.

The *baseline* or observation-only phase in your case analysis is referred to as A. This observation-only phase can occur at any point during service, although there are good reasons for trying to have this frame of reference before you begin the intervention. For clarity sake, we'll use the term *baseline* to refer to the before-intervention observations that make up this frame of reference. Then, we can say the practitioner can return to an *observation-only phase* any time during the intervention period, so as to provide a new frame of reference for some later intervention, as in the ABAB design, which we will discuss in Chapter 13. Baselines involve rigorous and systematic observation collected as data for our evaluation.

Some writers consider an A-only design, where careful watching is sufficient, with no *intervention* necessary. For example, a parent watches as an instructor teaches his or her infant to swim by preliminary playing-in-the-water games. While watching may ensure compliance with teaching (or just the enjoyment of watching the child play), it does nothing to the teaching intervention as such. We doubt the usefulness of this designation, and we do not use it in this book.

Baselines focus on a limited number of *targets*, those portions of the client or the client's life situation that need change. Ordinarily, the practitioner needs to know as clearly as possible what is to be accomplished, so that it will be recognized when it has been accomplished. That's why it is generally a good idea to start your practice with a clear *operational definition* of the targets to be addressed and to which you and your client agree as the baseline or frame of reference of your future intervention. Baselines are only one frame of reference in conducting an intervention. Sometimes social norms or rules can be used to recognize when the *goal* has been attained, such as finishing the number of community service hours required under judicial order. Other times, the content of the target may be sufficient, such as learning enough in practice sessions to get a passing grade on the test. Passing is itself the achievement of the goal. (Under some circumstances, you may not have the luxury to begin with a baseline, but we'll discuss that in Chapter 13.)

These targets are listed on the vertical line on graphs drawn up to monitor what happens to these objectives over time. Under most conditions, put one target on one graph. Study the graphs in this book carefully, as you'll be constructing many by yourself. (See Figure 12.1, in which we will emphasize the basics of a graph in connection with a case study presented shortly. And review Figure 1.1 for interpretations.)

Values, both the client's and the society's, are incorporated into the agreement of targets in this case. Values are what the client wishes would happen and what the society permits to happen in this situation. These values are indicated at the top and bottom of the vertical line. These ends are labeled plus + for something desired or minus − for something not desired and can be placed at either end of the vertical line, depending on whether we want more

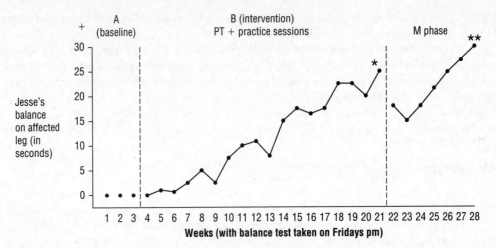

* At end of intervention phase, Jesse is asked if this experience represents attainment of his goal.

** At end of maintenance phase, Jesse is again asked if this self-controlled experience represents attainment
    of his goals.

FIGURE 12.1 Jesse's balance on affected leg (in seconds) using physical therapy and practice
sessions

of something (e.g., + would mean obtaining more desired skills) or less of something (e.g., + would mean obtaining lower levels of stress in the client's life). Be very careful in assigning the plus or minus; these have to match the content of the target. We often use just one symbol, and have the other symbol understood.

We distinguish a practitioner's good efforts at establishing *rapport* with clients (and engaging the clients in the process of change; Alpert & Britner, 2009), in contrast to some well-planned interventions set within the context of good rapport. A good relationship between client and practitioner is like the energy for engaging a client in planned changes; the intervention is the vehicle that gets you there. You need both energy and vehicle together.

The entire graphing is set within a theoretical context that says, in effect, if we appropriately perform certain interventions identified from the evidence in the scientific literature—this is evidence-based general practice—then we are likely to show desired outcomes in our case, similar to those reported in that literature. We need to use evaluation methods like single-system designs to provide evaluation-informed specific practice, indicating whether the general information, suitably adapted, is in fact leading to desired outcomes in the specific situation.

B refers to the planned systematic intervention that we construct, based on both the general evidence for this type of situation, and the detailed knowledge of the client's situation (within time constraints, and other constraints of the people involved). We often make use of a clear conceptual road map—a ***theory***—guiding the overall planning, but we always use socially and culturally sensitive actions suited to our clients and their situations. (See Chapter 1.) By obtaining ongoing feedback from our repeated measures of the targets, we may continually approach our client's ***objectives***—and we are able to document progress or a lack of improvement. There are a lot of things going on with the B intervention, but the alternatives of omitting any of these diminishe the possibility of good practice.

Some writers consider situations with only the intervention and no baseline to be a special situation: B design. We have sympathy for this idea, but we do not recommend it, as it is subject to many dangers. First, people sometimes say that they can observe when desired changes occur—surely the depressed person, who says he no longer feels depressed, is an adequate proof of satisfactory change. Unfortunately, Worten and Lambert (2007) note that practitioners, especially in mental health areas, tend to overestimate improvement and underestimate deterioration in relation to client reports of change. We say: Welcome the client's report of positive change, but also substantiate it with solid evidence (as in an AB design). This is especially true in the many areas where funders of social and health services demand documented evidence of improvement. This really takes the option of not evaluating our practice out of our hands however much we may appreciate clients informing us of their improved situation. We say: Use client reports of satisfaction and success, but provide the solid evidence as well.

The little hatch marks on the vertical line on the graph represent equal intervals or degrees of that target. (See Figure 12.1.) Events move the client up or down on that line, and we assume that each happening in the real world is clearly represented by a dot for a given time on a vertical line. Then, following those dots over time (indicated on the horizontal line), we get our moving picture of the changing target events. Things get better (that is, they move in the direction of the valued desired end of the vertical line) or worse (they go in the other direction), or sometimes they don't move at all. (Depending on the target condition, not moving can be good or bad: for example, a dying person not getting any worse; or, a truant not going back to school, respectively.)

We have to know exactly when the baseline period ends and the intervention begins (and ends) because we will be comparing patterns of the former against the ongoing pattern of the latter to assess our progress and, ultimately, the outcome of our service. Equally important, we have to know explicitly what is meaningful change in the life of the client and to that client. These two kinds of situations often go in tandem, but not always. For example, a hyperactive young boy may have learned some ways of staying calm in the classroom, but in public, he still appears to be wild and uncivilized.

We may want to annotate the graph on which we are plotting data, so as to indicate why some extreme score appeared in contrast to the regular pattern of the other scores. For instance, a child gets sick and stays home for several days, and her grades drop significantly. Otherwise, we might get thrown off course by averages that include extreme scores, when, in fact, the general thrust of the data may support our service goal.

The A phase can use any or all of the observation or measurement methods discussed in Chapters 3 through 7. They all have the common property of getting clear information on the target without changing events in the process, at least to the extent possible. (If some measure changes the event it is measuring, then we can't tell what is true of the event or what part the measure played in capturing the change.)

The B phase needs to be as carefully operationalized as was the target event, so that we will know exactly what we did, should the outcome prove successful, and we wanted to use these successful methods again. Yes, of course, if things don't go well, we need to know what not to do again in like circumstances. It is easier to operationalize in some situations than others, like instituting a time-out procedure versus instituting a meaningful activity schedule for a client. But do the best you can so that you and the client will both recognize when that activity is being conducted.

Logically, the AB design permits us to evaluate whether change occurred in the target. We need some external perspective or benchmark to indicate whether that change is socially or personally important. However, knowing that there is a positive change compared to the baseline is the great advance over the case study method. It is based on systematic efforts using reliable and valid measurements over repeated times. Equally important for the practitioner is that ongoing monitoring permits us the enormous advance of making adaptive corrections, as needed, especially when the intervention is not working. Monitoring means repeatedly making comparisons of the cumulated intervention effects with the baseline and the goal. That is, have things improved, and how much further work is needed to reach the client's goal?

Strengths of AB Designs

The logical structure of the AB design assumes that the (undesired) conditions in the A phase will continue unchanged, if nothing interfered with these events. (This is sort of a social version of Newton's second law of thermodynamics. Tell that to your roommate.) Of course, the B phase introduces a planned intervention that tries to interfere with the problematic situation in order to get it back on the right track. If the problematic events change for the better, then, logically, we should look for the cause or causes.

Limitations of AB Designs

Unfortunately, with the AB design, there can be other factors than the intervention that logically could have caused the change, such as inheriting a million dollars or having an adult child return home after a disastrous relationship ended. So, in the next chapter, we'll discuss other evaluation designs that try to sort out such alternative explanations for the outcome of a case. With the AB design itself, be satisfied for the time being that improvement was observed. If you need to document causal efficacy of your intervention, then study Chapter 13 with care.

GO: AB*M** DESIGNS

With this section, we enter new territory in evaluation of practice in field settings. We introduce several new structural elements beyond the conventional evaluation with single-system designs. The first of these elements is the *M phase* in which the practitioner teaches the client to take full control over what appears to be a successful change in a given target. That is, the pattern of target events from baseline to intervention shows a change in the desired direction. The practitioner asks the client to interpret this change, as to whether it represents the attainment of the goal the client was seeking. This client's interpretation is independent of the statistical or procedural analysis that we'll discuss in Chapter 14.

Let's say that the client agrees; the changes recorded on the graph do represent the attainment of the client's goal for this target, or something quite close to it. (We'll indicate this "asking the client about goal attainment" by an * [asterisk].) This is an important statement because it represents a client-centered interpretation, not something emanating from the practitioner or the data *per se.*

Moreover, even though the client and the practitioner agree that the visible change represents a goal attainment or its close approximation, there is another critical step. Can the client continue to maintain this goal achievement on his or her own? The practitioner will not be around forever, and eventually, the client has to take over completely. The maintenance phase is the testing ground for this eventuality. The practitioner trains the client to do for himself or herself whatever it was that was involved in the intervention. Then the practitioner turns over all of the machinery of the intervention to the client, and then steps back to let the client operate on his or her own for a reasonable period of time. (What is the reasonable period of time? It depends on the issue. We'll discuss some details of this decision later.)

Let's assume again that the results are positive. The practitioner again asks the client if these results are representative of what the client seeks to attain—and now adds—by his or her own efforts? If the client again agrees, then this AB*M** design provides two tests of the effects of the intervention, including one in which the client is in full control, and two tests of the client's interpretation of the results as being what he or she desired to attain.

But what if the results do not look encouraging on the graph? Then the practitioner would not likely ask the client if this pattern represents an attainment of client goals.

If the results on the graph do look encouraging, but if the client says, no, these do not represent his or her goal attainment, then the practitioner has some important rethinking to do. Is there clarity on exactly what target the client is seeking to attain? Is the intervention sufficiently strong to facilitate movement to attain that goal? This amounts to a reconstruction of the plan for practice and will likely require further intervention and evaluation.

What if the client is unable to attain or maintain the desired results during the M phase? Again, this is important information because it tells the practitioner that no matter what the statistical or procedural results are, the client cannot repeat them independently, which is the ultimate name of the human services game. It may require another approach to teaching the client how to be independent in using the intervention experience, and further testing of these results.

As you can see, the information gained by asking the client's interpretation of goals attained, and whether the client can sustain positive results on his or her own, represent a whole new evaluation ball game. We have put the client in the center of evaluating practice.

For this reason, we are calling the AB*M** design the basic design for practice. It fulfills the practitioner's ethical obligations ("help if you can, but do no harm") and the professional obligation of demonstrating the efficacy and efficiency of the intervention, while the client provides the fundamental interpretation of whether any outcome is really an attainment of his or her desired objective. By giving the client total control over the intervention, he or she may be seen to take back his or her life.

Case Study

Using an AB*M** Design—Jesse, the Runner

Jesse loved to run. He ran in college on the track team; as a young adult, he ran in local marathons for fun; and he kept up long-distance jogging well into his 70s. Then he had a stroke, and his doctors told him that he would have to hang up his running shoes. Jesse wasn't quite ready to do that, especially when he heard about a special rehabilitation project for older people who had experienced a stroke.

With his running background and general good state of health, he was admitted to the project, and what you are about to read is a brief overview of his experiences, very much adapted for purposes of this chapter from a study by Miller and colleagues (2008).

From the start, Jesse had his heart set on running again, and this is the overall goal. "Running" for Jesse did not mean track races, or marathons, but rather being able to get outside and run around his neighborhood and through a nearby park for some time each day without undue pain or health risk.

The project directors had other objectives as intermediary steps toward Jesse's goal, such as building up strength in his body and legs, especially on his affected side where the effects of the stroke were most visible; improving his balance to where it was before the stroke;

(continued)

and to increase his endurance for exercise. Each of these objectives had an empirical proxy, that is, a scale with observable measures from low to high, on each of these targets (strengthening; balance; and endurance). These scales are the vertical lines on the graphs. We'll use balance as the least complicated of these targeted objectives, as an illustration of the AB design. Then, we'll raise some other issues that will complicate the case, as you shall see.

Balance is actually a complicated matter involving the entire body cooperating with internal and external signals. The cochlea (or organ of balance in the ear) quickly sent signals to the muscles and nerves in the body to adjust to what was happening to the legs. In the case of rehabilitation, this involved standing on two legs, and then eventually on one leg for a number of seconds. The goal was to maintain one-leg balance for 30 seconds. Try it; it is no easy matter for people of any age.

Slowly, along with the other aspects of the rehabilitation program, Jesse began to stand, and then to try to balance on one leg (his good leg at first). He quickly got the idea of balance, that continual adjustment to internal signals of being upright, on his good leg. Then with considerable anxiety, he tried to balance on his affected leg. For him, the matter was both maintaining his weight on one leg even when holding onto a bar at the wall of the clinic, and then eventually, letting go of the bar.

It is interesting to speculate on what part Jesse's own motivation to succeed plays a part in his eventual mastery of the one-leg balance; motivation was not measured, but time in balance was, and Jesse was generally encouraged with the progressive results. As you can see in Figure 12.1, it was not an even progression, but the long-term trend was quite visible and eventually attained the rehabilitation team's objectives of 30 seconds (along with success on their other objectives as well).

The first two phases of Figure 12.1 are the conventional pictures of an AB design, with one important exception. (We want to emphasize that we are making up these data, so don't attribute any of the following to the article authors Miller et al., 2008.) At the end of the B phase, the directors of the project specifically asked Jesse whether these successes (in all of the strengthening, balance, and endurance objectives) meant to him the attainment of his own defined goal. Jesse gave a qualified yes answer because he was in fact doing the kinds of physical activities he needed to do when running on his own, but he wasn't yet actually running on his own around his neighborhood and nearby park. (Let's call this B*.)

The third phase of Figure 12.1 now introduces something quite different, what we call the AB*M** design. In the M or maintenance phase, the project directors took what had been successful aspects of the project and put them together in such a way that Jesse had to practice them on his own in his own environment, his neighborhood and park. They taught Jesse to use the methods on his own that they were using in the project, such as warm ups, gradual movements, pushing himself a little bit each time without pain, and the like. Jesse nodded that he understood what they were saying and demonstrated to them how he would do it.

This launched Jesse on his own, although the project team continued to collect objective data as before. As you can see from the data on Figure 12.1, Jesse was a bit anxious about running on his own at first, but gradually gained confidence by observing his own mastery of the situation. He was able to sustain his record, and at the last interview, he happily reported that this graphed record was an attainment of his overall goal. (This is the M** part of the AB*M** design.)

What do we have in Figure 12.1? First, we have the visual pattern of a sharp difference from baseline running, A, to intervention running, B. This pattern is so clear that we don't have to use statistical methods to determine its success (but see Chapter 14). Moreover, at the end of the B phase, the project team asked the client whether these results represented attainment of his goals, and he gave a qualified yes, as described above. We are going to denote this asking as an official part of the design with an * (asterisk).

The third phase of Figure 12.1 shows the M or maintenance data, when Jesse has learned to perform the relevant actions on his own in his own home setting. These data suggest that he is maintaining his performance about as well as he did under the direct guidance of the project team. This represents a second positive replication of the results of B, which is good, especially because Jesse did it all on his own, which is how he will live his life after termination from the project.

A final addition to the AB design is another question to Jesse as to whether these M data constitute the attainment of his original goal, and he gives an unqualified yes. We will indicate this with two ** (asterisks). This gives what we see as the basic single-system design, the AB*M** design.

Unfortunately, things in real life don't work out as well as textbook examples, and it may be that the B never succeeds in exhibiting sharply desired results. This is an occasion when you can use statistical procedures to determine the likelihood that these obtained results did not happen by chance alone. (See Chapter 14.) If the analyzed results are still not positive, then consider a new or stronger intervention, and keep evaluating. If the analyzed results are positive, then go on to the M phase.

Again, things may not go well in the M phase. Jesse may not be able to maintain the pace that he set in the clinic for one reason or another (unknown). This means that whatever success the project team had in the clinic has not held up in the client's natural environment, and by our reasoning, should not be considered a successful outcome. We suspect that Jesse might be somewhat discouraged by his own poor showing compared to what he used to be able to do, but he might also be grateful to recover from his stroke sufficiently to run at all. Life is complex, and "success" is never a simple matter.

But we textbook writers are an optimistic lot, and we prefer to leave Jesse running happily at home, and the project team writing up their report for publication.

Source: Based on Miller, W. W., Combs, S. A., Fish, C., Bense, B., Owens, A., & Burch, A. (2008). Running training after a stroke: A single-subject report. Physical Therapy, 88, 511–522.

Chapter Summary

As you can see from Jesse's case, all of our constructions or designs are arbitrary. Here is how to construct your own AB*M** design. Come as close as possible to the ideals set forth below, but adapt as necessary.

1. Identify the client in this situation, and obtain a statement of the client's goals. Clarify these goals in operational terms, so that client and practitioner can know exactly when a goal is attained (or not).

2. Break down the broad goals into specific intermediate objectives, for which empirical proxies are constructed by the practitioner (the targets of the intervention). This will also help client and practitioner know when objectives have been attained. The numbers on the vertical axis present possible degrees of the target on any given occasion. For example, 5 may represent the highest level of contentment on a repeatable standardized scale, and 1 may represent the lowest. At one point in time, the client may be at a 2 level; at another, at a 4 level. These would be plotted on the graph. Annotations may be added to the graph to explain different circumstances that may bear on the data.

3. When it appears to the practitioner that the data show positive change, then he or she should ask the client to look at the data and/or comment on whether changes in the situation reflect attainment of the client's objective. If yes, then go on to a maintenance phase where the client is taught how to use the intervention by himself or herself; the same data continue to be collected. If no, then the practitioner should continue the intervention, suitably adapted as needed, before repeating the question to the client.

4. The maintenance phase is exactly like the other phases except that the client is conducting the intervention all by himself or herself, and data are collected as before to reflect these new outcomes. If positive outcomes continue, then again the client is asked whether these results, now self-directed, reflect attainment of desired objectives. If yes, this provides the basis of a successful conclusion of a client-centered evaluation in which the client is shown to be able to perform an intervention deemed the attainment of client objectives. If the results of the client-controlled intervention are not positive, the practitioner should reconsider the intervention and the training, and repeat the process until successful.

CHAPTER 13

Advanced Designs

INTRODUCTION TO SIMPLICITY IN TALKING ABOUT COMPLEX SUBJECTS

We have been dancing around the term *causation* for many chapters, promising you the promised land of logic sometime later. The time has come to deliver on this promise. In the traditional literature of **single-system design** (Bloom, Fischer, & Orme, 2009), advanced evaluation designs like ABA, ABAB, and multiple baseline were offered as grounds to infer causation. (You'll see why this was so in a minute.) Unfortunately, we have to demur because we see the situation as much more complicated than previously expressed. Given this apparent reversal in thinking, we owe everyone an explanation on why we see causation differently. This explanation begins with the basic AB design.

Take any basic AB design on some client target. Rather than getting involved with specific details of content, let us say instead that the term *good* means that the current status of the client is desired by the client. And *bad* means that the current status of the client is undesired by the client. So, this would mean that in a typical AB design where the data on the graph improve from baseline to intervention, we would observe a pattern of data change like that in Figure 13.1, meaning that the baseline data, A, are problematic, and after the intervention, B, the data are more desirable to the client. Let's call this Scenario #1 (Figure 13.1). Let us ignore the situation when the intervention B does not change the problem for the better, because this is an incomplete intervention, and presumably, the helping professional would try another intervention, C, or a greater intensity of the B intervention.

Given this picture, we have said that the logic of AB designs permits us to say that B is different (in the positive direction) than A. We could not say why there is this difference. That is, we could not infer causality because there were many alternative explanations why the results turned out as they did. For example, something could have happened during the intervention time that had a stronger impact on the client than the intervention did, in either a positive or negative direction, like getting a pay raise or losing a job, and so on. (See Chapter 12 for other alternative explanations.)

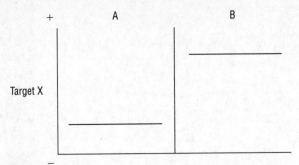

FIGURE 13.1   Scenario 1. General format for AB design (hypothetical data). No causality can be inferred from this design.

From the point of view of client-centered evaluation, we can say that the client and practitioner are happy with the results in the first scenario, so far as they go, while a researcher (or logician) is not happy because there is no logical basis to infer causality. Ideally, what we would want is to have client, practitioner, and researcher all agree on the positive nature of the outcome. Let's see how to attain this.

ABA DESIGN

We'll start with the ABA Design, the simplest of the advanced experimental *designs*, with regard to some client *target*. At *baseline*, A1, the problem situation is clear. And at the end of *intervention*, B, matters have improved considerably. So far, this is an AB design. But logically, if you remove the successful B intervention to see what happens—this phase would be A2— there are two possibilities: Things can go back to the problematic status at A1, or they can continue in a positive status as it was in the B phase. Let's talk about these alternatives:

Scenario #2 (Figure 13.2): This is the basic ABA textbook model in which the researcher (or the logician) is happy because he or she has shown that "when and only when an intervention is applied, do positive outcomes occur." This is the logical basis for inferring causality of the

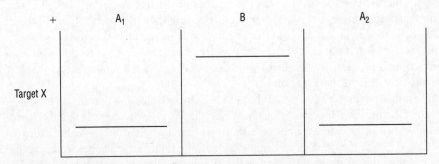

FIGURE 13.2   Scenario 2. General format for ABA design (hypothetical data). From this pattern of data, causality can be inferred, but the client is left in an undesirable position.

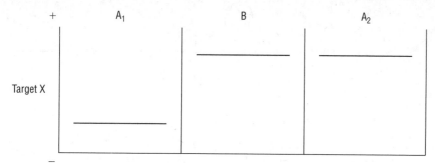

FIGURE 13.3 Scenario 3. ABA design (hypothetical data) from which causality *cannot* be inferred. Client and practitioner are in a desired position, but researcher or logician is not.

B intervention in this situation, and thus has been the textbook model of the strength of the ABA design. However, the client and the practitioner are not happy; a bad situation has returned and the client is no further ahead than when he or she walked in the door. The practitioner (like the researcher) recognizes the likelihood that B is causal, but this is not a successful outcome for client or practitioner.

Scenario #3 (Figure 13.3): In this scenario, the client and practitioner are happy, because it suggests that whatever happened in the B phase has carried over to the A2 phase. This is, after all, what we hope for in practice, that the client learns the effective behaviors from the intervention and carries on in her or his own life. But the researcher is not happy. There is no way to assume causation of the B intervention because the same positive results occurred when no intervention was present.

What we have here is a conflict between the ideals of logic and the practical world of client and helping professional. Ideally, we would want both groups to agree on a positive outcome. It is too bad to leave either the client, the practitioner, or the researcher feeling unhappy, so let's see what we can do to solve this dilemma.

THE M PHASE ADDED TO THE ABA DESIGN: THE ABAM DESIGN

You will recall from the Chapter 12 that we recommended that a *maintenance phase* be added to all *single-system designs* to make sure that the client had complete control over the successful intervention method when on his or her own, wherever possible. An M phase is not a logical addition to designs as we will be using it, but it is important in a new way. A good outcome in the M phase of an AB design would show that regardless of the actual cause involved, the client could produce the same positive outcomes on his or her own using the training from the B intervention. Now, the client and practitioner are happy, while the researcher is left rubbing his or her head—why are the practitioner and client happy when we still don't know the logical cause of this outcome? We think the answer is that the researcher is interested in statistical and logical outcomes while the practitioner and client are interested in practical outcomes. This dichotomy reflects the nature of research (abstract, generating general empirical statements) and evaluation (practical, solving immediate problems).

Let's apply a maintenance phase to two scenarios of the ABA design, and call it an ABAM design, with two possible outcomes in the M phase, as shown in Scenarios #4 and #5. (See Figures 13.4 and 13.5.)

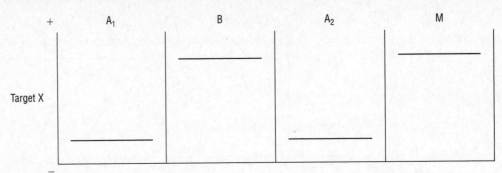

FIGURE 13.4   Scenario 4. General format for ABAM design (hypothetical data). Causality can be inferred logically (from ABA), and practically (from M phase). Client, practitioner, and researcher are all pleased.

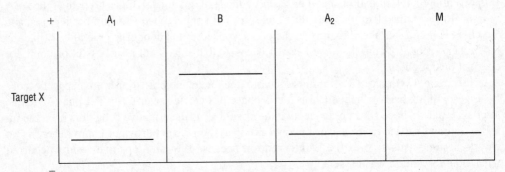

FIGURE 13.5   Scenario 5. ABAM design (hypothetical data). Causality can logically be inferred from the ABA design but it is fatally flawed in this scenario because the client cannot attain the same positive outcome on his or her own.

Scenario #4: Ah, now everyone is happy. The client is left in a positive outcome status, one which he or she produced himself or herself in the M phase. The practitioner is happy for the client and has a good hunch that this intervention might be added to his or her repertoire for another client with a similar problem. The researcher is happy that causation can now be inferred (from the ABA part alone), and moreover that the client can do it on his or her own as well (from the M part—researchers are not heartless beasts after all).

Scenario #5: Drat, now no one is happy. The client is left in a negative outcome status at the end of the M phase, especially one that he or she learned to do from instructions from the practitioner. The practitioner is unhappy about this outcome and confused as to why M was unsuccessful, whereas B was successful. And the researcher is unhappy because what was the apparent cause of positive behaviors in B turns out not to be effective when the client uses the same method himself or herself. What kind of causal information does an ABA design provide, if it doesn't show positive results when the client performs the intervention in the real world?

What have we learned from this exercise, so far? Causal inference is not all that it is cracked up to be; it is more complicated than we had expected. And it may leave the primary actors—clients, practitioners, or researchers in different states of happiness or unhappiness over the same outcome. However, this exercise once again suggests that an M phase can be very important in understanding the dynamics of the case, from the perspective of a client-centered evaluation. This is a different perspective from a purely logical point of view.

ABAB AND ABABM DESIGNS

The ABAB design is a powerful tool in the single-system design family, and you can see why: In the textbook outcome of the ABAB design, positive results are seen when and only when the intervention is applied by the practitioner, and never in the observation periods. Let's diagram this textbook ABAB design in Scenario #6 (Figure 13.6).

Shouldn't everybody be happy? The client ends right side up on the positive zone; the researcher and the practitioner have two occasions to infer causality (A1B1A2 and B1A2B2) on grounds that when and only when an intervention is introduced do good results occur. We don't want to be killjoys, but there are other scenarios. (See Figures 13.7 and 13.8.)

In Scenario #7 (Figure 13.7), we have some important points to make. First, we should never have gone into the B2 phase because the A2 phase violates the logic of both the ABA and the ABAB design. Let's argue this point. The logical rule is "when and only when an intervention occurs should positive results occur." This is broken in Scenario #7 when A2 shows good results,

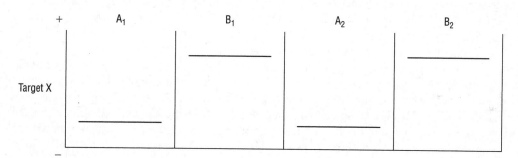

FIGURE 13.6   Scenario 6. General format for ABAB design (hypothetical data). Causality can be inferred from the ABAB design.

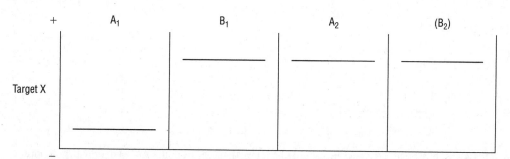

FIGURE 13.7   Scenario 7. Causality cannot logically be inferred from this ABAB design because A2 is at the same (desired) level as B1 (and B2, which should not have been started). However, it may be that the client has learned from the B phase how to perform at desired levels—a practical outcome. The client and practitioner are happy; the researcher is not. (See Scenario 9 in Figure 13.9.)

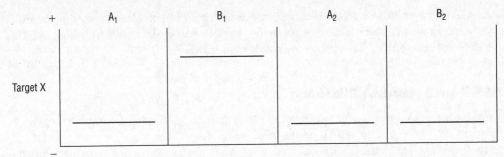

FIGURE 13.8   Scenario 8. Causation cannot be inferred from this ABAB design because B2 is at the same undesired level as A2, so that the intervention B is not reliably positive. The client, practitioner, and researcher are not happy with these results.

and therefore there are no (undesired) baseline positions for a second intervention to seek to change in the positive direction.

However, what if, in fact, the Scenario #7 client has learned to do things in a positive manner (reflected in results in A2, when no practitioner intervention was going on). Don't these good empirical results (where the client appears to have learned some intervention for his or her own good) overrule the logical principle, and make moving into a B2 phase perfectly sensible? With regard to the ABAB design: No, no, a thousand times no. Actually, only two times no, in B1 and A2. These are both positive already, and there is little one can learn by going back to B2 (the same B intervention as in B1, but occurring at a later time).

However, if you are going to an M phase after a situation like the first three results in Scenario #7 [A = bad; B = good; A2 = good], then what you are doing now is to see if the client can perform these successful results (as occurred in both B1 and A2) on his or her own (ABAM design). This is a completely different question from the standard ABAB in which the practitioner is in charge of the B1 and B2 interventions. See Figure 13.9, which is an ABAM design, and not an ABAB design, as shown in Figure 13.6. We'll return to the ABAM shortly.

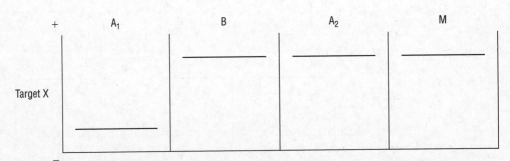

FIGURE 13.9   Scenario 9. Causality cannot be inferred logically from this ABAM design (hypothetical data), but it has practical implications that the client learned desired behaviors in B, repeated them in A2, and then again in M on his or her own. The practitioner was betting on positive results in M (based on results in A2), and this was confirmed. Compare this interpretation with Scenario 7 in Figure 13.7.

In Scenario #8 (see Figure 13.8), we are left in the same unhappy state as in Scenario #4 (Figure 13.4), maybe worse, because the researcher has a perfectly sound basis for inferring causality in the initial ABA part of this ABAB design, and now the B2 doesn't work. How frustrating, that the B intervention worked at time 1 but not at time 2. The client and practitioner are in the same boat because there is not much left of the B intervention, and they may have to consider some completely new C intervention or a change of intensity of the B intervention (from B1 to B2).

In Scenario #9 (Figure 13.9), causality cannot be inferred logically from this pattern of an ABAM design, but it has practical implications. The client seems to have learned how to perform the intervention in A2 without any intervention from the practitioner. The practitioner is happy as well, but feels for the researcher who cannot claim any basis for inferring causality. Compare this Scenario #9, an ABAM design, with Scenario #7 (Figure 13.7), an ABAB design. They look somewhat alike—but they are very different.

If we add the M phase to the ABAB design, let's see what happens: In the basic ABAB textbook model, adding an M phase leads to two different scenarios:

Scenario #10 (Figure 13.10) is perfect. The researcher is delighted because he or she has two versions of inferred causality (A1B1A2 and B1A2B2 plus an M phase where the client repeats the same results on his or her own). The client is delighted because he or she knows that the B intervention really works in this situation, and that he or she is able to control the intervention on his or her own. The practitioner is delighted over the delights of the client and the researcher, and to his or her good fortune to have an interventive tool that works in this kind of situation.

Scenario #11 (Figure 13.11) is very problematic. Yes, the researcher has his or her two clear inferences of causality (A1B1A2 and B1A2B2), but even this breaks down when the client can't manage to achieve the same level of success in the M phase. The client's hopes had risen sharply, but are now dashed to the ground because he or she can't repeat the success. The practitioner is in the same sinking boat. Yet it is still critical to know that the client cannot manage to produce the same results on his or her own, in spite of how good the evaluation results may be. This is what client-centered evaluation of practice helps us to understand on the differences between the points of view of the researcher and the practitioner.

So life isn't always fair, nor is practice, nor is evaluated practice. Make the best of it.

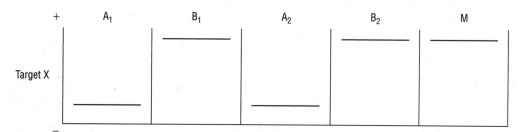

FIGURE 13.10 Scenario 10. General format of an ABABM design (hypothetical data). Causality can be inferred from this design, both on the logical basis (in the ABAB portion) and in the practical situation (in the M phase), in which the client has learned how to achieve the same desired outcome on his or her own that the practitioners achieved in B1 and B2. The researcher is also pleased with the support of the causal inference.

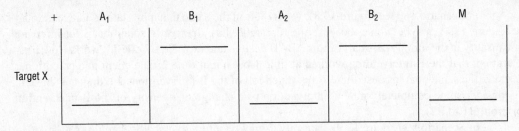

FIGURE 13.11   Scenario 11. Causation can be inferred in the ABAB portion of this design, but it is fatally flawed in this scenario because the client cannot attain the same positive outcome on his or her own. This ABAB portion may be good news for the researcher, but it is bad news for the client (and practitioner) who has demonstrated an inability to repeat positive outcomes when on his or her own.

MULTIPLE BASELINE DESIGNS

With the multiple baseline design, we have a design made in heaven for practitioners who do not want to remove a successful intervention from clients, even to be able to infer causality. Let's illustrate it in Scenario #12 (Figure 13.12.). Every symbol, line, and position on the page is important, so study this pattern carefully:

What we see in Figure 13.12 are two targets, X and Y, viewed at the same time for one client. Each has a baseline, A, but in target X, it is a short stable baseline, whereas in Y, the baseline is longer and stable as well and at the same time as interventive changes are being made in X. Note that nothing changes in target Y as the target is improving in target X. When the desired level is attained (and sustained) in target X, then the *same* intervention B is applied to target Y. As you can see, the Y target also improves after intervention, and we are able to infer that intervention B caused this improvement. Why? Because when, and only when, the same intervention B is applied to two different targets with stable baselines, does the outcome improve.

Now it is time to talk about those three elements: persons, problems, and places. This is where things really get interesting because the multiple baseline is the only design that lets us address:

1. two different persons with the same problem in the same setting, or
2. two different problems with the same person in the same setting, or
3. two different settings, with the same problem and the same person.

The logic of multiple baselines fits any of the three equally (see Figure 13.3; Scenario #13). Let's give some examples of this:

1. Here are Bob and Bobbie, neither of whom can do statistics, in the same class. Let's work with Bob (first, the target x) and then with Bobbie on this subject (target y).
2. Bob can't do statistics (target x) but he also is having trouble with math (target y) in the same class. Let's work with Bob on these two subjects, first the statistics, and when that is improved, then on mathematics.
3. In statistics class and in methods class, Bobbie can't handle abstract ideas. Let's work with Bobbie on her difficulties in each of these two classes (target x in statistics class, and target y in methods class), one at a time, using the same method to help her.

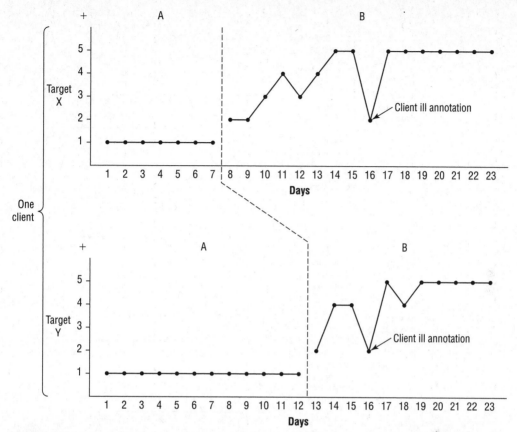

FIGURE 13.12 Scenario 12. General model for multiple baseline design illustrated by hypothetical data. Two target graphs on same client viewed simultaneously. Positive ends of axes indicated. Data entered as usual, including annotations on unusual data.

Rule: When and only when the interventions are applied do positive changes occur for the client. The diagonal dashed line connects the two graphs to show that the positive effect of intervention B on target X does not occur in target Y, until the intervention is also applied in target Y. The same intervention B is applied to two (or more) different targets.

We put in the same hypothetical data for each of the three situations (studying persons, problems, and settings) in Figure 13.13. In the first, we are trying to help both Bob and Bobbie with the one statistics class being offered at their school. In the second, we are trying to help Bob with both statistics and math, in the statistics class where both occur. In the third, we are trying to help Bobbie with both statistics and with methods, because both involve abstract thinking in different class settings. The logical model is the same in each case: When and only when the same intervention is introduced with a target does that target improve, and the other targets remain about constant.

MULTIPLE BASELINE DESIGNS WITH MAINTENANCE PHASES

As we've said, this multiple baseline design does supply the logical ingredients to infer causality when all of its components are fulfilled. However, this does not tell us whether the client can duplicate these successes when he or she is on his or her own. So, let's add a maintenance

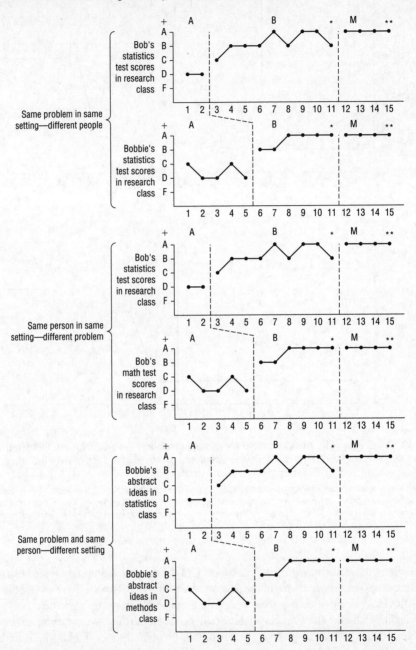

FIGURE 13.13   Scenario 13. Three types of multiple baseline designs illustrated.

Note: The symbol * refers to the question the practitioner asks the client at the end of the B phase. ("To what degree has the work we have done together so far attained the specific objective you were seeking here?")

The symbol ** refers to a similar question asked of the client at the end of the M phase. ("To what degree have you attained your objective, now that you have been working on your own to attain it?")

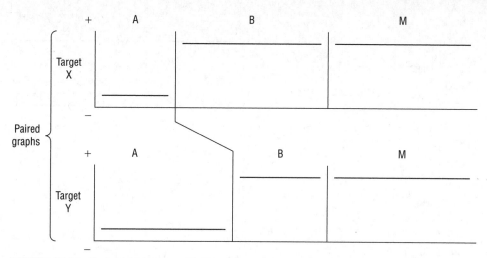

FIGURE 13.14 Scenario 14. General format of a multiple baseline with M phase (hypothetical data). Causality can be inferred from this design pattern as positive results occur when and only when the same intervention is applied to either different problems (targets), two different persons, or two different places—assuming the same unit in the other two factors (e.g., the same client and place in both target X and target Y). The M phase also shows the client can maintain both successful results on his or her own.

phase, but now watch what might happen. Remember, we are looking at the pair of targets at one time:

With Scenario #14 (Figure 13.14), all is well with the world. The researcher has his or her perfect multiple baseline, and even can enjoy the sweet delights that the client can reproduce results on his or her own. The client is thrilled for the same reasons, and the practitioner is pleased as well.

Scenario #15 (Figure 13.15) presents some real problems. It says that the maintenance phase of either target X or target Y may be bad, even if the other target is good. The multiple baseline design demands that *both* targets end in successful changes. This shakes the logic of multiple baselines by making the maintenance phase the final determiner of what is successful (namely, whether the client can reproduce all of the interventions for all of the targets).

So it turns out that client-centered evaluation is a tough taskmaster, making mush of some parts of what researchers had assumed to be the case with advanced designs (see Scenarios #9, #11, and #15). In other cases, the maintenance phase fully supports the logic of inferring causality, but now it is causality where it counts, namely, in the hands of the client. We have combined statistical and practical success (in Scenario #10 and #14).

THE BAB AND BABM DESIGNS: EMERGENCY DESIGNS

Sometimes, in spite of all the good advice you have received from practice methods instructors and field supervisors, as well as your teachers in these kinds of evaluation classes, you won't have the luxury of collecting baseline information before going to a carefully designed intervention. Emergencies happen. Get to work immediately.

What does getting to work immediately mean? It means that you have to make a lot of assumptions of what is happening in your client's life situation in order to have your intervention make any sense at all. These assumptions are based on your prior experiences as helping

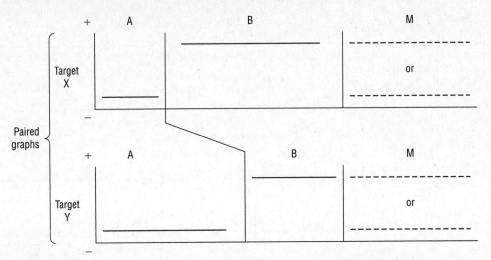

FIGURE 13.15   Scenario 15. Multiple baseline with M phase (hypothetical data) where one M phase is positive and the other M phase is negative. Causality can be inferred from this design pattern (using only the multiple baseline AB portion) but is fatally flawed with a mixed outcome in the two M phases, meaning the client on his or her own cannot reproduce the results at this later time.

professional and as a mature human being. And yet, you also realize how your perspectives may distort the actual client events, and so you recognize the need for ongoing evaluation to make sure you are in the right ballpark. Here is how to "have your cake and eat it, too."

Let's introduce a case situation, and follow along in these suggestions:

Ted Orlafsky walked into your office at school during the middle of the day, when he probably should have been in class. You're a school counselor intern, and have been dealing only with truancy, bullying, literacy, failing students, depression, and other minor issues, but you were not prepared for Ted Orlafsky who announced as he walked in your door, "I'm going to kill myself."

Do you know how long 5 seconds are? You suddenly learn as you stare at Ted without saying a word for 5 seconds, to let what he said sink in. Then you take a breath and gesture to a chair. "Sit down, Ted."

In spite of our good efforts to get you to take a baseline for at least a week or 10 days, you decide (absolutely correctly) that this is no time to practice all those marvelous designs and measurements you learned in your evaluation class. Instead, you lock your eyes on Ted and ask "Want to tell me about it?" while trying to hold still and act professional.

We are not going to discuss practice in this emergency situation, but would direct your attention to training that helping professionals get in hotline situations: make immediate human contact, ask for details of the stress, what methods are being considered, and can the client hold on a bit longer while you and he or she think it through and get help (e.g., Mishara & Daigle, 1997). Instead, we'll discuss some evaluation principles in emergency situations, which will parallel some views on practice in these difficult situations.

First, help if you can, but do no harm. (Thanks, Hippocrates.) What seems to be the cutting edge of the client's presenting emergency? And what would it take to repair the damage, at least to a point where one would have more time to consider reconstruction or prevention of further problems? If this involves breaking agency rules or tackling a client about to leave your office, do so—but make sure your agency has contingency rules for emergency actions and that you have professional insurance (or your agency will defend you if there is a law suit)—before emergencies occur!

Ted starts to tell you, then breaks down in tears. You let him cry for a few moments, offering a box of tissues from your desk. He starts again. Goes silent. Then he says, it's no use, and starts to get up. You race around the desk and get to the door, blocking his way. (You think briefly about client freedom of choice, and then put it out of your mind.) You firmly say, "Ted, go sit down. We need to talk." You don't move from the door. He is waving back and forth, probably wondering whether his 180 pounds will be enough to push your 120 pounds out of the way, then he finally goes back to his chair. You return to your place, all the while looking at him intently (and thinking frantically, what do I know about suicide and prevention?).

Second, take action. Do what you think is appropriate in the presenting situation, based on whatever knowledge you have at that moment. (No one is ever really prepared for the array of emergencies that present themselves, except to do first aid—mental health first aid or physical health first aid—so that possibly other helping professionals might come in to do the full service as needed. (Yes, do take that Red Cross emergency first aid class; it will serve you on many occasions.)

You ask whether he has taken any substances, obtained any lethal weapon, or made any other plans. He replies no. Then you suggest that he tell you about the several pieces of the story, one by one, so you and he can think about them separately and together. He sighs, and with his head down, starts talking about his girlfriend (break up), parents (prying into his affairs, grounding him, no use of the family car, etc.), school (grades sinking), job (fired last week for poor attendance), siblings (younger ones very annoying, older ones very successful, more than he could ever hope for), and so on.

Third, take notes toward an eventual measurement of the situation, while you are spending most of your time on direct emergency intervention. You listen intently, making some inconspicuous notes. As he appears to be ending his litany of problems, you nod your head and say, wow. (What class did you learn to say "Wow" in? You don't remember much class work at this time, and you are going on your human experience including whatever class work has filtered through to your consciousness.) "Ted, those things sound really rough. But let me go through them, one at a time, and let's discuss them. . . ." And so you do. Girlfriend. (What can you learn from this? Are there other girls in whom you are interested—and don't have to repeat the same things that bothered the first one? etc.) Parents. (Is another word for "prying" showing interest in their teenage son, as parents are supposed to do? Was Ted in any mental state to be driving a car—so was this a protective act on the part of the parents? etc.)

Ted reluctantly admitted that he had one strong and negative perspective on each of these social interactions, but the whole set of them were pretty discouraging. You admitted this, and Ted looked at you as if he had found an ally. But you were not going to ally yourself to any suicide, and told him directly that you thought that he could adapt to most of these situations, rough as they were. You point out, for example, with the girlfriend, that she had her rights as well as he, and that he may have been treating her like his property, which offended her royally. Ted looked like he had been socked in the solar plexus. "No, that's not so," he denied. You said nothing but just looked at him. "Do you really think that's what she thought?" You said nothing. Ted sighed, and was silent. After a time, when you felt that this emergency seemed to be under temporary control, you went on to other topics, including more background information: How long was this happening? What did it look like? How serious was it?—whatever questions that might help you establish a *reconstructed baseline*. You finally remembered your practice methods instruction, not to ignore the positive events, the goals desired, and such. What was Ted looking for in a girlfriend? Something casual, something more committed? . . .

Ted finally looked at his watch and said that he had better be going to his next class. You agreed, and asked him to come in again tomorrow during his study period. He agreed.

Let's truncate this case and say that you and Ted met for the next few days, each time discussing and defusing the situations, and that Ted seemed to be regaining his equilibrium. He reported a cooling off between himself and his parents, and his siblings, although he still was grieving over his lost "perfect" girlfriend. You told him that you would be away for the next week (holiday vacation) and that you thought it might be useful for him to consider his ways of dealing with all of these situations. You asked him to keep track of these various interactions—on forms that you can imagine from the measurement chapters—so that when you returned, you could pick up on the discussions (= intervention) that you and he had been having. He agreed and walked off with measurement plans in hand.

In fact, it was 2 weeks before you met; you contracted a bad case of influenza and were bedbound for the second week. In any case, Ted brought in the measures you and he had agreed on, and it didn't look as good as you had hoped. He was still quite depressed over his former girlfriend, and with his family, things had gone up and down the emotional scale. So, you began again to have the discussions (= intervention), but this time, you asked Ted to continue these same measurements.

We interrupt this case to bring you your textbook discussion of the BAB Design. (1) The initial emergency intervention, B (discussions on each target in turn and how it might be reconsidered as "unfortunate but changeable"). (2) The A phase (when you were away on vacation and then sick, but with Ted collecting objective data). (3) Then the B2 phase, with renewed intervention along with concurrent data collection. Let's illustrate this in Scenario #16, Figure 13.16 (BAB), with annotations to explain what was done when.

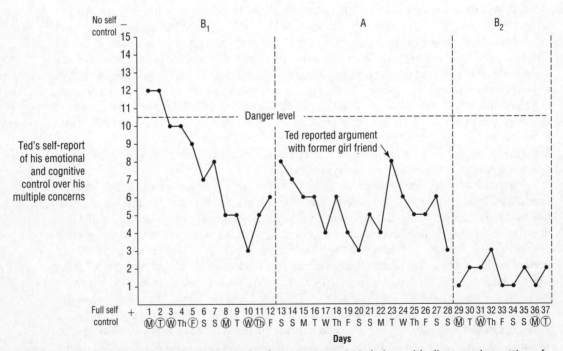

FIGURE 13.16 Scenario 16. Hypothetical example of an emergency BAB design, with client–worker setting of a danger level (serious thoughts of or preparatory actions regarding suicide) using client's self-reports called in daily. Office visits indicated by circled days. In the A phase, when the worker is away for school holiday and sick leave, client continues to call in to school clinic, which keeps records.

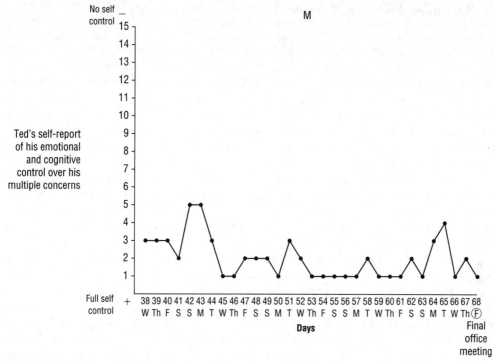

FIGURE 13.17   Scenario 17. Continuing the hypothetical example from Figure 13.16, here showing the maintenance phase in which client learns the skill of self-discussion regarding his multiple concerns in order to increase his adaptive ability to have control over his emotional and cognitive life.

Let's say that the BAB figure looks reasonably good, at least when and only when the intervention is being delivered. But as we discussed in this chapter, and especially something as serious as potential suicide, we want to make sure the client can manage to incorporate the intervention approach into his own self-discussions, and thereby to defuse what looks explosive, especially when all of the issues seem to come together exponentially. This is the M phase, and because of the seriousness of the situation, we would extend it for as long a time as school was in session (and perhaps with a contingency plan for summer).

In Scenario # 17, Figure 13.17 (BABM), we can see that Ted was willing to continue his data collection, with the results as shown. Ted appears to be able to manage his emotional and social states relatively well. You terminate the case, but give Ted a card for various emergency numbers if needed.

OTHER ADVANCED DESIGNS

When we said that all you could do with single-system designs was to vary the baseline phases and the intervention phases, we lied. It was a tiny white lie to prevent confusion because there are situations where we do strange things to interventions that don't look at all like our nice clean-cut AB*M** designs. However, these designs are so useful that we had to confess.

The Changing Intensity Design

The *changing intensity design* takes one baseline and one intervention, and then changes that intervention by degrees to see if more of it (or sometimes less of it) will move the client toward a goal. Here's an example, in Scenario #18 (Figure 13.18). Frida is in a sheltered workshop for developmentally delayed individuals where she is being taught to do simple work, toward a long-term goal of becoming economically self-sufficient. Recently, she has been putting small curtain weights or the like into small boxes, hour after hour, day after day. This is what she is capable of doing. Lately, she works for a short time, and then turns around and talks with her neighbors, stopping her work and interfering with theirs. You are asked to figure out how to get her back to learning to be an employable worker.

You recognize how powerful talking with friends is to her, so you make a deal: If she will work steadily for 10 minutes on her assigned task, she can come to the front of the room and talk with you for one minute. She loves this idea, and as the data in Figure 13.18 show, after a reconstructed baseline showing very poor work quotas, she quickly manages to work for 10 minutes to get her minute reward. You set a small kitchen timer for the 10 minutes so she can monitor her work time.

Then you tell her that now that she has the idea of working steadily, and also because you have lots of things to do at the workshop, Frida will now have to work for 15 minutes at a time to get her one minute reward. She ponders this for a moment and goes back to work. As the data show, she rather quickly gets to this 15 minute mark. Over a 4-hour work day, that is still a lot of talking to you, so your supervisor asks you to continue boosting the ante. And you do. Now Frida has to work 25 minutes to get her reward. She is not happy about that—we'll come back to some ethical issues here—but she obeys and now as the data show, she works 25 to 30 minutes. In fact, sometimes Frida works 40 minutes at a stretch, ignoring the timer going off. She still enjoys her one minute conversation with you, and is progressing to more complex work experiences that will help move her closer to her (and her guardian's) goal.

Ethical aside: What about the *ethics* of manipulating the client in order to get that person to do things she doesn't even like to do? This is a tough ethical question, but we have to place this

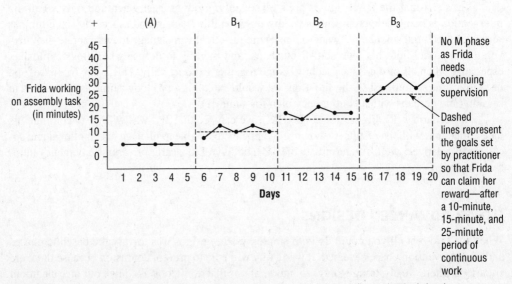

FIGURE 13.18 Scenario 18. Illustration of a changing intensity design (hypothetical data)

question in a larger context: Are there less-harmful alternatives to move Frida into an employable position? Do the long-term values of employability supersede the short-term interests in being sociable (and annoying to others)? We believe that this method is one of the least harmful to Frida, and potentially, one of the most beneficial to her, so that we are aware of the ethical issue, but have made a judgment call that some harm (not doing whatever she would like to do, i.e., talk to neighbors) is worth the potential benefit of learning how to work well, in terms of her long term goal.

Our point in bringing up this ethical issue is to remind readers that ethical issues are everywhere, and whenever we choose to do X rather than Y to help our client achieve his or her goal, we are skating on ethical thin ice. By being continually aware of these issues, we can seek to fulfill the Hippocratic code of ethics, help if you can, but do no harm. Helping and harming can each cut both ways, so consider carefully the ethical implications of your professional actions.

The Alternating Intervention Design

In the *alternating intervention design*, we alternate two or more interventions randomly. (Ain't titles grand?) Let's say that time is short, and you need to come up with a workable solution to a practice situation. So, you develop the two interventions that are described in the literature as potentially effective, and then randomly alternate when they will occur, when dealing with the same target. Here's an example, in Scenario #19. (See Figure 13.19.)

The grade school is about to revise its curriculum, and needs to know soon whether technique T is better than technique Q in teaching fifth graders to learn spelling words. The techniques are quite different, so you introduce one or the other on a random basis over a 2-week period, perhaps by using a table of random numbers. Figure 13.19 presents these data.

Remember we really do not know what exactly is causing the differences in correct spelling, but it is clear from this little experiment that the T method is better than the Q method, and consequently, was adopted for the new curriculum. Without other more rigorous information, we make an informed guess about T vs. Q, and our clients (the curriculum committee) accept our evidence as being reasonable given their circumstances and time demands.

What about maintenance phases in changing intensity designs or alternating intervention designs? As these examples suggest, an M phase might impose a harm or detriment in these cases. Frida may not ever be capable of mastering a changing intensity process for herself, and if

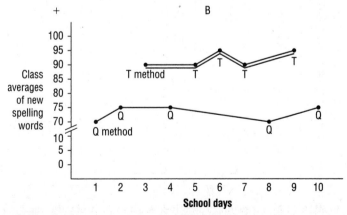

FIGURE 13.19 Scenario 19. Alternating interventions design rapidly comparing Method Q and Method T on randomized days to identify the apparently better method (hypothetical data).

you told the school committee that they should repeat the experiment themselves to see if they could control the situation like you did, you might be out of a job. Well, life isn't always fair, nor is practice, nor is evaluated practice. Make the best of it.

The Multiple Target Design, a Fake Advanced Design: Careful, But Keep Using M

We have found that students love this following design because it relaxes some of the requirements of the multiple baseline that are inconvenient, like having the *same* intervention applied to two *different* targets. Let's say, for example, you are leading an older middle-aged men's group composed of singles, divorced, and widowed gentlemen at a senior center. After a slow beginning, they agree to discuss how to deal with sexual issues for unmarried men, and with economic issues related to the stock market, and you bring in two different experts, one of whom shows some films and has an open discussion; the other lectures and hands out information sheets. You decide to measure how much information the men have on these issues before the experts come to the senior center, and how much information they absorb in the weeks after the experts speak. The group members mention to you how different these methods are, some liking the one, some the other.

Let's say that the measurements look like those in Scenario #20 (Figure 13.20). What do you observe? Like a multiple baseline design, the baselines are problematic, and the intervention phase data are quite good, and follow the pattern of staggered interventions like multiple baseline designs. Can you infer causality?

Not at all. Look carefully at the format of this example, and you will see that two *different* interventions were used, not the *same* one as required by the multiple baseline design. So, all you have here are two AB designs, performed on overlapping times, signifying no causal information at all—especially since two different interventions were used. A *multiple target design* are two AB designs dressed up to go the multiple baseline ball, but Security recognized them as merely AB designs, and refused to let them in to claim causality. But they lived happily ever after because they were useful AB designs and added important information, but not causal information, on the case.

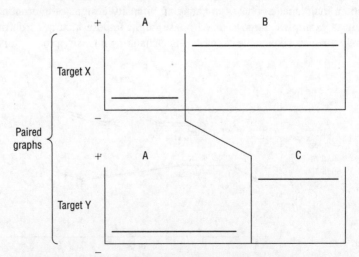

FIGURE 13.20 Scenario 20. Multiple target or Different intervention design (hypothetical data). Causality cannot be inferred from this design pattern because two different interventions were used with two different targets for the same client group.

Chapter Summary

To wrap up this chapter, we remind you about how to construct an advanced evaluation design.

1. Advanced designs take a different cast of mind, asking yourself what else is possible beyond our basic AB*M** design. All that you can vary are the baseline (or the ongoing observation phases) and the intervention phases with the same or different targets in certain time sequences. (So the answer to any test question your teacher throws at you on creating an advanced design is to make changes in these basic elements.) The logic is the same: Use the basic AB*M** design, and then add, intensify, return to an observation-only phase, as circumstances dictate. The designs we named above are just a few basic models, which cover a goodly bit of the territory. So start with them.

2. Ask yourself what you want to understand in this client situation: (a) What are the desired goals and objectives that the client wants to achieve at the end of the intervention? (b) What specific targets do you need to monitor to see if you are getting to those goals or moving away from them? (c) What time periods are reasonable in order to collect ongoing data? (d) Is your intervention reasonably likely to change these targets? (e) Can you train the client sufficiently to be able to replicate the successful intervention on his or her own? If you can answer each of these five points, you have the basic AB*M** design.

3. Ask yourself is it worth the extra effort to demonstrate that your intervention actually caused the specific change so that the client will feel as if he or she is investing in a successful intervention during the maintenance phase? (This is evaluation-informed specific practice using an advanced design.) If the answer is yes, then go on to some advanced design.

4. Begin surveying available advanced designs by asking yourself these questions:

a. Can I ethically remove a successful intervention, going back to an observation-only phase so as to assess the causal implications as in experimental replication designs ABAM or ABABM?

b. Can I arrange timed sequences of the same intervention for different settings, different problems, or different clients (with the other two conditions held constant)? If the answer is yes, this would be a multiple baseline design.

c. Can I change the intensity of the demanded client behavior to gain a fixed reward, or can I decrease the intervention and still demand the same level of client behavior? If the answer is yes, this would be a changing intensity design.

d. If I need to know which of two interventions is more effective and time is short, can I randomly employ one or the other intervention and observe what happens with regard to client behavior? If the answer is yes, this would be an alternating intervention design.

e. Can I arrange independent AB designs for different targets viewed at the same time with *different* interventions? If the answer is yes, this is a multiple target design, which really is not an advanced design in terms of logical power; it simply permits one to look at several targets and changing events at the same time. Be careful of a mistake that new evaluators sometimes make by confusing this multiple target design with its *different* interventions with the multiple baseline design which uses the *same* interventions.

5. Are you ready to take an advanced evaluation course? If yes, we have a wonderful book to recommend (Bloom et al., 2009).

Analysis of Data: A Systemic and Holistic Approach

Martin Bloom, Kimberly J. Vannest, John L. Davis, and Preston A. Britner

OVERVIEW OF SIX METHODS OF ANALYSIS

There are always multiple perspectives in the analysis of data from the practice situation. These perspectives reflect the stakeholders in the situation—the client, the practitioner (and agency), and significant others (including the community, which often pays part of the bill). This situation is parallel in some ways to the Rudyard Kipling story of the blind men of Hindustan and the elephant: each man touched a different part (e.g., tail, ear, trunk), and each claimed (rightly) that what they "saw" was an elephant. Which was the right claim? There is no logical ground for asserting that one way is more nearly right than another. In our opinion, they are all right—in contributing important pieces to the whole systemic picture of the elephant or a client's progress. We need to consider all of them, to the extent this is possible, and figure out what they mean as multiple perspectives on a single *target* event. This is what we mean by a holistic orientation to analysis.

So, this chapter will present a brief overview of these methods of analysis, along with the details on how to perform them. We'll conclude with a discussion of putting all of the pieces together.

METHOD #1 ANALYSIS INVOLVING TARGETS: FROM THE CLIENT'S PERSPECTIVE

Much of what we have discussed in this book has concerned asking the client (or making pertinent observations) about whether specific targets of the intervention are changing in such a way as to be achieving their *objectives*. This is true even if we consider internal feelings or thoughts, because practitioners can help bring these inside feelings or thoughts into sharper perspective. For example, Engel, Jensen, and Schwartz (2004) used an 11-point Likert Scale to help the client quantify the intensity of pain being experienced, in a study devoted to reducing chronic pain. In general, evaluators figure out ways to ask these questions related to specific targets. Are the client concerns still present after *intervention*, or has there been some change—such as fewer problems, or more objectives achieved? We attach numbers to these changes so as to see objectively what the client feels or does, using the various methods from Chapters 6 to 9.

Practitioners should recognize that a client "concern" can be either a *problem* (or "target complaint" as it sometimes appears in the literature) or a *potential* (i.e., what the client hopes to achieve in a positive sense). One example of a problem would be when a single parent reports feeling stressed out concerning her two active and healthy twin infants; the goal would be to reduce those feelings of stress. A potential *goal*, or a positive goal, for this client would be to learn relevant child rearing skills. Sometimes the two may be related, like helping the single parent reduce her feelings of being stressed out by teaching her some effective child rearing skills with her healthy, happy, rambunctious babies. You would tackle each targeted concern separately but eventually look at the simultaneous patterns of change, ideally with the record of the number of self-rated stress events going down and the observer-rated ability to use effective child rearing practices going up.

METHOD #2 CLIENT ANALYSIS OF GOAL ATTAINMENT: FROM THE CLIENT'S PERSPECTIVE

We've argued that the client's views on goals are central in any analysis of a helping program. *Client analysis of goal attainment* involves considering the client's views on how the entire intervention program is working with his or her concerns to date. In the *design* chapters (Chapters 12 and 13), we introduced the notion of formally asking this question—"To what degree has the work we have done together so far attained the specific objectives you were seeking?" This was indicated by an asterisk in the AB* design. Remember that the sum of these objectives represent the client's goals. If the objectives have been met, then we could ask the *global question*: "To what degree has the work we have done together so far attained your overall goal you were seeking?"

Then, at the conclusion of the *maintenance phase* (M) when the client was on his or her own, we recommended the AB*M** design, when the client again assessed the overall results produced under the client's own initiatives.

It may be that even if we knew the client's views on *specific* targets (from Method #1), we might miss something equally as important: the overall goal attainment from that client's point of view. For instance, we could have measured some specific targets on a client's health, nutrition, social supports, and the like, but still miss the big picture from the point of view of the client. Consider the case of an older person in need of protective services, who may have told us—had we asked—"Yes, I am well fed here; the room is very clean; and the staff are always nice to me. But I still hate being in a nursing home and losing all of my independence." This is a global assessment made by the client and a key component to achieving *client validity* in an evaluation of practice.

We need to see the forest even when we have carefully observed and measured many trees. How do we ask these global questions? It may be a part of any good practice in which helping professionals ask "how are you doing?" type questions. What we propose here is that:

1. These questions should be considered carefully in advance so as to capture the big picture from the client's perspective. It may be useful to have the client direct us, either verbally or from information obtained in structured logs. "I get the sense, from hearing what you say (or from reading your log), that this __X___ is what is central to your concerns. How has it been going in the past week?" Keep the question fairly general, and don't ask about specific targets.

2. It is also important that these global goal-oriented questions be repeatable, so we can get a reading on progress (or lack thereof) each time we meet with the client. The more natural the question is, the easier it is to ask it repeatedly.

METHOD # 3 TREND ANALYSIS: WHAT GRAPHED DATA PATTERNS HAVE TO TELL US ABOUT THE COURSE OF AN INTERVENTION

What is most likely to occur after we measure a *baseline* and do nothing else (except continue those measures)? The answer is more of the same, assuming we began with enough data points to create a reliable trend. One or two are clearly not enough, but 100 are too many. As a guideline, 6 to 8 data points may be reasonable to show a trustworthy trend. These are naturally decisions to be made in the context of the setting, the intervention and client needs, and no guideline is a definitive rule. There are certainly times when a shorter baseline is needed so that treatment can be initiated, and there is a distinction to be made between applied science of behavior and pure science. Whether the pattern of data at baseline is increasing (case a), level (case b), or decreasing (case c), what we can expect is more of the same from baseline projected into the next time period (if there had been no intervention). (See Figure 14.1.)

An important note: Sometimes there is a jump up or down between when baseline ends and intervention begins. (The technical name for this is a *discontinuity*, or change in level between phases.) This enlarges other observations made above, making an improvement in scores (positive) and a decline in scores (negative) even more meaningful. For example, Margaret's client caught onto the idea of assertive actions as soon as she discussed them with her client, not to be passive, not to be aggressive, but to stick up for one's fair rights. This showed immediately in the intervention phrase, where the client started out on a higher level

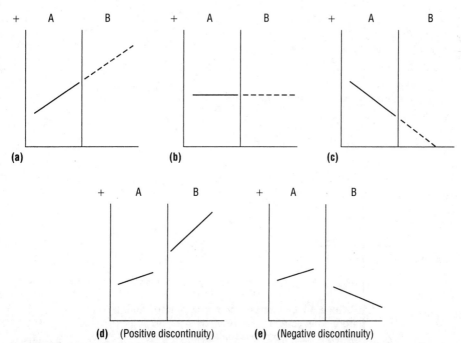

FIGURE 14.1 Three examples of continuous data, and two examples of discontinuities, between baseline and intervention periods

and took off from there. (See Figure 14.1, case d.) This would be an example of a positive discontinuity. Unfortunately, Gregory had no such luck with his group of spousal abusers who had been mandated to attend these sessions on reduction of violence. In fact, it seemed that the more he talked about being violent with one's partner, the more these men went home and became angrier than before (and more abusive, according to accounts provided by these partners). (See Figure 14.1, case e.) In this latter example, there is a negative discontinuity where average abuse scores dropped immediately, and even got worse as the weeks passed.

What about when something different happens in the intervention pattern compared to the baseline pattern? We've presented some logical patterns in Figure 14.2. The first batch of cases

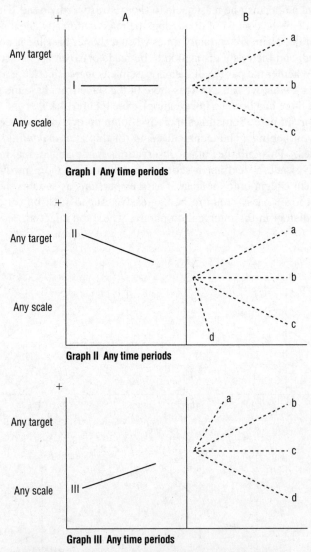

FIGURE 14.2 Illustration of basic patterns of intervention trend lines compared to level, decreasing, or increasing baselines. See text for detailed discussion of the logical possibilities

(graph I) start with a baseline that is level, but with changes during intervention in which (a) scores improve; (b) there are no change of scores; and (c) scores worsen.

But notice what happens in the second batch (graph II), in which all baselines show a deteriorating pattern (II.a., II.b., II.c, and II.d.). II.a. shows that the downward trend in baseline is turned around during intervention. This double turnaround means that we can call this "much improved." II.b. shows a leveling off during the intervention, which is an improvement from the downward trend at baseline. II.c. shows no change from the downward pattern; the client is continuing the downward decline, even in the intervention period. II.d. data take a sharp turn to deterioration during intervention. This is doubly problematic for the intervention that is supposed to make things better, not worse.

Something similar happens when the baseline pattern shows overall improvement toward a desired goal. III.b. shows an intervention pattern with no change from baseline; the data continue to show improvement but not more so than were shown before in baseline. III.c. shows a level pattern in intervention, but coming after improvement in baseline, this means that intervention period is worse than baseline. Indeed, in III.d., in which the baseline pattern is reversed in intervention, matters are getting "much worse" because of that double change, going from an improving situation in baseline to a deteriorating situation in intervention. However, look at III.a. In this case, the data show marked improvement over baseline data, which is doubly good because the trend had been improving in the first place.

We aren't ready yet to look at the details, but the big picture is clear. Other things being equal, the comparison of patterns of data between baseline and intervention periods can show the situation is getting better, staying the same (which means remaining problematic), or getting worse. The degree of improvement or deterioration depends on where the client started from in baseline—better or much better, worse or much worse. Use words carefully, so as not to exaggerate the improvement or deterioration during the intervention period. Discontinuities exaggerate all of these trends.

Of course, you will rarely get such neat straight lines. Often client data will show considerable variation within a single baseline or intervention phase. What we need to do is create a line that summarizes how the client is doing. This is done by creating a single straight line in a phase that best reflects its direction. Here's how:

Step 1.   Divide a phase, such as the baseline phase, into two equal parts and draw a vertical construction line dividing them. (See Figure 14.3.)

Step 2.   Divide each half into two equal parts, and draw dashed lines dividing then.

Step 3.   Find the median score of each half, and put a point on the one quarter and three quarter line, respectively, representing the median each half of a phase. (Reminder on finding the median: For an odd number of scores, it would be the score where half of the other scores are above, and the other half below. For instance, 1, 3, 4, 7, 46, the median score would be 4. For an even number of scores, it is average of the two middle scores. For example, given scores 1, 3, 4, 7, 10, 46—the two middle scores are 4 and 7; 4 plus 7 is 11, divided by 2, gives a median of 5.5.) For example, if the median of one half of the baseline was 4, and the median of the second half of the baseline was 5.5, in connecting these points with a straight line, you would find an accelerating line reflecting the entire set of baseline data. This is the baseline trend line.

Step 4.   Repeat steps 1 to 3 for the other phase, and project the *baseline trend* into the intervention phase. This projection represents what the trend would likely be if nothing

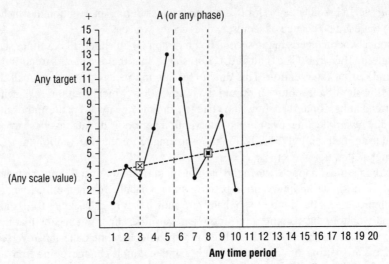

FIGURE 14.3 Constructing a simple straight trend line in baseline using medians with odd numbers of scores

Step 1: Divide a phase, such as baseline, into two equal parts. In 14.3, the line is at 5.5.

Step 2: Divide each half into two equal parts and draw dashed construction lines. No scores are lost in calculations with dashed lines.

Step 3: Find median score of each half by putting numbers in order:

1 3 4 7 13—the middle score is 4. Enter as ⊠ on $\frac{1}{4}$ construction line

2 3 5 8 11—the middle score is 5. Enter as ⊠ on $\frac{3}{4}$ construction line

Step 4: Connect the two median scores with dashed line and project into next phase.

intervenes to change it. Then you can look at the trend line of the intervention data, compared to the baseline trend line, as in Figure 14.3, showing an odd number of scores, and in Figure 14.4, showing an even number of scores. Is the *intervention trend line* better than, the same as, or worse than the baseline trend lines?

Let us make some general comments on comparison of patterns of baseline and intervention data:

a. For there to be real improvement, the trend in the intervention period has to be better than the baseline pattern and not merely more of the same. Say you are measuring the strength of a stroke victim's arm for two weeks before she is able to get into a rehabilitation center. There was mild and irregular improvement during baseline, and in the intervention period (after a training period to learn the rehabilitation methods) you saw a continuation of that gradual improvement. Did rehab help beyond what was already occurring in the client's improvement? Knowing the baseline trend that was theoretically extended into the intervention period will help to make this decision. With a positive baseline trend, illustrated in the stroke victim's situation, one cannot attribute the continued improvement to the intervention. Because the same trend continues from baseline to intervention, a plausible argument would be that the improvement may be due to something other than the intervention.

b. The intervention pattern should be reasonably positive and stable, over a reasonable length of time. Many factors influence any behavioral outcome, and so regardless of

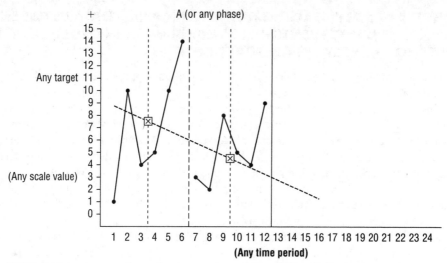

FIGURE 14.4 Constructing a simple straight trend line in baseline using median with even numbers of scores

Step 1: Divide a phase, such as baseline, into two equal parts. In 14.4, the line is at 6.5.

Step 2: Divide each half into two equal parts and draw dashed construction lines. No scores are lost in calculations with dashed lines.

Step 3: Find median scores of each half by putting numbers in order:

1 4 5 10 10 14—the middle two scores of the first half are 5 and 10, which total 15; 15 divided by 2 equals 7.5. Enter as ⊠ on ¼ construction line

2 3 4 5 8 9 —the middle two scores of the second half are 4 and 5, which total 9; 9 divided by 2 equals 4.5. Enter as ⊠ on ¾ construction line

Step 4: Connect the two median scores with dashed line and project into next phase

how good the intervention may be, there will likely be some variation in client scores over time. However, the positive changes that occur during intervention should eventually be relatively stable and stay in place for the time the client is on his or her own (during the M phase). This would be as close as we can come to predicting how the client will perform after termination of the case.

c. Use your common sense in evaluating data patterns and trend lines. Sometimes the baseline trend line plunges into the horizontal axis so that the client cannot show any improvement (or deterioration) when in fact those changes are continuing to occur. Look at the new data, even if the trend lines are going off the graph, and imagine the most unfavorable trend possible to compare with the new data. The intervention data should become more positive relative to that worst case scenario.

Even when some data points during the intervention are in the negative zone, the client may see these events differently than the practitioner: "Oh, those low points were when my in-laws came to visit and tensions were high. But in general, when things were normal around my house, the intervention training worked fine for me." The practitioner might have caught this point when annotating the data the client reported—"Anything unusual going on at your house during the past week (when the data were worse than usual)?" Or maybe the point was missed.

In any case, the client should be involved, when possible, in the interpretation of hard data such as appears on graphs. These "hard data" may not be as firm as they first appear.

METHOD #4 ANALYSIS USING NON-OVERLAPPING DATA BETWEEN BASELINE AND INTERVENTION: STANDING BACK IN ORDER TO GET CLOSER TO UNDERLYING ABSTRACT ENTITIES

Human society has long used numbers, symbols, and their manipulation to discover abstract entities and their relationships that cannot be observed directly with our five senses. Ancient Egyptians used a form of mathematics to identify factors in their study of the heavens, such as epicycles (the imaginary paths of the planets), so as to make their observations of the paths planets took over time to come out accurately. It worked, and the ancients could predict heavenly events with great accuracy. There are no such things as epicycles, but they were created to make visible reality more comprehensible. We in the modern era are also interested in change, and scientists have developed various ways to measure it—not by epicycles, but rather with abstract mathematical tools, which magically reveal underlying relationships (which we think is what the ancients were trying to do with epicycles, as well).

Recently, scientists have used measures of *effect size* (ES) as a way to quantify the amount of improvement from one phase of a single-system evaluation to another (Bloom, Fischer, & Orme, 2009; Parker et al., 2005). This is an abstract way to think about how similar or different two numbers are, either within the same study (baseline and intervention phases) or from different studies of the same kind of problem. ES provides a standard measure of change in order to do this.

However, abstractions are hard to pin down, and there has been considerable debate about how to quantify effect size, just as the followers of the ancient Egyptian astronomers were debating with the new astronomers like Galileo and Kepler (who threw out epicycles with their new ideas, numbers, and symbols explaining the movement of planets). See Shadish and Rindskopf (2007) for a discussion of different ways to look at single-system data from a mathematical perspective.

A promising recent development in the ES area has been the systematic work of Parker and his colleagues (e.g., Parker & Brossart, 2003; Parker, Vannest, & Brown, 2009). This procedure is called the Improvement Rate Difference (IRD). It is a relatively easy method to use, compared to the other methods that require more statistical manipulations. And it can be hand scored, as we will detail shortly.

For now, we want to emphasize how abstractions can help us understand the underlying relationships among clients, events, and circumstances. We have to stand back, so to speak, in order to get closer to the underlying abstract entities. Take something as familiar as the normal curve with its very explicit characteristics, such as the area under that curve occupied by two standard deviations above and below the mean, namely, 95% of that area. If some event falls outside this 95% area of the normal curve, then we had better pay close attention to it—especially if it is something we intended to happen out of the ordinary.

Parker, Vannest, and Brown's (2009) IRD procedure emerged from a study of 166 outcome patterns from a search of the relevant literature on *single-system designs*. From this study, the authors suggest that when your client analysis shows that there is a non-overlap of 90% or more of the data points favoring intervention over baseline, then your results are like the top 25% of their study of successful outcomes. This is a probabilistic statement: It does not tell you that your results are statistically significant as such, but that this kind of result (90% or more non-overlap of data points) is like the top 25% of their study sample. It is relatively easy and fast to determine the percent of non-overlapping scores and then to compare your results with a chart constructed from Parker et al. (2009).

TABLE 14.1 Model for calculating the IRD		
	Baseline	**Intervention**
Desired Scores	A	C
Undesired Scores	B	D

However, this procedure can be a tough taskmaster because it is difficult to attain 90% of non-overlap, or even 80%. Benchmarks for judging your IRD scores are given by Parker et al. (2009), and these suggestions can be helpful when evaluating client change. The benchmarks are as follows: .50 or below are considered a small effect, or one that could have happened by chance alone; .50 to .70 are moderate effects; and IRD scores of .70 or higher are considered high. Here's how to do the non-overlap method: *The basic idea is to remove the smallest number of data points in either phase or both phases in order to eliminate any overlap between these two adjacent phases.*

Consider the following table (Table 14.1, in which we will place data from Figure 14.5, and then illustrate the steps to calculate the IRD).

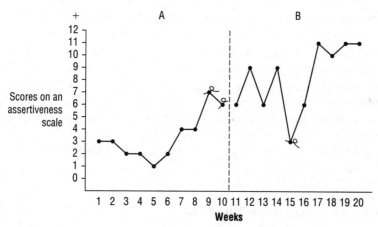

FIGURE 14.5   Illustration of the non-overlapping data approach

Step 1: Remove the least number of data points to achieve non-overlap of A and B phases (or any adjacent phase). Removing weeks 9 and 10 in baseline (A) and week 15 in intervention (B) best accomplishes this.

Step 2: What proportion of data points were *removed* from baseline? Take that number (2 in this case) and divide by the total number of baseline observations (10), and get .20 or 20%.

Step 3: What proportion of data points are *remaining* in the intervention phase? Take that number (9 in this case) and divide by the number of observations in the intervention phase (10), and get .90 or 90%.

Step 4: Subtract step 2 from step 3 (.90 − .20 = 0.70) and compare to chart at step 5.

Step 5: > .70 = strong results

　　.50 − .70 = moderate results

　　< .50 = small effects, or could have happened by chance

Step 1. As shown in Figure 14.5, we removed two data points from the baseline and one data point from the intervention, so as to find the graph with no overlapping data points between the two phases. Notice that the two baseline data points removed were the most positive of all baseline data, which happened without any intervention. This represents the possibility that intervention may not be needed at all. We have to check this by means of the calculations below. Notice also that the one intervention data point is the least positive of all the intervention data points. What is left after we remove these three data points from Figure 14.5 becomes the working data for the IRD calculations. In general, remove as few data points from the two phases as possible to achieve this non-overlap.

Step 2. In the baseline phase, the number of data points remaining indicates "undesired scores," and that number goes in Cell B. In Figure 14.5, that number is 8, indicating low levels of the desired goal of assertiveness. In Cell A goes "desired scores" that occurred without any intervention, and represent relatively high levels of the desired goal of assertiveness. This number is 2. (For ease of calculation, we have 10 baseline points.)

Step 3. In Figure 14.5, the Intervention phase shows 9 data points in the desired area; this number goes in Cell C. There is 1 data point in the undesired area, and that number goes in Cell D. (See Table 14.2.)

Now we are ready to calculate the IRD between baseline and intervention.

Step 4. Divide the number in Cell A by the numbers in Cells A and B combined. In our example, this means dividing 2 by 10, which yields .20. This is the baseline improvement rate.

Step 5. Divide the number in Cell C by the numbers in Cells C and D combined. In numbers, this means dividing 9 by 10, which is .90. This is the intervention improvement rate.

Step 6. Subtract the baseline improvement rate (.20) from the intervention improvement rate (.90) to obtain a .70 IRD. How good is the IRD in this particular case? It's a fairly strong effect, according to tables from Parker et al. (2009). This relatively simple mathematical procedure reveals the probability in this situation, even though it is invisible to our eye. Put this piece of information together with the other aspects of analysis.

METHOD #5 STATISTICAL ANALYSIS

Statistical methods of analysis are also available, including some that are on computer programs for ease in doing statistical analyses. Those who are interested may see Bloom, Fischer, and Orme (2009), Parker and Brossart (2003), or Rubin (2010).We will leave these methods for an advanced evaluation course. You could say that we're emphasizing inferential non-statistics in this text.

TABLE 14.2   Adding data to the IRD model

	Baseline	Intervention
Desired Scores	A = 2	C = 9
Undesired Scores	B = 8	D = 1

METHOD #6 SUSTAINED TIME ANALYSIS: THE TEST OF TIME

Another consideration derived from the client-centered approach can be termed "sustained time of successful (self-help) intervention." It is clearly important to *attain* the client's goals, but it is equally important to *sustain* those independent achievements over time. How much time? Good question, for which there is no simple answer. But there are approximate guidelines.

a. If the target is of relatively low seriousness in the client's life—marital behavioral styles that don't mesh, problems with institutions like interacting with a child's school—then we would suggest an M phase time about as long as the B phase was. This is probably the default time in most cases.

b. If the target is of medium seriousness in the client's life—ones in which major disruption of life would be involved, like job changes or conflicts in family planning—then we would suggest an M phase time about twice as long as the B phase.

c. If the target is of high seriousness in the client's life—risk of violence, consideration of divorce—then we would suggest an M phase about three times as long as the B phase.

When in doubt, err toward a longer time for sustained accomplishment of client goals. This won't be a serious problem for clients who are, in effect, acting on their own without the practitioner guiding their actions in any case. But the results of the maintenance period data can make the client and the practitioner more confident of the sustainability of a successful intervention when the client is on his or her own.

Chapter Summary

Let's go back to the blind men of Hindustan, which is pretty much the position we are in as evaluators. We "touch" the targets and "see" that things are going pretty well for some and not so well for others. We "touch" the client's view of goal attainment and "see" that the client has given some global assent to attainment. We "touch" the graph where trend lines seem to be heading in the right direction (as illustrated in Figure 14.2), which is encouraging. We have hands-on contact with the procedure to find non-overlapping data between baseline and intervention (or any two adjacent phases); after working the several steps, perhaps we discover that our data are not as strong as the top-rated studies with their abstract ideas about significance, even though we see considerable non-overlap between baseline and intervention with our own eyes. We touched the calendar when the clients are running their own affairs, and we were gratified to see continuing positive results and the clients' affirmations that they have attained desired goals—on their own steam.

What are we to make of all these (imaginary) pieces of information, especially when (in our example here) all do not point in the same exact direction? That is a very good question that gets to the heart of evaluation of practice. Assuming that all of our calculations and observations are correct, we are left with the facts that, taken from different vantage points, we may arrive at a complex picture of results. We bring professional and personal values to these results, perhaps favoring one more than the other but honoring all. We really want the clients to feel their own success in attaining their goals, but we also really want to demonstrate—to our funders, agency, and the profession—that what we did with these specific clients matches up as well as what other researchers have reported in the literature.

Honest researchers will admit that it is very hard to get great results, particularly when they cannot control many of the factors influencing people in the real world. And so it is with evaluators. Be happy to find confirmation anywhere you can, especially from the client and relevant others in the situation. Try your best to demonstrate that these results did not happen by chance alone. What is the bottom line? You must make a determination of the effectiveness of your intervention with this particular client so as to take the next action step. Helping practitioners cannot live by abstractions alone; they must make decisions and take action in an all-too-imperfect real world.

CHAPTER 15

Decision Making

WHAT IS DECISION MAKING?

You have been making decisions all of your life, from putting on your sock first on your right foot or on your left foot, to deciding whether to commit to a relationship with this person or that person. On lesser decisions, you probably do not weigh the consequences—you just put on the sock. On greater decisions, you definitely seek all kinds of information to help with your decision. Decisions in the helping professions are generally of the greater variety, and the objective information you obtain from evaluation is one kind of information to help you weigh the consequences of some possible action—although such data are not the sole basis of your decision. (You will probably also consider the values of the interested parties, the likelihood of the success of one *intervention* or another, the costs to all parties involved, etc.)

In fact, you will likely make decisions at every step of the way in dealing with a client, only some of which will involve the collection of data on matters that no one knows for certain. (This is, of course, why we go through all the effort to collect the data.) In this chapter, I will reconstruct a case study told to me [MB] by a helping professional dealing with the client, in which I will give you some vicarious experiences with both the data and the non-data kinds of decisions, partly to show how these two may work hand in hand.

Decision making is the next logical step after evaluation, in which some problematic concern is assessed, a helping program selected and used, and outcomes identified. What is the helping professional to do with these relatively objective results in terms of deciding what to do next? This question is important when the results are positive, but it is critical when the results are negative or neutral.

Decisions come in clumps. (It is rare for a helping profession to decide only the equivalent of whether to put on a sock first on this foot or that foot.) Rather, one decision usually involves related decisions. (Should I wear my striped socks with my business suit?) So, in deciding to take one course of action, you will likely have to consider what this will do with regard to other concerns that would be affected by a decision in the first area. You can *guess* at likely interaction effects, but you can only *know* what will happen by evaluating changes in all relevant events as they occur. We will distinguish between the ordinary everyday decision making from the kind that uses numerical evidence. Ordinary decisions will be called *ordinary decisions*, and the kind that use numerical evidence will be called *numerical decisions*.

Both kinds of decision making are (or can be) a shared activity for clients and helping professionals, because the decisions will presumably affect the life course of the client (to a greater or lesser degree). Indirectly, the decisions also affect the helping professional as well, in building a reservoir of effective helping tools that might be used with future clients in similar situations. Decision making is just as much a part of the helping process as any other component, but with the numeric decisions, there are some more or less objective pieces of information—usually in the form of data on graphs—that the client did not have at the start. Because we don't usually have these kinds of objective data, we will emphasize the question: How are any objective data to be used in making subjective decisions?

Decisions ultimately relate to one of only several categories: (1) continue doing what was being done; (2) do more of, or less of, what was being done; (3) try some new method to achieve the goal; or (4) terminate this service (or this part of the service) as having satisfactorily attained the goal.

There is a process involved in arriving at the making of a decision. Let us illustrate this process by using a decision you made in coming to school.

Most important decisions about our personal lives begin with some sort of (1) **goal** or end in view (such as first getting a BMW, and then maybe an MSW later), about which we locate.

(2) as much *information about alternatives* (there are also counseling degrees, and the possibility of getting a teaching credential, etc.) and the likely *costs and benefits* of these alternatives (one or two years at a university vs. getting a welfare or teacher's aide position immediately, but not being able to get other jobs that require credentials, etc.).

(3) Then we might *prioritize* which alternatives seem best, given our information, our available resources, and our valued goals (for example, investing in advanced education as the best insurance for a future career).

(4) Next we *assemble all of the ingredients necessary* to make a decision (such as financing for college, grade records, references, but also social pressures and personal desires and hopes), and when everything we think we will need is at hand, we (5) *commit* ourselves to the highest-priority path (i.e., we put all the forms into an envelope and mail it), all the while (6) *evaluating* how the whole process seems to be moving toward attaining our goals. If we interpret the facts available to us as indicating that we have met this objective, then we can turn to other issues in the case (or termination of the case). However, if we interpret the facts available to us as not meeting the objectives, then we have to go back in our thinking to see where we can improve the intervention or make the evaluation more sensitive.

You, no doubt, have your own personal take on this list of events in your decision to be in a helping profession, but these general ideas will do as introduction to professional decision making, where what you decide has strong bearing on another person's life and situation. Let's look at a case example, and follow these six steps in the decision making process, albeit from the outside looking in. We'll break into the story, on occasion, to ask what you think the practitioner should do next—that is, what decision the practitioner should make and for what reasons.

Case Study

Family Repercussions of Military Deployment

The war is not over for the Allen family because Sergeant Roger Allen has been redeployed to a combat zone for another long period of service, leaving his wife, Patricia Allen, to care for their two children, Lucy, 7 years old, and Andy, 12 years old. After struggling with problems related primarily to Andy and his schooling, Patricia made an appointment with a counselor at a family agency near the base where Roger had been stationed before his deployment. This is where you meet.

You invite them to the agency "family room," where interviews are held. It is a large comfortable room; in the middle is a cluster of chairs, couch, and coffee table. There are brightly colored walls, and a lemon tree in a tub in the corner. There are also some video cameras and equipment in the corner, for those occasions when the interviews are recorded. You invite everyone to be seated. Mrs. Allen sits on the couch; she is an attractive, well-dressed 36-year-old African American woman. Lucy sits next to her, dressed in her pinafore dress and holding tightly to her mother's hand. Andy makes a beeline to the video equipment, and Mrs. Allen shouts for him to sit down. He does. He looks very uncomfortable in a button-down shirt.

You repeat your name and ask the children what grade they are in and what sort of things they like best to do in school and at home. The children answer perfunctorily at first, but they grow more relaxed when you tell them about your brother's children, somewhat the same ages as Lucy and Andy, and the recent play they put on at school. They ask you questions about the play, and soon you have an excited interchange with the children. Mrs. Allen looks on with interest at how happy the children seem. She, herself, looks crumpled up, as if exhausted.

Then you ask Mrs. Allen if she would like to tell you about the concerns she had in coming to the agency. Like a cork pulled from a champagne bottle, Mrs. Allen erupts, spouting angry words, waving her hands, crying. It is all Andy's fault, she says. He never obeys. He takes things. (Indeed, Andy was caught last week stealing money from a locker of another student at school.) And he is mean and talks back to her. All the time Mrs. Allen is reciting Andy's faults, he is shaking his head, making negating statements. Finally, he gets up and goes to the window and stares out, as the stream of invectives continues.

You probably are a bit overwhelmed by the flood of strong feelings and the events they describe, but you take advantage of a moment of silence as Mrs. Allen wipes away some tears, to sympathize with how difficult it must be to raise a family when her husband is on the war front. Mrs. Allen takes a deep breath and regains a bit of composure. "Yes," she admits, and describes her situation, living in a small rented house, near uncongenial neighbors, mostly White, who seem to talk about trivial things all the time. Mrs. Allen and her husband are from the rural south, both went to college on scholarships, met and married and started their family. He joined the National Guard, partly out of patriotism, but partly for the pay. He was surprised to be deployed, but went gladly to serve his country. Money was always a problem; although Army pay was regular, it was still a stretch, she believed, and she took a job at a local store. The money helped relieve some stress, but it took her away from the children after school. Her husband wrote her e-mails complaining about this—another source of tensions in the family. Now she felt overwhelmed that things were spinning out of control.

(continued)

This is just the time to stop and ask you some questions about what decisions the practitioner might have reached at this stage of the story. To make life simple, let us offer the following alternatives, each of which leads to a different scenario.

Alternative #1:   Mrs. Allen should be helped to focus on the problems with Andy, because the school is concerned about the theft. Officials at the school are aware of Mrs. Allen's family situation, and they have offered her as much help as they can provide.

Alternative #2:   Mrs. Allen should be helped to address the money and work situation, because it involved both lessening stress financially and increasing stress within the marital situation. The military chaplain volunteered to help Mrs. Allen think through this situation.

Think of why you made a decision between alternatives 1 and 2—even though you may think we should have offered better alternatives. In fact, this disguised case is partly based on a real situation, and these were, in fact, the choices facing the counselor at this time, so go with the flow and think of this as an exercise in decision making. What criteria were driving your choice?

The *goals* of each alternative are both positive and reasonable—solving a school situation of which the authorities are very concerned, or solving a family situation when one partner is overseas, and the state-side partner has no family or friends nearby.

How much *information* do you have on each alternative? There would likely be considerable information about the school and theft situation, while details about the spousal dispute would be difficult to manage with one partner overseas. Can you get information on the client's problems to be resolved at the same time you obtain information on client strengths (and social supports) to be used to resolve those problems?

How do you see the *prioritization* between these two goals—the school problem with Andy and the family tensions? Some possible thoughts you might have had include: Which problem seems to demand immediate attention? Which is the easier problem to resolve quickly? What's the connection between the two presenting problems? Would a solution to one problem make a difference in the other as well? Other ideas?

Can you see how it would be possible to *assemble a large amount of the needed information* on one or the other goal option in order to make an informed decision? This would include what strengths the client brings to the situation, as well as what concerns she has that are burdensome to her. Also, in this kind of situation, keep in mind what your agency rules require you to do, as contrasted with what you might be permitted to do without violating agency rules.

Let's say you make a choice between these two options. Do you think you could gain a *commitment* to work on this priority item from the client (and her family)?

Assume you made your choice and are planning some action strategy; can you see how you might *evaluate* whether or not you are reaching some resolution of that problem? What possible evaluation design might be employed? What kinds of measures might be used in this situation? Who could be involved in the data collection? How might the data be analyzed on an ongoing basis, so as to get corrective feedback in your plan of action if need be?

Yes, you clever reader, the italicized terms above are exactly the terms of ordinary decision making, but the huge difference is that you are involved in making decisions that affect the lives of other people. Notice also how many places in this process the client is involved—another aspect of client-centered evaluation of practice. And notice how difficult it is to be clear and certain about any of the questions above.

Moving right along, let's say that the social worker decided to work on the school problem first. In a client-centered evaluation of practice, the social worker would ask the client to identify her goals. Mrs. Allen is not very specific. She says that she "... just wants to have peace in her family and to have her children grow up to be good people." When pressed to clarify these goals, Mrs. Allen explains that she wants her children to keep out of trouble with the law (probably in reference to Andy's recent problems with taking money). Mrs. Allen recalls wistfully how much easier it was when the children were younger, and she and her husband lived back in their old home town where she could consult any number of relatives for advice on how to handle some incident with the children. Now all that is gone while Mr. Allen is deployed, the children are older, and the Allens have made a home up north.

You nod in understanding of what Mrs. Allen has told you, but you say that you would like to get some information from Andy's perspective, too. Mrs. Allen looks a little concerned, but agrees. You notice that Andy is very attentive and it making little nods of approval as well. So, you go on, in a calm and warm manner:

"Andy, what was going on in your mind when that situation about the money occurred at school?" Andy gulped, and said in a very quiet voice that he needed the money because he never gets any at home. Mrs. Allen interrupts and says "That's not true. I do, too, give you money." Then Andy yells: "No, you don't." Mrs. Allen turns to you and says, "See, see how he is." And she begins to cry. You sense the high tension, but decide not to diffuse it. You say, in a calm voice, that yelling doesn't seem to get to the bottom of the situation. You ask Mrs. Allen if Andy gets a regular allowance, and she responds that he is supposed to, but sometimes she just doesn't have the money, especially near the end of the month. Andy says he doesn't get his allowance most of the time, and that his mom is always buying things for herself. And Lucy speaks up hesitantly that she doesn't get her allowance either. There is a very long silence. (You let the silence work for you.)

Mrs. Allen speaks first, very quietly, almost as if talking to herself: "Can it be that Andy took that money because I didn't give him his allowance?" You say that this may be one factor, and there may be others as well, but allowance seems to represent a clear objective in this situation. Andy is shaking his head in agreement and says to his mother, tearfully: "I tried to tell you that, I did try."

Time for another decision making challenge: What you probably observe here is a mother who is under stress from her husband being away in a war, leaving her without aid from family or friends. She admits to impulse buying when stress is high—"It's better than drinking," she notes, "like a lot of military spouses do." She seems to you surprisingly immature as a parent, and seems to swing between lectures on values and religiosity versus harsh punishments for each of Andy's violations, neither of which seems to work for long.

So, here are your alternative decisions; assume for the moment that you have to work on one alternative:

Alternative #3:   Focus on Mrs. Allen and her impulse buying habits and lack of a careful budget, in order to guarantee that Andy and Lucy get their regular allowances.

(continued)

Alternative #4:   Focus on Mrs. Allen's child-rearing skills regarding Andy's growing independence (as a young teenager) and her losing the battle of control of his behaviors.

Your turn. Look over the several steps in decision making as listed above, and see what you decide to do—and why. For your information, we'll list these steps again:

What are the goals? What information do you have on the alternatives, especially the probable costs and benefits of each? What priorities do you see in each alternative—that is, assuming both are important, which one should come first? Can you see how you might assemble as much of the relevant information about each alternative, especially employing the strengths of the client and her supporting resources? Can you obtain a commitment from the client (and relevant others) to work on a plan to resolve this concern? Who is to do what with whom toward what end?

And, because this is, after all, a textbook on evaluation, can you think of ways to define targets, measure them on a repeated basis, employing at least a basic *AB*M** design*, and then plotting data on a graph and interpreting it? So, what did you decide? What was your thought process?

Of course, Mrs. Allen values both regular allowances and giving Andy a growing sense of teenage independence. You point out that giving allowances irregularly is a kind of compromise to allowance giving and retaining control over her son, a solution that satisfies neither. Teenage independence should not include theft to make up for allowance. (Andy frowns at this point.) But the decision in the case of allowance should be mutually arrived at—Andy smiles broadly—because it involves privilege and responsibilities for all parties—Andy looks somewhat suspicious.

What might be helpful in this situation is a kind of family contract, where the rules are spelled out: Who? Is to do what? With whom? For what goal? Where? When? Under what circumstances (social and physical contexts)? And how will everyone concerned know when the action has been completed as intended?

For example, Mrs. Allen is to give Andy and Lucy their full allowance every Saturday at breakfast time when she has the funds. But also, Mrs. Allen will make out a budget where she sets aside all fixed expenses, including the children's allowance—pre-written checks for rent, and so on, but envelops with money for allowances—so that funds will be available as needed. Extra money may be spent on one small luxury a month, not to exceed X dollars. When this has been done as intended, the mother and children will write a letter to Mr. Allen telling him about the new arrangement and how it is working. Andy will tell his father how he is spending (or saving) the money. And he promises never to take anyone's money ever again. The children are nodding yes.

Mrs. Allen studies the contract, and finally looks up and smiles. Yes, she says, yes. The children are smiling. And Andy gives his mother a big hug.

Wait, the case is not over yet. Remember that you have a mother who is under great stress, is somewhat immature in making child-rearing decisions, and has shown a pattern of dealing with the stress in ways that, unbeknownst to her, create other stresses. You've offered a well-constructed plan to remove one set of stressors (on Andy and Lucy), but no one knows for sure whether Mrs. Allen will be able to implement the plan, nor what effects it will actually have on the children. So you suggest a trial period of one month, during which time Mrs. Allen and the children carry out the plan and record the results. For simplicity, you propose an evaluation plan that consists of a big chart to be taped to the refrigerator door.

	Week 1	Week 2	Week 3	Week 4
	Circle D for done or ND for not done and signed by all parties			
Checks written for routine continuing expenses	D ND	D ND	D ND	D ND
Allowance money given to Andy each week	D ND	D ND	D ND	D ND
Allowance money given to Lucy each week	D ND	D ND	D ND	D ND
Andy has not been involved in any problems with school or the law	D ND	D ND	D ND	D ND
INITIALED by Mrs. A,	_____	_____	_____	_____
Andy,	_____	_____	_____	_____
Lucy	_____	_____	_____	_____

What happened? Look at three hypothetical cases in Figure 15.1 and see what you think. Let's discuss this in terms of how you would use the numerical information from the graph to make a decision on next steps in the case. Notice that in this situation, the **intervention** is entirely under the control of the participants, and hence, is like an **M phase**.

In Case #1, you can observe a perfect condition, where Mrs. Allen and Andy complied with the agreement. Now the question is what to do with this numerical information. Is it strong enough, consistent enough, long-lasting enough to decide to terminate the case?

In Case #2, you can observe that the first week went well, and the second week, almost as well, but then things went seriously out of control. You might have explored what happened in the third week: this is where some annotation of the chart would have been helpful, to see if these results were part of a negative trend, or due to some special stresses that occurred that month.

In Case #3, you can observe that things did not go well at first, but after 2 weeks of trying, Mrs. Allen got her act together and things went as planned. Even so, what are you to do with these data as part of your decision making?

The answers to these questions are "it all depends." No, we are not trying to weasel out of giving answers to these questions, but it really depends on other non-numerical factors going on at the same time. With Case #1, we would be willing to accept the Allen Family's agreement that the concerns were resolved, but we would prefer to have their agreement with that decision. Think back to the discussion of an AB*M** design. So, perhaps the practitioner would meet with them on the fifth week and have them all sign a statement that the new situation fulfills their goal expectations, thus reinforcing the public nature of family decisions.

With Case #2, we suspect that we do not know all of the dynamics of the situation and our intervention does not succeed in resolving the problems. Data like these offer a good point of departure to ask: What is going on that we did not consider in our first meeting? How can we address these new issues? In short, these data tell us clearly to revisit the situation, change the apparent causal factors, and try another evaluation.

With Case #3, we have a mixed situation in the sense that we may not have initially offered Mrs. Allen all of the support she needs to resolve her problems. Fortunately, she

(continued)

seems to have resolved them herself in the third and fourth weeks. We can ask what was happening that produced these good results, and try to reinforce this, either in continuing contact with the family, or, based on Mrs. Allen's testimony, that she thinks she will be able to continue successfully on her own. This is a situation in which you might want to have a follow-up phone call to see if the results of the past 2 weeks have continued into the next few weeks.

In short, it all depends. But what is clear is that data are involved in thinking about decisions, along with values and other pressures, all within the client-centered evaluation approach (see Figure 15.1). We give meaning to these data by putting them into the value context of the client situation. We provide starch to decision making by providing relatively objective data as one basis for action.

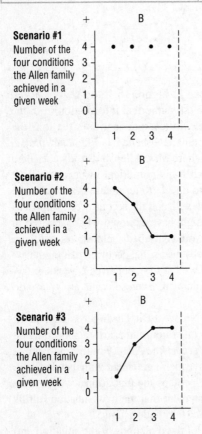

FIGURE 15.1 Three scenarios regarding the Allen family meeting four conditions related to the proposed intervention. Note that intervention B is actually under the control of the Allen family and thus constitutes an M phase in evaluation design

Chapter Summary

This summary is different from the others, in as much as it is also a summary for the entire book.

We started out with a new conception of evaluation of practice, one in which the client is front and center in our thinking. To the extent possible, we had the client define her or his own goals in coming into the helping situation (even if she or he did not start the process voluntarily).

We saw the helping professional's role as being one of identifying specific ***objectives***, the sum of which would represent that client's goals. Then we used the conventional graphing procedures on conventional evaluation designs—until we realized that there were problems in the conventional way.

We decided that the best way to reduce these evaluation problems would be to include the client's voice and behaviors in the maintenance phase (after the intervention phase showed some improvement over the ***baseline phase***). This really blew us away, and we started seeing stars. Actually, we started to put stars (asterisks) in the basic design formulas to indicate the importance of clients in voicing their judgment on whether their own goals had been attained or not.

Then, the ***analysis of evaluation data*** turned into something new, a systemic and holistic analysis incorporating various aspects of the evaluation: specific targets attained, a global assessment made, an interpretation of trend lines, and an analytic study of non-overlapping data between baseline and intervention (as parallel to findings in a large study of single-system evaluations).

We also began to recognize the importance of timing. How long should a maintenance period run, in order to make sure the client really was able to carry on by himself or herself?

In this final chapter, we discussed decision making, the pulling together of all of the information pertinent to a decision, including the client's contributions, the practitioner's analysis of trends in the graphs, and a comparison of our work against the general standards from the literature. Exactly how do we combine these disparate elements?

A decision = information from the evaluation + values of all relevant parties + pressures positive and negative + guess or luck or unknown or error factors. . . . ***Single-system designs*** are just part of the mix in making a decision.

Clearly, it depends on who is doing the weighing of the elements: If it is strictly up to the client, then listen to the client's judgments (* and ** in our AB*M** design). If your agency is required to post objective evidence of outcome, then emphasize the trends and the non-overlapping data. If the profession (and society at large) have opinions and values on this kind of case, then enter their ideas into the formula. There is no one right answer, unless it is Hippocrates': "Help if you can, but do no harm," to which we would add: All things considered.

GLOSSARY

AB*M**: We introduce this expanded AB design as the fundamental design for client-centered evaluation of practice. The asterisks represent times when the client is directly asked about how well her or his goals are being achieved—regardless of what the objective measures say (although the practitioner would not conclude an intervention phase unless it appears that a goal had been attained). Clients take charge in deciding whether some outcome does achieve what the client had sought to achieve. In particular, the M or maintenance phase, when the client has been taught to conduct the "intervention" on her or his own, is an acid test of client-centered outcome because it is very much like the situation when the client is entirely on her or his own. (See DESIGNS)

Analysis of Evaluation Data: The data collected with great care on client targets over periods of time have to be analyzed, that is, they have to be put into certain patterns so that the information they provide may be used to make decisions. We take the point of view that the five patterns we discussed in Chapter 14 should all be performed so as to obtain a systemic or holistic perspective on the situation, as no one form of analysis has any logical priority over any other.

One pattern concerns changes in the client's targeted objectives. From the client's perspective, are there more or fewer problems than initially?

A second pattern concerns asking the client whether specific goals have been attained. This question is made into an official part of the helping process, as indicated by the *AB*M*** design notations.

A third pattern concerns the overall trend of the graphed data, especially when we distinguish data collected before and after an intervention is made. There are a small number of basic patterns comparing baseline data with intervention data, which give us the big picture on how the client's targeted concerns are changing.

A fourth pattern using a simple mathematical procedure to analyze the pattern among non-overlapping baseline and intervention data, so as to observe how like published studies our data are, a rough indicator of statistical significance.

A fifth pattern assesses how our results stand the test of time, as we need to be relatively comfortable with results that are not simply a random event, but which have some stability over time. This is further discussed in the maintenance phase as M**.

Statistical tests of significance can also be used. Your instructor may choose to introduce you to some of them.

Archival Records: Many kinds of information are recorded by other professionals for their own purposes, such as taking blood pressure readings to indicate health status. This same recorded information might be used for an entirely different purpose, such as indicating how often a patient in a public hospital (as contrasted with a private hospital) was seen by the RN. This archival record would not intrude in the life of either client or RN, while serving an important purpose for an evaluator of programs.

Baseline (A Phase): A baseline represents a client's starting position with regard to a given concern, before any intervention occurs. It is an operationalized statement or definition of how much, how often, what size, and so on the target pattern presents itself before service begins. It is as objective as possible, but as relevant to the client's overall concerns as well. By convention, the baseline is indicated on graphs as A.

There are two general types of baselines: A CONCURRENT BASELINE is obtained in some period of time before intervention begins, whereby the plan of action is constructed based on the nature and extent of baseline assessment. Enough information is obtained ideally to represent the stable presenting concerns of the client, so that it is possible to know whether or not the baseline pattern is different during the intervention period. A RECONSTRUCTED BASELINE occurs when there isn't enough time to obtain a concurrent one, and it is used as a quick point of reference to compare to intervention data. It is indicated by (A), and one must be cautious about its veracity.

Some evaluation designs remove an intervention to see whether the target returns to a prior (undesired) state, as part of the process of investigating causality in advanced evaluation designs. In order to distinguish pre-intervention baselines from those times when intervention is intentionally removed, we will call the latter Observation-only Phases, but they refer to the exact same data collection methods being applied to the same target.

Behavior: Behavior refers to what people do, in contrast to what characterizes people. For example, a woman may be crying, bent over in her chair, speaking about being very unhappy, not be able to perform her ordinary activities, and such. These are actions. Practitioners may characterize her (by the sum of her behaviors) as being "depressed." Others might wonder about that person's physical illness. These characterizations depend on the theory (or ideology or professional perspective) that gives an interpreted meaning to a group of behaviors.

Behaviors include overt actions, but also covert feelings and thoughts—which can be observed only by that individual who may report these feelings and thoughts to a practitioner. The basic point is that a behavior must by observable and measurable by someone, either the client or some observer. When the client observes and records her or his own behavior, we term this self-monitoring. When an outside observer records the behavior, we call this direct observation. All behavior takes place within a physical and social setting. The possible effects of these situational factors may influence or distort the behavior to be observed. Clear operational definitions of the behavior in question will help reduce distortions.

Behavioral Products: Sometimes, the effects of some behavior may be used in a new way. For example, a sign-in sheet in a nursing home may indicate the number of people going to see particular clients. If the number is low, this may activate the practitioner to get a "friendly visitor" program started at the nursing home. A librarian's records of the number of books or books-on-tape borrowed in a nursing home might indicate need to encourage residents to take advantage of this service.

Client Validity: We introduce this type of validity (see VALIDITY) to reflect the client-centered evaluation of practice. It refers to the client agreeing (or disagreeing) that a given state of the target attains (or does not attain) what the client is seeking. This agreement is solicited by the practitioner at the end of an intervention phase and again at the end of a maintenance phase when it appears that a stable objective has been attained. In fact, only the client can testify to this state because only the client sees the situation from the inside point of view, rather than from the perspective of an outsider like the practitioner.

Concept: A concept is an arbitrarily constructed general term derived from some class of events (such as how a client presents herself and the troubling situation that brought her to your agency—she may seem "depressed" to you). Concepts serve as building blocks for larger conceptual terms (e.g., propositions, theories) and as links to the information network where you can find evidence-based practice ideas. Concepts are neither true nor false, but merely better or worse guides to reality. For example, the concept "depression" refers to some but not necessarily all of these physical (e.g., slumped posture), psychological (e.g., persistent unhappy feelings, unpleasant thoughts), and social factors (e.g., ineffective in ordinary social roles), and so on. Having this concept enables you to locate effective methods of intervention, although you should evaluate the specific outcomes with your client. Keep open to other relevant concepts that more fully describe your client situation.

We note that the term *construct* often appears in the literature as a kind of concept; we do not make any distinctions between them in this book.

Decision Making: Decision making is a process by which a number of facts and values are combined in such a way as to perform one given action, rather than some alternative actions. This is not as simple a matter as adding all of the known facts to arrive at some decision, because values (a person's persistent preferences) may increase or decrease or nullify the facts of the matter.

However, the thrust of this book is to help the practitioner consider whatever objective evidence is available (from the evaluation process) as one important source of information in making a decision. Ignoring factual evidence is risky and may play into your biases—"don't confuse me with the evidence; my mind is made up"—which is harmful to the client in the long run. It may feel good to you, but it doesn't help solve client problems.

We have indicated six steps in decision making that should help you to minimize biased decisions. (See Chapter 15.)

Designs (or Evaluation Designs): Designs are logical arrangements of measurement (or observation) phases and intervention phases that can inform clients and practitioners whether or not desired changes have occurred in the targeted objectives. In some cases of advanced designs, it is also possible to infer whether or not the intervention caused the observed changes.

We introduce some designs that combine logical and psychosocial arrangements in which the client is involved in interpreting whether the change has attained his/her objectives. The first such opportunity occurs after the practitioner has guided the intervention, in the B phase. In B*, the client is asked a global question assessing the outcome from her or his point of view. Then, in a maintenance phase, when the client is in complete charge of the intervention on his or her own behalf, there is a second opportunity for the client to assess the outcome, in the M** phase. Asking the client these global questions is not part of the logical design, but it complements such designs in important ways, which only the client can provide. Thus, we propose that an AB*M** design is the basic design for client-centered evaluation of practice. Adding the maintenance phase to other designs likewise strengthens the psychosocial import of the results, where the client's point of view is incorporated into the basic fabric of the evaluation.

Conventional designs, such as the AB, the ABA, the ABAB, and the multiple baseline design, all may likewise benefit from a maintenance phase in which the client interprets results from his or her point of view. On some occasions, the changing intensity designs and alternating intervention designs may likewise benefit.

We want to call attention to the differences among the ABAB, ABAM, and the ABABM designs. They look somewhat alike, but there are important differences as described in Chapter 13.

Effect Size: There are many ways of comparing numbers, such as by comparing their means, or variations from means, and observing visual trends across phases. These descriptive statistics are the content of basic statistics books. Effect size is one way of using more of the available information in making such as comparison, and it also allows us to make comparisons across different studies. However, these comparisons take us into abstract realms where it is difficult to visualize manipulations of means and standard deviations except in mathematical terms. The formulas used in constructing various effect sizes are operational definitions, literally. The meaning of a numerical result is given by the operations used to generate it. We have chosen not to use these abstract numerical formulae, giving preference to what clients and practitioners can do with empirically meaningful terms before them, and suggesting that multiple perspectives on the meaning of data will provide all of the information needed for a beginning practitioner.

Ethics: Ethics are the set of rules defining when some behavior is in or out of compliance with some value system or its codification into laws and procedures. Helping disciplines develop professional codes of ethics to specify when their members are acting according to the guidelines—and when they are not. There are consequences for violating the ethics of a profession (and a society).

Follow-Up Phase: There may be occasions, even after a client-conducted intervention during the maintenance phase, when the helping professional makes contact with the client after a formal termination, so as to check on the progress or continuation of the service outcome. Follow-up is not intended as a continuous collection of information, as was conducted throughout the service period (baseline and intervention), but as an occasional and usually unannounced contact with the former client to see how things are going under "normal" (that is, non-therapeutic) conditions. The hope is that the former targeted event is still in a desired zone for the client. If not, the practitioner might introduce the idea of a client's return to treatment.

Goals: Helping professionals seek to help the client attain her or his goal, which is a long-term desired outcome, often combining intermediate objectives, like stepping stones, which lead to that goal. For instance, achieving the goal of fiscal solvency would involve obtaining requisite education, job training, and assertiveness to locate appropriate positions that offer adequate pay, fringe benefits, safe working conditions, and so on. One obtains fiscal solvency when all of these other intermediate steps are attained (and maintained). Goals are frequently complex entities, understandable as broad abstract ideas (like fiscal solvency), but which require specification as to what concrete steps (objectives) are needed to attain those goals. (See OBJECTIVES.)

Group Measure (or Measurement of Group Behavior): These are measures that are distinctive of the whole group as a group, rather than characterizing any individual member of that group. For example, group morale refers to a group-level phenomenon, not to the morale or contentment of any one member of that group. Some group measures are additive, such as counting each person's attendance to indicate group attendance. Other group measures are qualitative, such as group problem solving ability, which reflects the synergistic interaction among members, not to any one person's ability to solve problems.

Individualized Rating Scale (IRS): Among the most flexible and useful of measurement tools, the individualized rating scales are constructed by helping professional and client interactions so as to reflect the dimensions on the client's specific target. If an aggressive youth is completing an IRS that he and his counselor worked out, the questions might include rating the degree to which the client felt angry before a fight (1 = very much angry, to 5 = not angry at all) or the degree to which the client perceived a racial insult to have instigated the fight (1 = a very bad insult, to 5 = no insult at all). With these kinds of questions directed to events that might have triggered the combat, the client and practitioner might reconstruct what was happening so as to reduce future incendiary events. In short, we look for the target complaints or the individual's identified problems or issues, then rate their intensity, so as to give a unique picture of this client in this time and place. Of course, we can use the same scale repeated over time to observe how these factors change, especially in relation to the overall goal of reducing fighting behavior.

Intervention (B Phase): Helping professionals apply a variety of services designed to augment desired changes regarding the client's concerns. In a word, interventions help clients help themselves. People don't become "clients" unless they need a spark to energize them into personal or interpersonal problem solving. So helping professionals have that role of sparking the client into thinking clearly and taking charge (i.e., acting decisively)—and recording the results of these joint actions. Rarely do practitioners conduct the entire intervention, and then usually only in institutional settings where clients may be unable to participate fully.

In addition, these interventive services and client targets need to be clearly operationalized so that helping professionals can know what worked and what did not, both for the sake of the current client and to build a practice repertoire. Conventionally, these are known by letters B, C, D, and so on, for as many letters as there are distinctive interventions (but not including some letters reserved for special purposes, like M for the maintenance phase). When the same intervention is repeated on different occasions, we indicate this by numbering them, as in B1, B2 (as in an A1B1A2B2 design, commonly written as ABAB with the 1s and 2s understood). When we change the intensity of the intervention, we indicate this by superscripts, like B^1, B^2, B^3.

In this book, we have introduced the suggestion that clients be asked a formal question at the end of a B phase: To what degree do these outcomes attain your desired goals and objectives? If a positive response is made, the helping professional is advised to go into the M or maintenance phase. This formal question and its answer is indicated by an asterisk * in the AB*M** design.

Logs: [See Structured Logs.]

Maintenance Phase (M Phase): This becomes a critical phase for client-centered evaluation of practice in which the helping professional trains the client on performing a feasible version of the intervention, and then steps back from any direct involvement with delivering services. The collection of ongoing data on targets continues as before. Should the client maintain something like the level of success achieved in the B phase when the helping professional was active, it would be a very close simulation of what client can do for himself or herself in the real world.

We also suggest that the M phase conclude with a formal question to the client (just like the formal question asked at the end of the B phase): To what degree do these outcomes attain your desired goals and objectives? This is indicated by the double asterisk ** in the AB*M** design.

Nonreactive Measures: These are measures (or observations) that in and of themselves produce little or no reaction on the part of the respondent. For example, an anxious client might chain smoke on breaks in the interview. A count of the cigarette butts left in the ash tray after the client has left might indicate a change in this nervous habit over a series of sessions. Such an unobtrusive count would in no way affect the client's behavior. (See UNOBTRUSIVE MEASURES.)

Objectives: Objectives are the necessary intermediate steps used to help a client attain her or his long-term goals. The helping professional breaks down a long-term complex goal into its constituent (and testable) parts and plans a sequence of actions intended to accomplish these objectives so as to enable the client to attain this long-term goal. For example, to attain the goal of fiscal solvency, a client would have to attain certain educational knowledge and skills suitable for given types of jobs—these would be intermediate steps, and they require a planned sequence of stages to attain them in order to achieve more advanced steps toward a goal. [See GOALS.]

Operational Definitions: We operationalize the meaning of a term when we supply the instruction manual on how to do whatever the concept suggests, and how to produce or reproduce the event being described. For example, being tardy at school is defined as being observed entering the school door after the time set for school to begin. A more difficult example is retardation. This term has been operationally defined at several times during its history of usage—a divine punishment; a stubbornness to conform; a mental illness for which there is no cure; a genetic and thus inborn condition; a cultural condition that reflects the degree of supportiveness available more than the person's abilities; and so on—reflecting the dominant ideological perspective sometimes more than objective facts of the condition. Therefore, just because a term has an operational definition does not make it true beyond the context in which that definition was formed.

It is helpful to distinguish operational definitions from connotative or dictionary definitions, which are terms defined by using other words, which in turn needs terms to define them.

Pattern of Targeted Events: As targets are plotted on a graph, the client and helping professional can observe changes over time. The benchmark represents the desired outcome of a given target, such as an objective of 130 pounds attained over the next three months. (This could be shown on the graph as a construction line drawn from the current weight to an ideal 130 pound weight, with the actual weight recorded by dots above, at, or below this construction line.) This could be through weight loss, or in some cases, through weight gain, depending on the client's objectives. In each case, the weight recorded each week would represent one point in a "moving picture" of that client's weight relative to the benchmark outcome being sought. This moving picture is a pattern of data points on the graph, and can be described roughly at ascending, remaining approximately the same, or descending, relative to some identified value (such as reaching the objective of 130 pounds). There are mathematical methods of describing the trends or patterns of data more accurately, if statistical measures are used to evaluate outcomes.

Physical Traces: These are unintended behavioral products that supply information. For example, where chairs are placed in a nursing home corridor may indicate how much social interaction is being encouraged (as in clusters of chairs in an arc) or discouraged (as when chairs are placed in long straight lines for ease of cleaning, not for social interaction).

Propositions: Propositions are sets of concepts related in such ways as to describe: (1) what we assume to exist, so we can get to the next logical steps of analysis; (2) what we hypothesize to exist and which we can test in the empirical world; or (3) something we prefer or value, for which there is no empirical test. Philosophers give wonderful names to these three classes of propositions: (1) assumptions or axioms; (2) hypotheses or predictions; and (3) values or preferences. (There are technical differences among these terms over which rivers of ink have been spilled; we'll leave well enough alone and stick with these definitions.) The important point is that hypotheses or predictions can be tested to discover the truth of a situation. Does X lead to Y? Can Z reduce the impact of X? These are the types of questions that lead to new information and measured results in the real world.

Reliability: Reliability means consistency in measurement, which we can determine by measuring the same client under the same circumstances on repeated occasions. We can use the same observer making independent observations over time, or two observers independently observing the same client at the same time. Independence or sameness are a matter of degree in the real world; we try to make observations in as similar ways as possible, even though different social situations or times are never exactly the same.

Self-Monitoring: Self-monitoring is a general term indicating that the client is taking part in observing and measuring some aspect about himself or herself. The behavior is likely to be internal feelings or thoughts, or possibly internal physiological reactions, which only the client can know. It can also include external events. All people self-monitor (without realizing it in a technical sense), such as by weighing themselves in the morning, assessing their feelings of road rage as a reckless driver zips past them, underlining an important date or event on the calendar, and so on. The task for the practitioner is to encourage the client to give an accurate, full report in the service of an intervention that is intended to help the client.

Single-System Design (SSD): Single-system designs refer to a family of logical arrangements of careful observations of problems or potentials, and the interventions related to them so as to evaluate practice in field conditions. They include at least one phase of objective measurement of the targets of intervention (either before or after any intervention), and one phase of intervention regarding those targets in which the same measurement procedures are continued. Logically more powerful designs have more than one of each phase observations and/or interventions. Single-system designs are based on the idea that we need both "before" and "after" measures on the same targeted problems to determine whether any real change has occurred.

Standardized Rating Scales: This type of measurement often involves scientists who are at a distance from your particular client, and yet their efforts in identifying a concept (such as depression or contentment or parent engagement in the foster care process) and finding statements (items) that indicate degrees or intensities of that concept, can apply to your client and many others as well. There is a great deal of effort that goes into the construction of such a scale, and in the process of constructing it, testing it out with known populations, and finding the smallest number of items that performs most effectively in distinguishing people with or without this condition, and identifying its validity and reliability. But when a standardized scale is completed, it may be used in many different places with many kinds of people, all of whom share the possibility of having what that scale measures.

There are a large number of such scales, and many places where they are located. We call your attention to the following reference books:

Aiken, L. R., & Groth-Marnat, G. (2005). *Psychological testing and assessment* (12th ed.). Boston: Allyn & Bacon.

Fischer, J., & Corcoran, K. (2007). *Measures for clinical practice: A sourcebook (Vol. 1, Couples, families, and children; Vol. 2, Adults) (3rd ed.).* New York: Oxford.

Hunsley, J., & Mash, E. J. (Eds.). (2008). *A guide to assessments that work.* New York: Wiley.

Maddox, T. (2008). *A comprehensive reference for assessment in psychology, education, and business* (6th ed.). Austin, TX: Pro-Ed.

Structured Logs: We introduce the idea of the structured log as another aspect of client-centered evaluation of practice, in which the client writes an interpreted discussion of some events of concern, following a practitioner-generated structure (presented below). Then the practitioner and client discuss what patterns appear to emerge for these reports. The idea of structure is important, as it is the practitioner's contribution to help the client zero in on what matters in that person's life. Sometimes a TARGET LOG is used to get a strong description of the problems; at other times an INTERACTION LOG is used to capture the flow back and forth between the parties involved in a problematic situation. TIME LOGS emphasize the unit of time that is the focus of attention and identify who is doing what to whom during that time. CRITICAL INCIDENT LOGS may be used to explore what are the significant elements of some unclear but problematic event. And a purely EXPLORATORY LOG is used when the situation is so unclear as to need some ingredients to formulate hunches about the problem and potential solutions.

Target: As used in this text, a target represents a specific objective that has been given an operational definition so that both the client and the helping professional know the exact status of this objective at each time during the helping process. For example, the general goal of a person coming to a physical trainer at a gym might be to be physically fit, given her age, health conditions, and so on. This would include intermediate objectives such as: (1) being at a certain healthy weight; (2) achieving a level of physical strength; and (3) attaining good balance and endurance. Various devices can operationalize these objectives. A scale can measure weight in pounds as compared to tabled values according to gender, height, physique, and so on. Exercise machines can be set at certain levels for certain numbers of repetitions that represent operational levels of endurance. Targets are the specific numbers the client sets as representing attainment of these objectives of exercise that represent gains in appropriate weight (benchmark at 130 pounds, for example), adequate strength (benchmark at 10 repetitions at 20 pound weights, then a new target with 25 pound weights), and the like.

Theory: Theories are systems of concepts and propositions that focus on a limited portion of the world, describe that portion, explain how it came to be and how it operates as it does, and predict what might be (i.e., future states of that portion of the world or sometimes a past state). People survive by being applied theoreticians who figure out how to move through the world and pass on the collective wisdom (or stereotype) to future generations.

We distinguish GENERAL THEORIES and local theories. General theories deal with large territories of the world, such as a Skinnerian behavioral or a Bandurian cognitive behavioral theory that could apply to any human behavior. The terms these kinds of theories use are, necessarily, abstract so as to apply to many topics. Such theories provide a powerful general background to think about how people behave in situations and physical environments. Often these general theories provide a likewise general set of directions on

changing behavior, such as Skinner's terms: reinforcement, punishment, and the like. General theories are not true or false; only hypotheses derived from theories can be tested for their truthfulness.

LOCAL THEORIES are systems of concepts and propositions that deal with specific situations (i.e., recognizing the peculiarities of the particular client context). If the local theory is to guide practice, it has to introduce the conceptual forces and structures faced by the client, so as to suggest how changes of these forces and structures can take place. Local theories are more limited in scope to the given client, yet richer in details of the fabric of life surrounding that client. Local theories operate with the same kinds of rules of logic as do general theories.

Unobtrusive Measures: When the questions we ask or the observations we make of a client's behavior do not intrude on, or change anything significant about the thing observed, then to that degree the measure is unobtrusive. Note that whenever we ask questions, there is always some effect, large or small, on the person asked. Likewise, to the extent that a person knows she or he is being observed, there is some effect on her or his behavior. We can minimize these potentially obtrusive effects by the way we ask questions (neutrally, not as if these are personal questions) or make observations (with as little awareness of being observed on the part of the client as possible). The ethical issue is raised if the information obtained is worth the deception used to get it; or whether there are alternative (and non-deceptive) ways to obtain the same information. (See NONREACTIVE MEASURES.)

Validity: Validity in scientific usage refers to whether a measure of something (like the term *depression*) really measures that thing and only that thing. In parallel language, lawyers speak of the truth, the whole truth, and nothing but the truth. It is difficult to be sure a measure is completely valid because we have to know what is in the measure and also what is the nature of that thing being measured in order to say that the measure truly reflects the thing being measured.

Scientists have constructed several ways of approximation: (1) Face (or faith) validity refers to whether, on the face of it, the items reflect the thing being measured. (2) Content validity refers to whether the items are a representative sample of the thing being measured. (3) Criterion validity refers to the ability of a measure to predict: (a) concurrent events or (b) future events accurately. Pragmatically, this is the best approximation of truth, especially when combined with (4) client validity (with its employment of the client to determine whether these changes, in fact, represent attainment of the client goals). (5) Construct validity refers to whether an operationalized measure reflects the construct or concept it intends to measure.

Values: Values are people's persistent preferences. The objects of these preferences differ by size (this dessert vs. that dessert, or this political position vs. that political position), by concreteness or abstractness (this blue hat or a favored color, blue), and by individual vs. collective preferences (this particular book vs. my country). When we share values with many others, we can speak of a common culture or value system. When we hold unique views, we can speak of personal attitudes toward objects.

REFERENCES AND OTHER SOURCES

Aiken, L. R., & Groth-Marnat, G. (2005). *Psychological testing and assessment* (12th ed.). Boston: Allyn & Bacon.

Alfassi, M. (2003). Promoting the will and skill of students at academic risk: An evaluation of an instructional design geared to foster achievement, self-efficacy, and motivation. *Journal of Instructional Psychology, 30,* 28–40.

Alpert, L. T., & Britner, P. A. (2009). Measuring parent engagement in foster care. *Social Work Research, 33,* 135–145.

American Psychiatric Association. (2000). *Diagnostic and statistical manual of mental disorders* (Rev. 4th ed.). Washington, DC: Author.

American Psychological Association. (2007). *Thesaurus of psychological index terms* (11th ed.). Washington, DC: Author.

Ayllon, T. (1963). Intensive treatment of psychotic behavior by stimulus satiation and food reinforcement. *Behavior Research and Therapy, 1,* 53–61.

Bandura, A. (1986). *Social foundations of thought and action: A social cognitive theory.* Englewood Cliffs, NJ: Prentice-Hall.

Bandura, A., Barbaranelli, C., Caprara, G. V., & Pastorelli, C. (1996). Multifaceted impact of self-efficacy beliefs on academic functioning. *Child Development, 67,* 1206–1222.

Bandura, A., Barbaranelli, C., Caprara, G. V., & Pastorelli, C. (2001). Self-efficacy beliefs as shapers of children's aspirations and career trajectories. *Child Development, 72,* 187–206.

Bernstein, B. E., & Hartsell, Jr., T. L. (2000). *The portable ethicist for mental health professionals: An A-Z guide to responsible practice.* New York: Wiley.

Blenkner, M., Bloom, M., & Nielsen, M. (1971). A research and demonstration project of protective services. *Social Casework, 52,* 483–499.

Bloom, M. (2010). Client-centered evaluation: Ethics for 21st century practitioners. *Journal of Social Work Values and Ethics, 7(1).*

Bloom, M. (1986). *The experience of research.* New York: Macmillan.

Bloom, M., Fischer, J., & Orme, J. G. (2009). *Evaluating practice: Guidelines for the accountable professional* (6th ed.). Boston: Pearson/Allyn & Bacon.

Chesebrough, E., King, P., Gullotta, T. P., & Bloom, M. (2004). *A blueprint for the promotion of prosocial behaviors in early childhood.* New York: Kluwer Academic/Plenum Publishers.

Concept. (n.d.). In *The American Heritage Dictionary of the English Language* (4th ed.). Retrieved May 28, 2010, from http://dictionary.reference.com/browse/concept

Dale, J., Caramlau, I. O., Lindenmeyer, A., & Williams, S. M. (2008). Peer support telephone calls for improving health. *Cochrane Database of Systemic Reviews, 2008,* Issue 4, Art. No. CD006903.pub2 doi:10.1002/14651858.

Dolgoff, R., Loewenberg, F. M., & Harrington, D. (2009). *Ethical decisions for social work practice* (8th ed.). Belmont, CA: Thomson Brooks/Cole.

Ehrenreich, B. (2009). *Bright-sided: How the relentless promotion of positive thinking has undermined America.* New York: Holt.

Engel, J. M., Jensen, M. P., & Schwartz, L. (2004). Outcome of biofeedback-assisted relaxation for pain in adults with cerebral palsy: Preliminary findings. *Applied Psychophysiology and Biofeedback, 29,* 135–140.

Erikson, E. (1950). *Childhood and society.* New York: Norton.

Fischer, J., & Corcoran, K. (2007). *Measures for clinical practice: A sourcebook (Vol. 1, Couples, families, and children; Vol. 2, Adults)* (3rd ed.). New York: Oxford.

Franklin, B. (1793). *Autobiography of Benjamin Franklin.* London: J. Parsons.

Friman, P. C. (2009). Behavior assessment. In D. Barlow, M. Nock, & M. Hersen (Eds.), *Single case experimental designs: Strategies for studying behavior for change* (3rd ed.) (pp. 99–134). Boston: Allyn & Bacon.

Gassner, J., & Dukore, B. F. (Eds.). (1970). *A treasury of the theatre.* New York: Simon & Schuster.

Gliner, J. A., & Morgan, G. A. (2000). *Research methods in applied settings: An integrated approach to design and analysis.* Mahwah, NJ: Lawrence Erlbaum Associates.

Greenstein, T. N. (2006). *Methods of family research* (2nd ed.). Thousand Oaks, CA: Sage.

Howland, J. L., Wright, T. C., Boughan, R. A., & Roberts, B. C. (2009). How scholarly is Google Scholar? A comparison to library databases. *College & Research Libraries, May*, 227–234.

Hudson, W. W., & Faul, A. C. (1998). *The clinical measurement package: A field manual* (2nd ed.). Tallahassee, FL: WALMYR.

Hunsley, J., & Mash, E. J. (Eds.). (2008). *A guide to assessments that work*. New York: Wiley.

Klein, W., & Bloom, M. (1995). Practice wisdom. Social Work, 40, 799–808.

Maddox, T. (2008). *A comprehensive reference for assessment in psychology, education, and business* (6th ed.). Austin, TX: Pro-Ed.

Maslow, A. H. (1943). A theory of human motivation. *Psychological Review, 50*, 370–396.

Miller, W. W., Combs, S. A., Fish, C., Bense, B., Owens, A., & Burch, A. (2008). Running training after a stroke: A single-subject report. *Physical Therapy, 88*, 511–522.

Mishara, B. L., & Daigle, M. S. (1997). Effects of different telephone intervention styles with suicidal callers at two suicide prevention centers: An empirical investigation. *American Journal of Community Psychology, 25*, 861–885.

O'Neil, J. M., & Britner, P. A. (2009). Training primary preventionists to make a difference in people's lives. In M. E. Kenny, A. M. Horne, P. Orpinas, & L. E. Reese (Eds.), *Realizing social justice: The challenge of preventive interventions* (pp. 141–162). Washington, DC: American sychological Association.

Parker, R. I., & Brossart, D. F. (2003). Evaluating single-case research data. A comparison of seven statistical methods. *Behavior Therapy, 34*, 189–211.

Parker, R. I., Brossart, D. F., Vannest, K. J., Long, J. R., De-Alba, R. G., Baugh, F. G., et al. (2005). Effect sizes in single case research: How large is large? *School Psychology Review, 34*, 116–132.

Parker, R. I., Vannest, K. J., & Brown, L. M. (2009). The improvement rate difference for single-case research. *Exceptional Children, 75*, 135–150.

Peterson, C., & Seligman, M.E. P. (2004). *Character strengths and virtues: A handbook and classification*. New York: Oxford University Press.

Pigliucci, M. (2010). *Nonsense on stilts: How to tell science from bunk*. Chicago: University of Chicago Press.

Poropat, A. E. (2009). A meta-analysis of the five-factor model of personality and academic performance. *Psychological Bulletin, 135*, 322–338.

Reik, T. (1948). *Listening with the third ear: The inner experience of a psychoanalyst*. New York: Grove Press.

Rogers, C. (1951). *Client-centered therapy: Its current practice, implications and theory*. Boston: Houghton Mifflin.

Rosenberg, M. (1965). *Society and the adolescent self-image*. Princeton, NJ: Princeton University Press.

Roseth, C. J., Johnson, D. W., & Johnson, R. T. (2008). Promoting early adolescents' achievement and peer relationships: The effects of cooperative, competitive, and individualistic goal structures. *Psychological Bulletin, 134*, 223–246.

Rubin, A. (2010). *Statistics for evidence-based practice and evaluation* (2nd ed.). Belmont, CA: Brooks/Cole, Cengage Learning.

Saleeby, D. (1996). The strengths perspective in social work practice: Extensions and cautions. *Social Work, 41*, 296–306.

Satir, V. (1964). *Conjoint family therapy: A guide to therapy and technique*. Palo Alto, CA: Science and Behavior Books.

Seligman, M. E. P., Steen, T. T., Park, N., & Peterson, C. (2005). Positive psychology progress: Empirical validation of interventions. *American Psychologist, 60*, 410–421.

Shadish, W. R., & Rindskopf, D. M. (2007). Methods for evidence-based practice: Quantitative synthesis of single-subject designs. *New Directions for Evaluation, 113*, 95–109.

Turk, D. C., Okifuji, A., & Skinner, M. (2008). Chronic pain in adults. In J. Hunsley & E. J. Mash (Eds.), *A guide to assessments that work* (pp. 576–592). New York: Oxford University Press.

Veach, R. M. (1981). *Theory of medical ethics*. New York: Basic Books.

Webb, E. J., Campbell, D. T., Schwartz, R. D., & Sechrest, L. (1966). *Unobtrusive measures: Nonreactive research in the social sciences*. Chicago: Rand McNally.

White, M., & Epston, D. (1990). *Narrative means to therapeutic ends.* New York: Norton.

Wiersma, W., & Jurs, S. G. (2009). *Research methods in education: An introduction* (9th ed.). Boston: Pearson/Allyn & Bacon.

Worten, V. E., & Lambert, M. J. (2007). Outcome-oriented supervision: Advantages of adding systematic client tracking to supportive consultation. *Counseling and Psychotherapy Research, 7,* 48–53.

INDEX

Pages including tables and figures are indicated as t, f